MW01493067

A Solutions Manual for General Equilibrium, Overlapping Generations Models, and Optimal Growth Theory

A Solutions Manual for General Equilibrium, Overlapping Generations Models, and Optimal Growth Theory

Truman F. Bewley

Harvard University Press
Cambridge, Massachusetts
London, England
2011

Copyright © 2011 by the President and Fellows of Harvard College
All rights reserved
Printed in the United States of America

ISBN 978-0-674-05829-3

Introduction

This *Solutions Manual* contains answers to all the problems in my book, *General Equilibrium, Overlapping Generations Models, and Optimal Growth Theory* (Harvard University Press, 2007). Almost all the problems were used in homework or examinations for courses on microeconomics, general equilibrium theory, and mathematical economics. Homework and exams were returned to students with the answers given here. These were intended to educate, and hence are longer and more detailed than might be the work of good students or what an instructor would need. The problems vary in difficulty, but students should be able to do all of them after reading the book carefully.

A Note to the Reader

By technical necessity this book was prepared from vintage files, which have been faithfully reproduced in order to make these solutions available to students.

Contents

A Solutions Manual for General Equilibrium, Overlapping Generations Models, and Optimal Growth Theory

Answer to Homework Problems for Chapter 3, Problem #1

Problem: 1) Consider the Edgeworth box economy where the endowment of consumer A is (1, 0) and the endowment of consumer B is (0, 1). For each of the following three cases, find and sketch the set of Pareto optimal allocations and the utility possibility set and find the allocations that maximize the sum of the utilities of the two consumers. By "sketch the set of Pareto optimal allocations," I mean find the coordinates of a few points on the utility possibility frontier and fill in the remaining part of the curve. In maximizing the sum of the utilities in part b, use the symmetry of the problem. In order to see where the sum of the utilities is maximized, it is important to have a fairly accurate sketch of the utility possibility set.

a) $u_A(x_1, x_2) = \sqrt{x_1 x_2}$ and $u_B(x_1, x_2) = \sqrt{x_1 x_2}$.

b) $u_A(x_1, x_2) = x_1^{1/6} x_2^{1/3}$ and $u_B(x_1, x_2) = x_1^{1/3} x_2^{1/6}$.

c) $u_A(x_1, x_2) = x_1 x_2^2$ and $u_B(x_1, x_2) = x_1^2 x_2$.

Answer: a) Because u_A and u_B are homothetic, the set of Pareto optimal allocations is the diagonal of the Edgeworth box, as shown below.

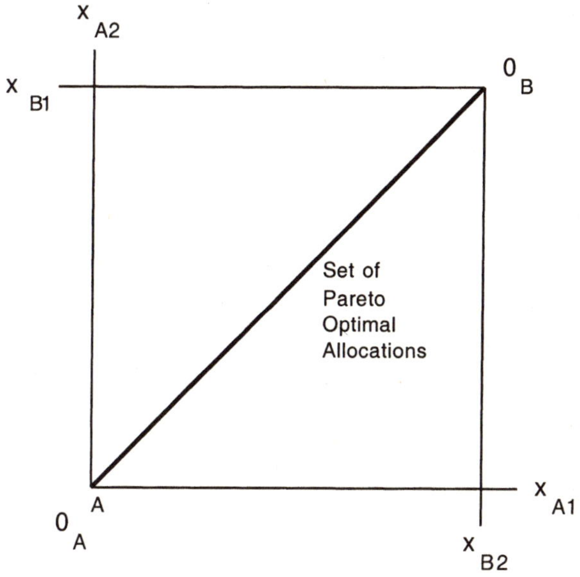

Because u_A and u_B are linearly homogeneous, the utility possibility frontier is a straight line as sketched below.

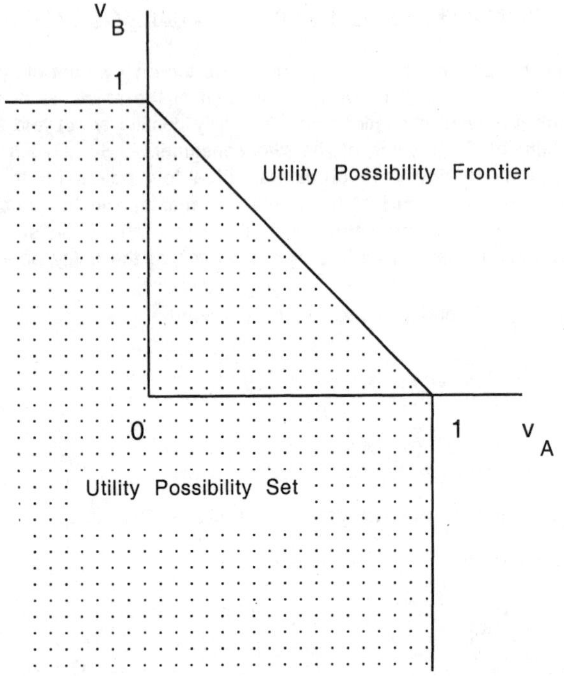

The allocations that maximize the sum of utility is the entire set of Pareto optimal allocations, namely, $\{(\mathbf{x}_A, \mathbf{x}_B) \mid x_{A1} = x_{A2}, x_{B1} = x_{B2} = 1 - x_{A1}\}$.

Answer: b) In order to find the set of Pareto optimal allocations, we must solve the equation

$$\frac{\partial u_A(x_{A1}, x_{A2})/\partial x_{A1}}{\partial u_A(x_{A1}, x_{A2})/\partial x_{A2}} = MRS_A = MRS_B = \frac{\partial u_B(x_{B1}, x_{B2})/\partial x_{B1}}{\partial u_B(x_{B1}, x_{B2})/\partial x_{B2}}.$$

Since the total endowment of each commodity is one, this equation becomes

$$\frac{\partial u_A(x_{A1}, x_{A2})/\partial x_1}{\partial u_A(x_{A1}, x_{A2})/\partial x_2} = \frac{\partial u_B(1 - x_{A1}, 1 - x_{A2})/\partial x_1}{\partial u_B(1 - x_{A1}, 1 - x_{A2})/\partial x_2},$$

which in turn becomes

$$\frac{\dfrac{1}{6}\left(\dfrac{x_{A2}^{1/3}}{x_{A1}^{5/6}}\right)}{\dfrac{1}{3}\left(\dfrac{x_{A1}^{1/6}}{x_{A2}^{2/3}}\right)} = \frac{\dfrac{1}{3}\left(\dfrac{(1-x_{A2})^{1/6}}{(1-x_{A1})^{2/3}}\right)}{\dfrac{1}{6}\left(\dfrac{(1-x_{A1})^{1/3}}{(1-x_{A2})^{5/6}}\right)},$$

which implies that

$$\frac{x_{A2}}{x_{A1}} = 4\left(\frac{1-x_{A2}}{1-x_{A1}}\right),$$

and hence that

$$x_{A2} - x_{A1}x_{A2} = 4x_{A1} - 4x_{A1}x_{A2}.$$

Solving this equation for x_{A2}, we see that

$$x_{A2} = \frac{4x_{A1}}{1+3x_{A1}}.$$

The set of Pareto optimal allocations looks approximately as in the drawing below.

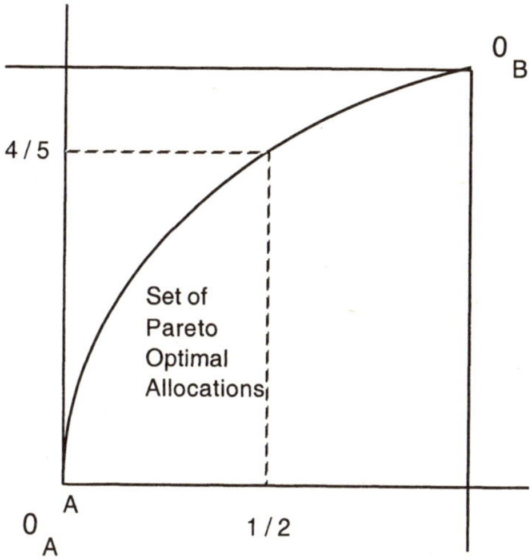

The utility possibility frontier looks approximately as follows.

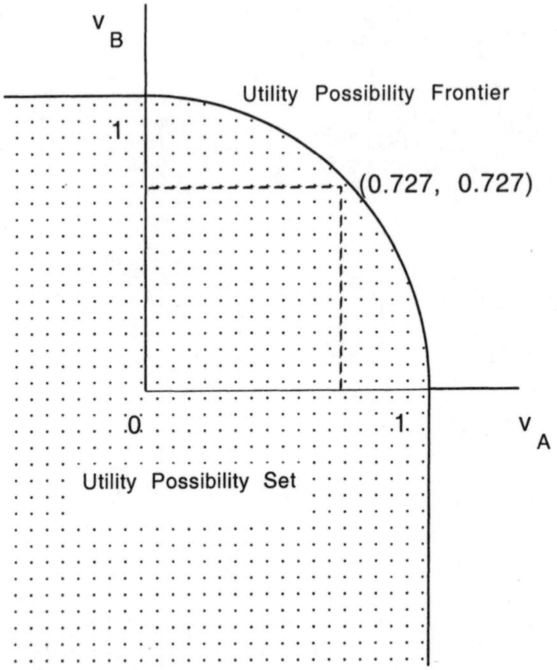

The point (0.727, 727) on the frontier may be found by letting $x_{A1} = 1/3$. Then $x_{A2} = 2/3$, so that $x_{B1} = 2/3$ and $x_{B2} = 1/3$. At these values for the allocation, $v_A = v_B = \frac{2^{1/3}}{3^{1/2}} \cong 0.727$.

The concavity of the utility possibility frontier is a consequence of the concavity of the utility functions. The symmetry of the utility possibility set with respect to the two axes follows from the symmetry of the problem. If the allocation

$$((x_{A1}, x_{A2}), (x_{B1}, x_{B2})) = ((\bar{x}_{A1}, \bar{x}_{A2}), (\bar{x}_{B1}, \bar{x}_{B2}))$$

is feasible and achieves utility levels $(v_A, v_B) = (\bar{v}_A, \bar{v}_B)$, then the allocation

$$((x_{A1}, x_{A2}), (x_{B1}, x_{B2})) = ((\bar{x}_{B2}, \bar{x}_{B1}), (\bar{x}_{A2}, \bar{x}_{A1}))$$

is feasible and achieves the utility levels $(v_A, v_B) = (\bar{v}_B, \bar{v}_A)$. From the symmetry and convexity of the utility possibility set, it follows that the point on the frontier where the sum of the utilities is maximized is the point where $v_A = v_B = \frac{2^{1/3}}{3^{1/2}}$. The corresponding allocation is $((x_{A1}, x_{A2}), (x_{B1}, x_{B2})) = ((1/3, 2/3), (2/3, 1/3))$.

Answer: c) The utility functions of part b are the sixth power of the utility functions of part a. Since the sixth power is an increasing function, the utility functions of part c are monotone transformations of the corresponding utility functions of part b. Therefore the indifference curves and hence the set of Pareto optima are the same in the two parts. The utility possibility frontier, however, differs, because it depends on the shape of the utility functions, not just on the indifference curves. In attempting to plot the utility possibility frontier, notice that the points $(v_A, v_B) = (1, 0)$ and $(v_A, v_B) = (0, 1)$ belong to the frontier. If we calculate the utility levels at the allocation $((x_{A1}, x_{A2}), (x_{B1}, x_{B2})) = ((1/3, 2/3), (2/3, 1/3))$, we find that $v_A = v_B = 4/9$. Therefore the utility possibility frontier is not concave and the utility possibility set is not convex. If we calculate more points, we see that the utility possibility frontier is convex. This is so because the utility functions are convex. The utility possibility set looks approximately as follows.

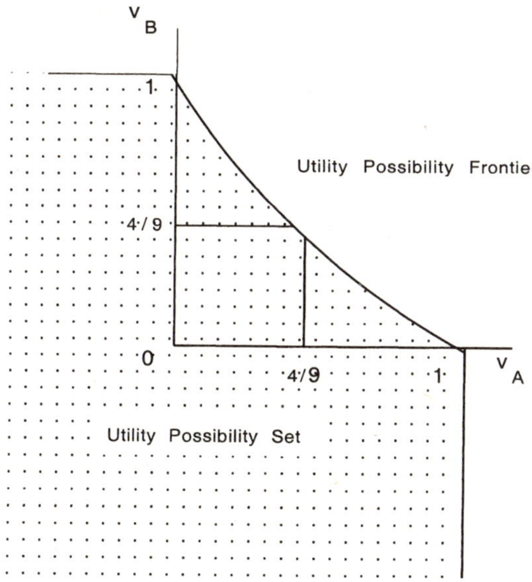

The allocations that maximize the sum of the utilities are the ones corresponding to the points (1, 0) and (0, 1) on the utility possibility frontier. That is, they are the allocations

$$((x_{A1}, x_{A2}), (x_{B1}, x_{B2})) = ((1, 1), (0, 0))$$

and

$$((x_{A1}, x_{A2}), (x_{B1}, x_{B2})) = ((0, 0), (1, 1)).$$

<u>Answer to Homework Problems for Ch 3, Problem #2</u>

<u>Problem</u>: 2) Find the optimum allocation and draw the feasible set for each of the following three Robinson Crusoe economies, where L is the input of labor, ℓ is the consumption of leisure, x is the consumption of food, and y is the production of food. Indicate Crusoe's indifference curves and the optimum on the drawing. In a commodity vector, the first component is labor-leisure time and the second is food.

a) $y = f(L) = 2L$, $\mathbf{e} = (1, 0)$, $u(\ell, x) = \ell^{2/3}x^{2/3}$.

b) $y = f(L) = L$, $e = (1, 0)$, $u(\ell, x) = \min(\ell, 2x)$.

c) $y = f(L) = 3\sqrt{L}$, $\mathbf{e} = (1, 0)$, $u(\ell, x) = \ell + 2x$.

<u>Answer</u>: a) The first order condition for an optimum is

$$\frac{\dfrac{\partial u(x, l)}{\partial l}}{\dfrac{\partial u(x, l)}{\partial x}} = \frac{df(L)}{dL},$$

which implies that

$$\frac{\dfrac{2}{3}\dfrac{x^{2/3}}{\ell^{1/3}}}{\dfrac{2}{3}\dfrac{\ell^{2/3}}{x^{1/3}}} = 2,$$

so that

$$\frac{x}{\ell} = 2.$$

Feasibility implies that

$$2\ell = x = 2L = 2(1 - \ell) = 2 - 2\ell$$

and hence

$$4\ell = 2$$

and so

$$\ell = 1/2 = L,\ x = 1 = y.$$

The corresponding diagram is as follows. The feasibility set is indicated by the letter $\mathfrak{F}$.

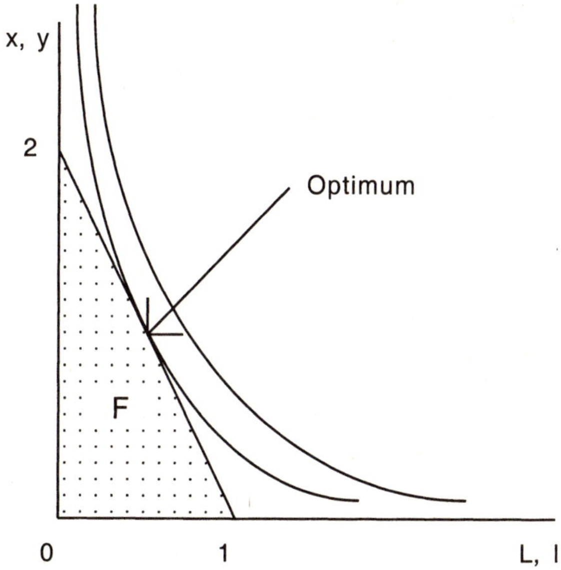

<u>Answer</u>: b) The diagram looks as follows. The optimum is at the point (1/3, 2/3), as is evident from the diagram. The indifference curves are the each made up of two half lines meeting at right angles at their endpoints.

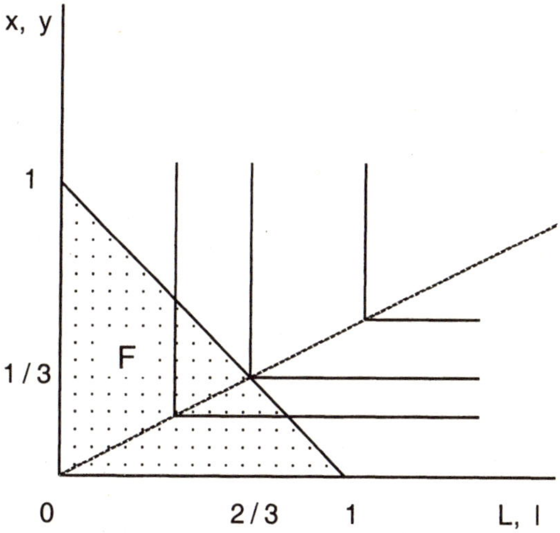

<u>Answer</u>: c) If we apply the equation

$$\frac{\dfrac{\partial u(x,\ell)}{\partial \ell}}{\dfrac{\partial u(x,\ell)}{\partial x}} = \frac{df(L)}{dL},$$

we find that

$$\frac{1}{2} = \frac{3}{2}\frac{1}{\sqrt{L}},$$

so that

$$L = 9,$$

which is infeasible. If L = 1, so that $\ell = 0$ and x = y = 3, then

$$\frac{df(L)}{dL} = \frac{3}{2} > \frac{1}{2} = \frac{\partial u(0,3)/\partial \ell}{\partial u(0,3)/\partial x},$$

so that we have a corner solution to the maximization problem. The optimum occurs at this point. The diagram is as follows. The parallel straight lines are indifference curves.

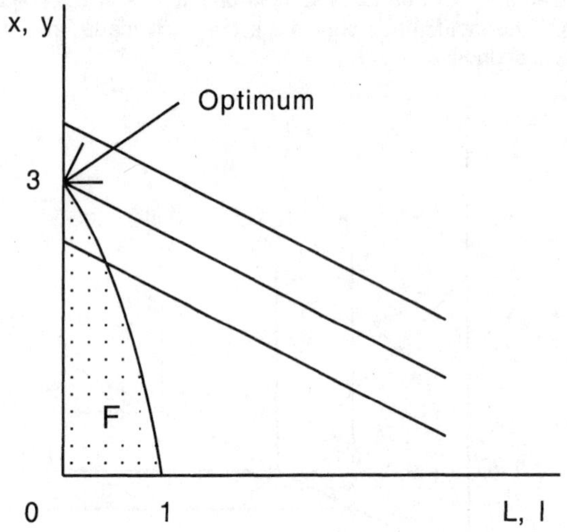

Answer to Homework Problems for Ch 3, Problem #3

Problem: 3) For each of the three following Edgeworth box examples, calculate and draw an accurate picture of the set of

$$V = \{(u_A(\mathbf{x}_A),\ u_B(\mathbf{x}_B)) \mid \mathbf{x}_A \in R^N_+,\ \mathbf{x}_B \in R^N_+,\ \mathbf{x}_A + \mathbf{x}_B = \mathbf{e}_A + \mathbf{e}_B)\}$$

and of

$$\mathcal{U} = \{(v_A, v_B) \mid \text{there is a feasible allocation } (\mathbf{x}_A, \mathbf{x}_B) \text{ such that } v_A \le u_A(\mathbf{x}_A) \text{ and }$$

$$v_B \le u_B(\mathbf{x}_B)\ \}.$$

a) $\mathbf{e}_A = (1, 0)$, $\mathbf{e}_B = (0, 1)$, $u_A(x_1, x_2) = 3x_1 + x_2$, $u_B(x_1, x_2) = x_1 + 3x_2$.

b) $\mathbf{e}_A = (1, 0)$, $\mathbf{e}_B = (0, 1)$, $u_A(x_1, x_2) = \min(x_1, 2x_2)$, $u_B(x_1, x_2) = \min(2x_1, x_2)$.

c) $\mathbf{e}_A = (1, 0)$, $\mathbf{e}_B = (0, 1)$, $u_A(x_1, x_2) = \sqrt{x_1 x_2}$, $u_B(x_1, x_2) = x_1 + 3x_2$.

Answer: a)

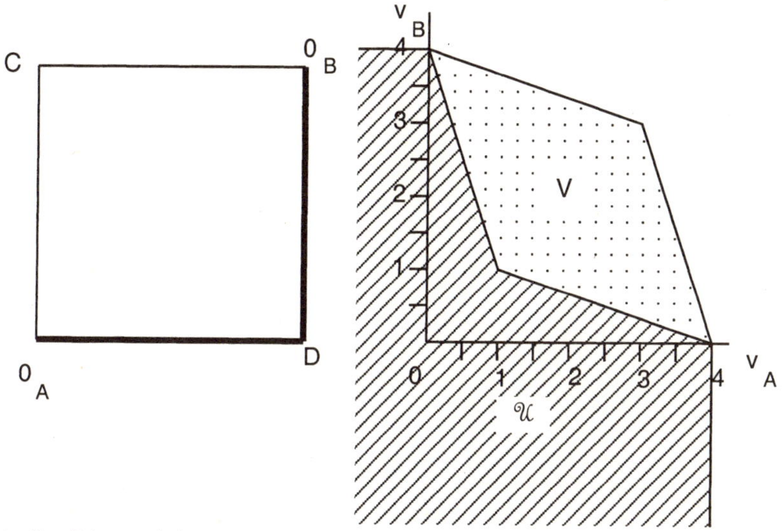

In the Edgeworth box to the left above, the heavy lines mark the set of Pareto optimal allocations. The box maps into the dotted area V at the right in utility space. The point O_A in the box maps to the point (0, 4) in utility space, the point C maps to the point (1, 1), the point 0_B

maps to the point (4, 0), and the point D in the box maps to the point (3, 3). Roughly speaking, the utility vector mapping rotates the Edgeworth box counter clockwise by 90 degrees, squeezes it into the diamond shape and places it on the diamond to the right. The set $\mathcal{U}$ is V together with everything to the southwest of it.

<u>Answer</u>: b)

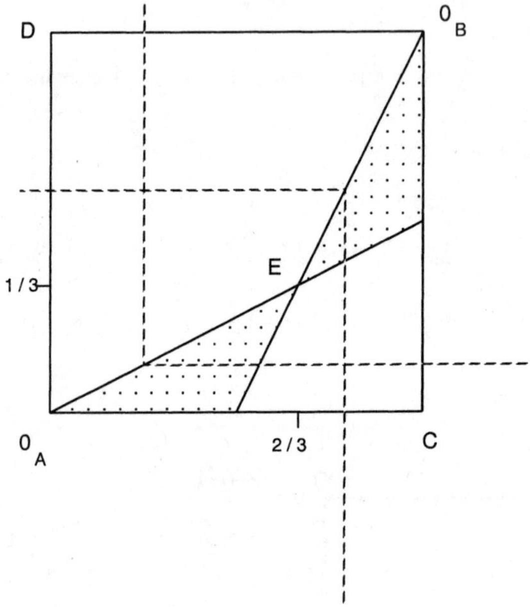

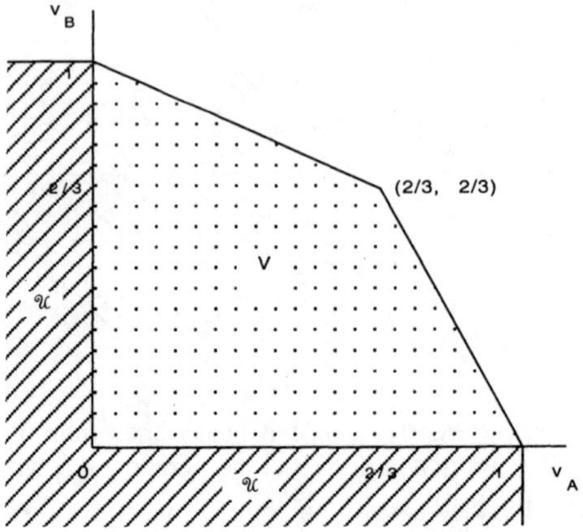

In the Edgeworth box above, the regions shaded with dots form the set of Pareto optimal allocations and the dashed lines are indifference curves. The dotted area in the bottom figure is the image of the box in utility space, the set V. The point E maps to the point (2/3, 2/3) in utility space. The point 0_A maps to the point (0, 1). The point 0_B maps to the point (1, 0). The points C and D map to the point (0, 0) in utility space. The left and bottom edges of the box map to the vertical axis from (0, 0) to (0, 1). The right and top edges map to the horizontal axis from (0, 0) to the point (1, 0). The shaded region from 0_A to E maps to the line from (0, 1) to (2/3, 2/3) in utility space. The shaded region from E to 0_B maps to the line from (2/3, 2/3) to (1, 0) in utility space. The set $\mathcal{U}$ is V together with everything to the southwest of it.

<u>Answer</u>: c)

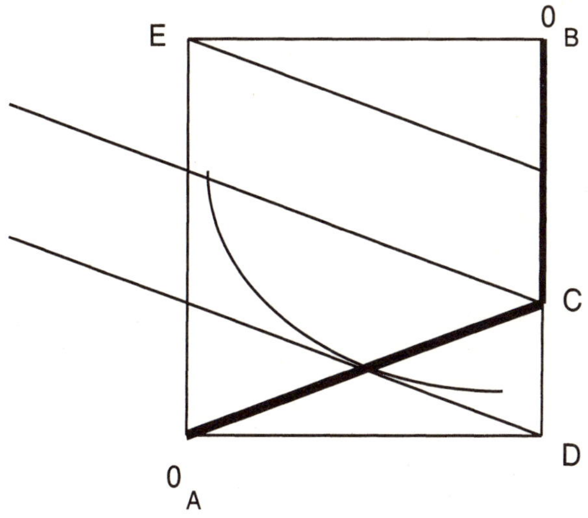

In the Edgeworth box above, the heavy lines mark the set of Pareto optimal allocations and the parallel straight lines are indifference curves for person B. One curved indifference curve is shown for person A. The point C has coordinates (1, 1/3) from the point of view of the origin for person A.

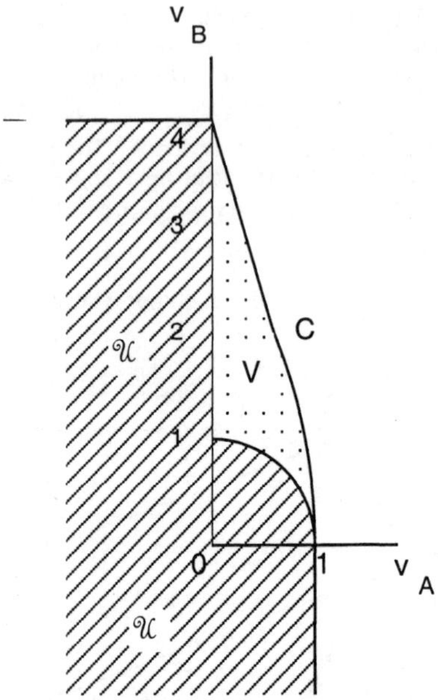

The image of the Edgeworth box is the dotted area V in the above diagram. The point 0_A in the Edgeworth box maps to the point (0, 4) in utility space. The point C maps to the point $(\sqrt{3}/3, 2)$ in utility space, which is labeled again as C. The line from 0_A to C in the box maps to the straight line from (0, 4) to $(\sqrt{3}/3, 2)$ or C in utility space. The right-hand side of the box maps to the curve $v_B = 3 - 3v_A^2$ in utility space going from the point (0, 3) through the point $(\sqrt{3}/3, 2)$ or C to the point (1, 0). The top edge of the box maps to the curve $v_B = 1 - v_A^2$ going from the point (1, 0) to the point (0, 1) in utility space. The bottom edge of the box maps to the straight line going from the point (0, 4) to the point (0, 3) along the vertical axis in utility space. The left-hand edge of the Edgeworth box maps to the straight line from the point (0, 4) to the point (0, 1) along the vertical axis in utility space. The utility possibility set $\mathcal{U}$ is V together with everything to the southwest of V.

In order to calculate the slanted straight line of Pareto optima in the Edgeworth box, use the equations

$$\frac{x_{A2}}{x_{A1}} = \frac{\sqrt{\dfrac{x_{A2}}{x_{A1}}}}{\sqrt{\dfrac{x_{A1}}{x_{A2}}}} = \frac{\partial u_A/\partial x_1}{\partial u_A/\partial x_2} = \frac{\partial u_B/\partial x_1}{\partial u_B/\partial x_2} = \frac{1}{3},$$

so that $x_{A2} = \frac{1}{3} x_{A1}$.

In order to calculate the curve $v_B = 3 - 3v_A^2$, notice that along the line from D to 0_B in the box, the utility of person A is $v_A = \sqrt{x_{A2}}$, and the utility of person B is $v_B = 3x_{B2} = 3(1 - x_{A2}) = 3 - 3v_A^2$. Similarly to calculate the curve $v_B = 1 - v_A^2$, notice that along the top edge of the box the utility of person A $v_A = \sqrt{x_{A2}}$ and the utility of person B is $v_B = x_{B1} = 1 - x_{A1} = 1 - v_A^2$.

In seeing what happens to points on the left-hand and bottom edges of the box, notice that person A has zero utility at every such point, so that it is only necessary to calculate the interval over which the utility of person B varies.

Answer to Homework Problems for Ch 3, Problem #4

Problem: 4) For the Edgeworth box economies listed below: i) find the set of feasible allocations and the set of Pareto optimal allocations and show them on a box diagram, ii) find a Pareto optimal allocation $\overline{\mathbf{x}} = (\overline{\mathbf{x}}_A, \overline{\mathbf{x}}_B)$ that gives the consumers equal utility, that is, is such that $u_A(\overline{\mathbf{x}}_A) = u_B(\overline{\mathbf{x}}_B)$, iii) indicate the endowment allocation $\mathbf{e}$ and the allocation $\overline{\mathbf{x}}$ on the box diagram, iv) find and draw the utility possibility set and indicate the utility vectors corresponding to the endowment allocation and to the allocation $\overline{\mathbf{x}}$, and v) find all vectors of the form $\mathbf{a} = (a_A, a_B)$, such that $\mathbf{a} > 0$ and $a_Au_A(\overline{\mathbf{x}}_A) + a_Bu_B(\overline{\mathbf{x}}_B) \geq a_Au_A(\mathbf{x}_A) + a_Bu_B(\mathbf{x}_B)$, for all feasible allocations $\mathbf{x} = (\mathbf{x}_A, \mathbf{x}_B)$.

a) $\mathbf{e}_A = (1, 0)$, $\mathbf{e}_B = (0, 1)$, $u_A(x_1, x_2) = \sqrt{x_1x_2} = u_B(x_1, x_2)$.

b) $\mathbf{e}_A = (0, 1)$, $\mathbf{e}_B = (1, 0)$, $u_A(x_1, x_2) = 2x_1 + x_2$, $u_B(x_1, x_2) = x_1 + 2x_2$.

c) $\mathbf{e}_A = (2, 0)$, $\mathbf{e}_B = (0, 1)$, $u_A(x_1, x_2) = x_1 + x_2 = u_B(x_1, x_2)$.

d) $\mathbf{e}_A = (1, 0)$, $\mathbf{e}_B = (0, 1)$, $u_A(x_1, x_2) = \min(2x_1, x_2)$, $u_B(x_1, x_2) = \min(x_1, 2x_2)$.

e) $\mathbf{e}_A = (1, 0)$, $\mathbf{e}_B = (0, 2)$, $u_A(x_1, x_2) = \min(x_1, x_2) = u_B(x_1, x_2)$.

Answer: a)

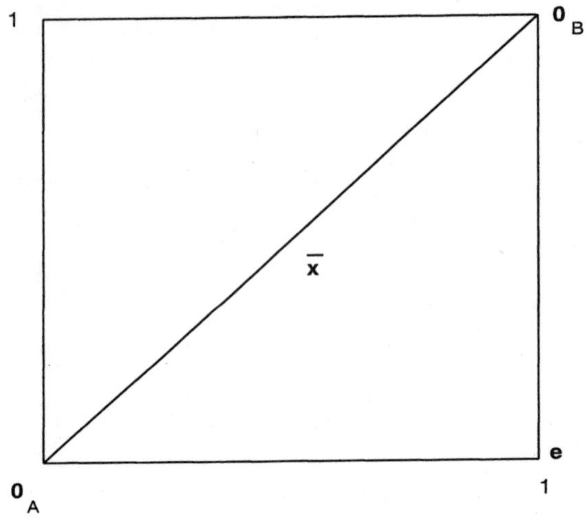

i) The set of feasible allocations is the box above. The set of Pareto optimal allocations is the diagonal, because both consumers have the same homothetic utility function. ii) The Pareto optimal allocation $\overline{\mathbf{x}}$ that gives both consumers the same utility is $(\overline{x}_A, \overline{x}_B) = ((1/2, 1/2), (1/2, 1/2))$. iii) The allocation $\overline{\mathbf{x}}$ is at the center of the box, and the endowment allocation, $\mathbf{e}$, is at the lower right-hand corner of the box. iv) The utility possibility set $\mathcal{U}$ is all the points on the line segment going from (1, 0) to (0, 1) in the diagram below together with all the points southwest of that line segment. The utility vector of the endowment allocation is at the origin and that of the allocation $\bar{\mathbf{x}}$ is at the midpoint of the line segment.

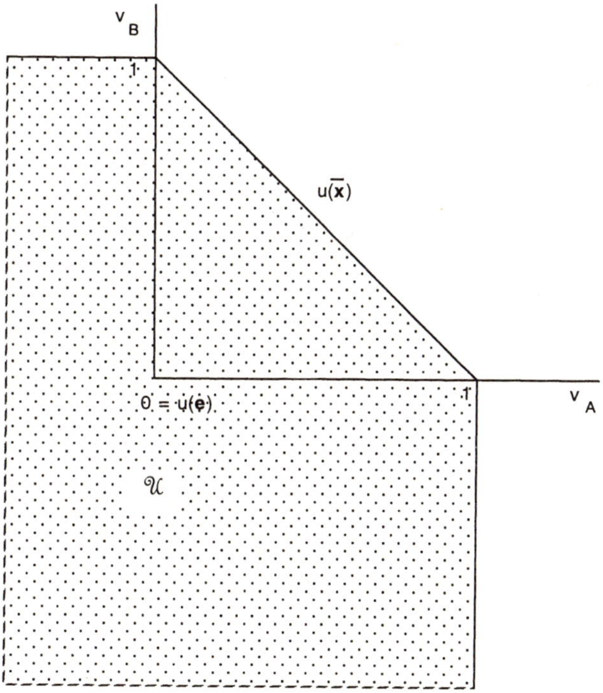

v) $\{\mathbf{a} = (a_A, a_B) \in R^2_+ \mid a_A = a_B > 0\}$.

Answer: b)

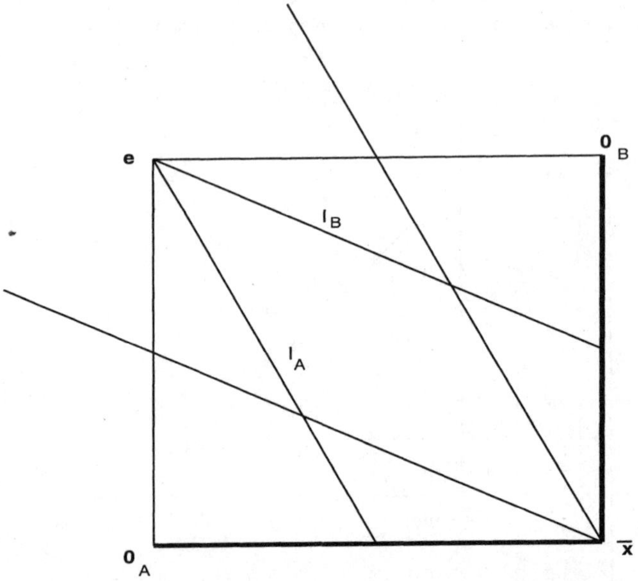

i) The set of feasible allocations is the box shown above. The Pareto optimal allocations are the thick lines at the bottom and right-hand edges of the box. Indifference curves of person A and B are indicated as I_A and I_B, respectively. ii) The allocation $\bar{\mathbf{x}}$ is at the lower right-hand corner of the box. iii) The endowment allocation is at the upper left-hand corner of the box. iv) The utility possibility frontier is the line going from the point (0, 3) to (2, 2) to (3, 0) in the diagram below. The utility possibility set $\mathcal{U}$ is everything on this frontier and southwest of it. The utility vector of $\bar{\mathbf{x}}$ is at (2, 2), and the utility vector of the endowment, $\mathbf{e}$, is at (1, 1).

iv)

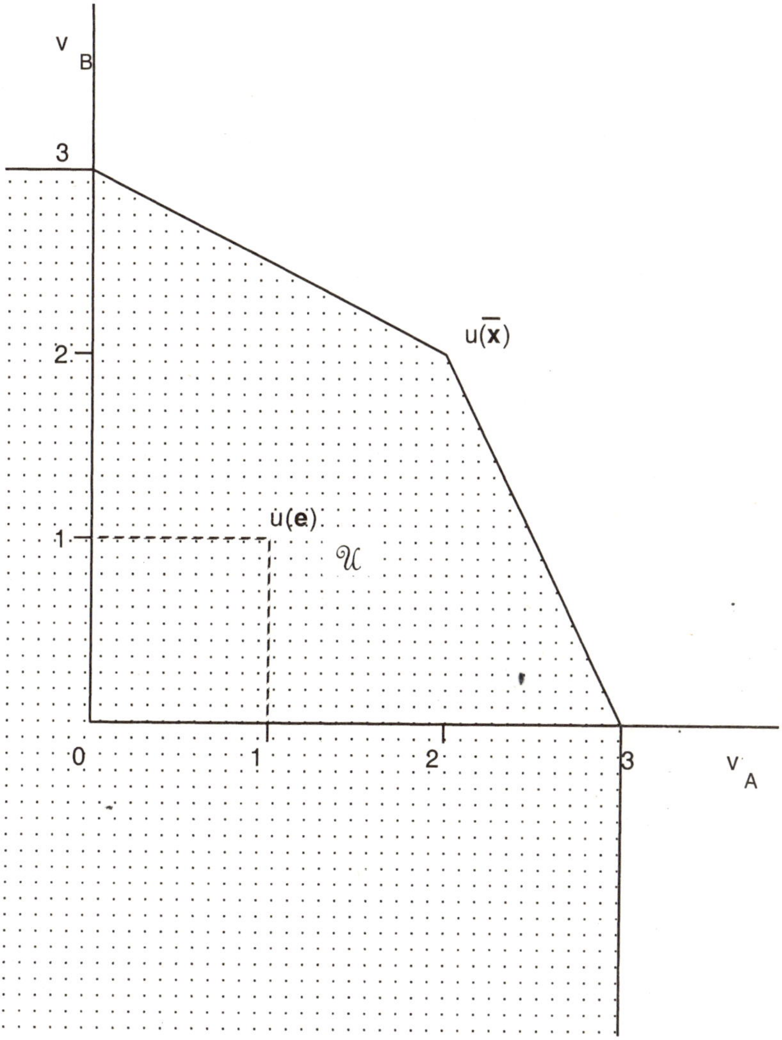

v) $\{(a_A, a_B) \mid (a_A, a_B) >> 0 \text{ and } \frac{1}{2} \leq \frac{a_A}{a_B} \leq 2\}$.

c) i) The set of feasible allocations is the whole box in the diagram below, as is the set of Pareto optimal allocations. (Because the consumers have the same linear utility functions, their indifference curves are tangent at every point in the box.) Indifference curves are straight lines of slope minus one. ii) An allocation giving the same utility to each consumer is $\bar{\mathbf{x}}$, where $\bar{\mathbf{x}}_A = (1, 1/2) = \bar{\mathbf{x}}_B$. iii) The allocation $\bar{\mathbf{x}}$ is at the center of the box in the diagram. The endowment allocation **e** is at the lower right-hand corner of the box.

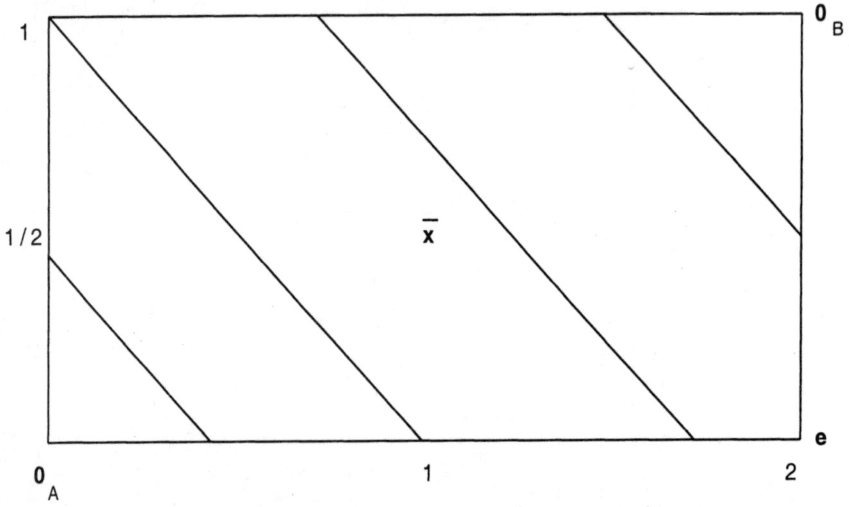

iv) The utility possibility frontier is line going from (0, 3) to (3, 0) in the diagram below. The utility possibility set $\mathcal{U}$ is everything on this frontier and southwest of it. The utility vectors corresponding to **e** and to $\bar{\mathbf{x}}$ are as indicated; $u(\mathbf{e}) = (2, 1)$; and $u(\bar{\mathbf{x}}) = (3/2, 3/2)$.

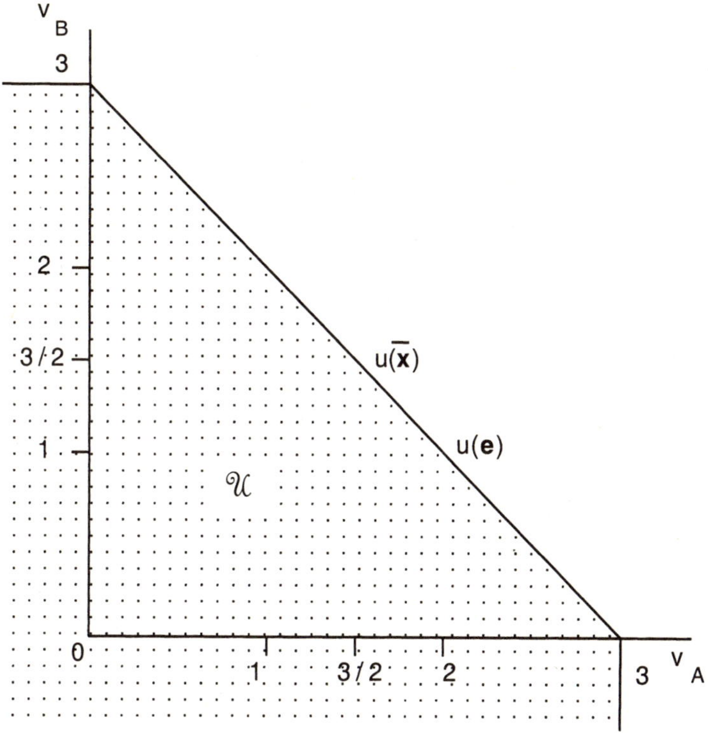

v) $\{\mathbf{a} = (a_A, a_B) \in R^2_+ \mid a_A = a_B > 0\}$.

Answer: d)

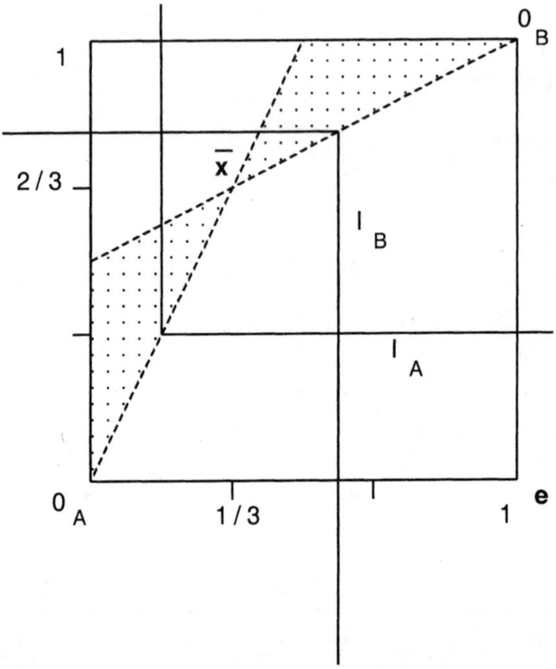

i) The set of feasible allocations is the box in the above diagram. The set of Pareto optimal allocations is shaded with dots. Sample indifference curves for persons A and B are labeled as I_A and I_B, respectively. The Pareto optimal allocation giving each consumer the same utility is $\bar{\mathbf{x}} = (\bar{\mathbf{x}}_A, \bar{\mathbf{x}}_B) = ((1/3, 2/3), (2/3, 1/3))$. It is shown in the box, as is the endowment allocation **e**. iv) The utility possibility set $\mathcal{U}$ is as shown in the diagram below.

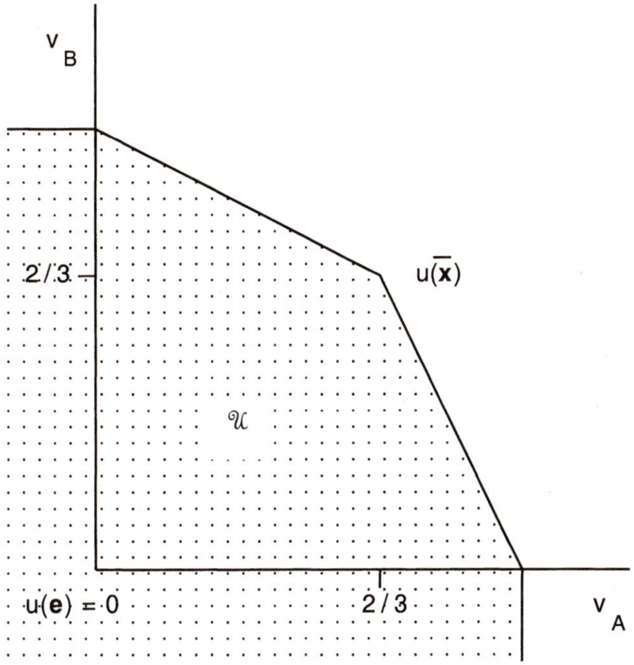

v) $\{(a_A, a_B) \mid (a_A, a_B) \gg 0 \text{ and } \frac{1}{2} \leq \frac{a_A}{a_B} \leq 2\}$.

Answer: e)

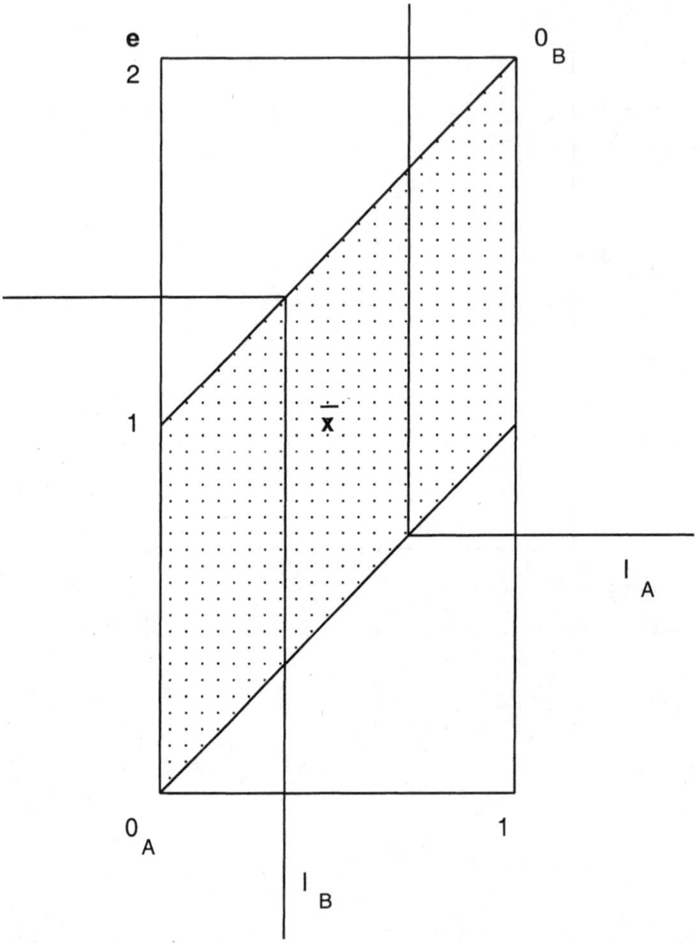

i) The set of feasible allocations is the box in the above diagram. The set of Pareto optimal allocations is the region in the box shaded with dots. Sample indifference curves for person A and B and labeled as I_A and I_B, respectively. ii) The allocation $\bar{\mathbf{x}}$ is the allocation $\bar{\mathbf{x}}_A = \bar{\mathbf{x}}_B = (1/2, 1)$. iii) $\bar{\mathbf{x}}$ and **e** are as indicated in the box diagram. iv) The utility possibility set $\mathcal{U}$ is as shown in the diagram below.

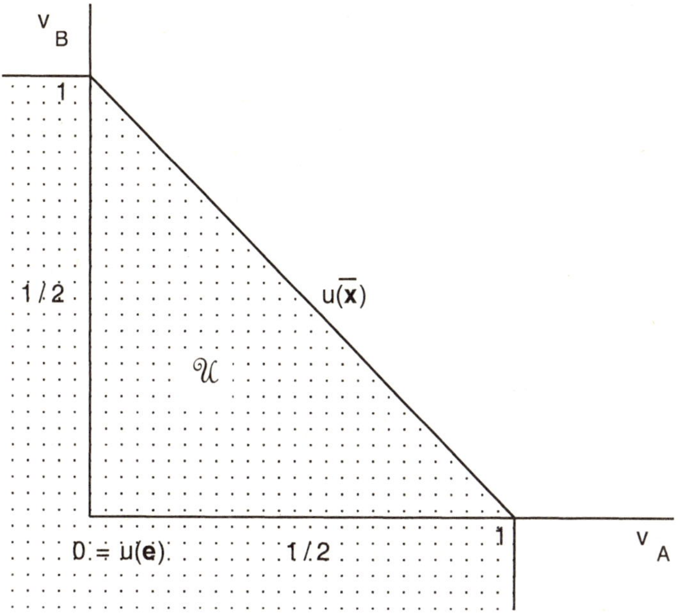

v B
1
1 / 2
u(x̄)
𝒰
0 = u(e)
1 / 2
1
v A

Answer to Homework Problems for Ch 3, Problem #5

Problem: 5) For the Edgeworth box economies listed below find a number a_B such that the Pareto optimal allocation with $x_{A1} = 1/2$ maximizes the welfare function $u_A(x_{A1}, x_{A2}) + a_B u_B(x_{B1}, x_{B2})$ among all feasible allocations.

a) $\mathbf{e}_A = (1, 0)$, $\mathbf{e}_B = (0, 1)$, $u_A(x_1, x_2) = 2\sqrt{x_1} + \sqrt{x_2}$, $u_B(x_1, x_2) = x_1 + 2x_2$.

b) $\mathbf{e}_A = (1, 0)$, $\mathbf{e}_B = (0, 1)$, $u_A(x_1, x_2) = x_1^{1/3}x_2^{2/3}$, $u_B(x_1, x_2) = \sqrt{x_1 x_2}$.

Answer: a) At the Pareto optimal allocation **x**,

$$a_B = \frac{\partial u_A(\mathbf{x}_A)/\partial x_1}{\partial u_B(\mathbf{x}_B)/\partial x_1} = \frac{1/\sqrt{x_{A1}}}{1} = \frac{1}{\sqrt{x_{A1}}} = \frac{1}{\sqrt{1/2}} = \sqrt{2}.$$

b) In order to do this problem, we first find the Pareto optimal allocation using the specification $x_{A1} = 1/2$ and the equation

$$\frac{\partial u_A(\mathbf{x}_A)/\partial x_1}{\partial u_A(\mathbf{x}_A)/\partial x_2} = \frac{\partial u_B(\mathbf{e}_A + \mathbf{e}_B - \mathbf{x}_A)/\partial x_1}{\partial u_B(\mathbf{e}_A + \mathbf{e}_B - \mathbf{x}_A)/\partial x_2}.$$

This equation becomes

$$\frac{\frac{1}{3}\left(\frac{x_{A2}}{x_{A1}}\right)^{2/3}}{\frac{2}{3}\left(\frac{x_{A1}}{x_{A2}}\right)^{1/3}} = \frac{\frac{1}{2}\sqrt{\frac{1-x_{A2}}{1-x_{A1}}}}{\frac{1}{2}\sqrt{\frac{1-x_{A1}}{1-x_{A2}}}},$$

which is

$$\frac{1}{2}\frac{x_{A2}}{x_{A1}} = \frac{1-x_{A2}}{1-x_{A1}}.$$

Hence

$$x_{A2} - x_{A1}x_{A2} = 2x_{A1} - 2x_{A1}x_{A2},$$

so that

$$x_{A2} + x_{A1}x_{A2} = 2x_{A1}$$

and so

$$x_{A2} = \frac{2x_{A1}}{1 + x_{A1}} = \frac{1}{3/2} = \frac{2}{3}.$$

Therefore

$$x_{B1} = \frac{1}{2} \text{ and } x_{B2} = \frac{1}{3}.$$

Now we may compute a_B as follows.

$$a_B = \frac{\partial u_A(x_A)/\partial x_1}{\partial u_B(x_B)/\partial x_1} = \frac{\frac{1}{3}\left(\frac{x_{A2}}{x_{A1}}\right)^{2/3}}{\frac{1}{2}\sqrt{\frac{x_{B2}}{x_{B1}}}} = \frac{2}{3}\frac{\left(\frac{2/3}{1/2}\right)^{2/3}}{\left(\frac{1/3}{1/2}\right)^{1/2}} = \frac{2^{11/6}}{3^{7/6}}.$$

Answer to Homework Problems for Ch 3, Problem #6

Problem: 6) Let $\mathbf{y} \in R^N$. Prove that $||\mathbf{x} - \mathbf{y}||$ is a continuous function of $\mathbf{x}$. (Hint: Use the triangle inequality. That is, use the fact that $||\mathbf{x} + \mathbf{y}|| \leq ||\mathbf{x}|| + ||\mathbf{y}||$.)

Answer: By the triangle inequality,

$$||\mathbf{x}' - \mathbf{y}|| = ||\mathbf{x}' - \mathbf{x} + \mathbf{x} - \mathbf{y}|| \leq ||\mathbf{x}' - \mathbf{x}|| + ||\mathbf{x} - \mathbf{y}||,$$

so that

$$||\mathbf{x}' - \mathbf{y}|| - ||\mathbf{x} - \mathbf{y}|| \leq ||\mathbf{x}' - \mathbf{x}||. \qquad \text{A)}$$

Similarly

$$||\mathbf{x} - \mathbf{y}|| = ||\mathbf{x} - \mathbf{x}' + \mathbf{x}' - \mathbf{y}|| \leq ||\mathbf{x} - \mathbf{x}'|| + ||\mathbf{x}' - \mathbf{y}||,$$

so that

$$||\mathbf{x} - \mathbf{y}|| - ||\mathbf{x}' - \mathbf{y}|| \leq ||\mathbf{x} - \mathbf{x}'|| = ||\mathbf{x}' - \mathbf{x}||. \qquad \text{B)}$$

Inequalities A and B imply that

$$\big|\,||\mathbf{x}' - \mathbf{y}|| - ||\mathbf{x} - \mathbf{y}||\,\big| \leq ||\mathbf{x}' - \mathbf{x}||$$

and hence that

$$\lim_{\mathbf{x}' \to \mathbf{x}} ||\mathbf{x}' - \mathbf{y}|| = ||\mathbf{x} - \mathbf{y}||.$$

That is, $||\mathbf{x} - \mathbf{y}||$ is a continuous function of $\mathbf{x}$.

Answer to Homework Problems for Chapter 3, Problem #7

Problem: 7) Prove if that $\mathbf{y} \in R^N$ and C is a closed set in R^N, then there is a point in C that is closest to $\mathbf{y}$, that is, there is a vector $\mathbf{z} \in C$ such that $||\mathbf{y} - \mathbf{z}|| \leq ||\mathbf{y} - \mathbf{x}||$, for all $\mathbf{x} \in C$.

Answer: Let $\underline{\mathbf{x}}$ be an arbitrary member of C and let

$$K = \{\mathbf{x} \in C \mid ||\mathbf{y} - \mathbf{x}|| \leq ||\mathbf{y} - \underline{\mathbf{x}}||\}.$$

K is closed and bounded and so is compact. By the previous problem, the function $||\mathbf{y} - \mathbf{x}||$ is continuous with respect to $\mathbf{x}$. Therefore the problem

$$\min_{\mathbf{x} \in K} ||\mathbf{y} - \mathbf{x}||$$

has a solution, $\overline{\mathbf{x}}$. Then $\overline{\mathbf{x}}$ solves the problem

$$\min_{\mathbf{x} \in C} ||\mathbf{y} - \mathbf{x}||,$$

since any point in C that is not in K is at least as far from $\mathbf{y}$ as is $\overline{\mathbf{x}}$.

Answer to Homework Problems for Chapter 3, Problem #8

Problem: 8) Suppose that C is convex and closed. You know from the previous problem #7 that if the vector **y** in R^N does not belong to C, then there is a vector **z** in C which is closest to **y**. Let **x** be a vector in C not equal to **z**.

a) Show that $\left.\frac{d}{dt}||\mathbf{y} - [\mathbf{z} + t(\mathbf{x} - \mathbf{z})]||^2\right|_{t=0} \geq 0$, where the notation means that the derivative is evaluated at t = 0.

b) Use part (a) to show that $(\mathbf{y} - \mathbf{z}).\mathbf{z} \geq (\mathbf{y} - \mathbf{z}).\mathbf{x}$, for all **x** in C.

c) Use part (b) to show that $(\mathbf{y} - \mathbf{z}).\mathbf{y} > (\mathbf{y} - \mathbf{z}).\mathbf{x}$, for all **x** in C.

You have shown that if C is compact and convex and **y** does not belong to C, then there exists a non-zero N-vector **w** such that $\mathbf{w}.\mathbf{y} > \mathbf{w}.\mathbf{x}$, for all **x** in C. This is a special case of the Minkowski separation theorem.

Answer: a) If $0 \leq t \leq 1$, then $\mathbf{z} + t(\mathbf{x} - \mathbf{z})$ belongs to C, since C is convex. Because **z** is the point in C closest to **y**,

$$||\mathbf{y} - [\mathbf{z} + t(\mathbf{x} - \mathbf{z})]|| \geq ||\mathbf{y} - \mathbf{z}||,$$

if $0 \leq t \leq 1$. Therefore

$$||\mathbf{y} - [\mathbf{z} + t(\mathbf{x} - \mathbf{z})]||^2 \geq ||\mathbf{y} - \mathbf{z}||^2,$$

if $0 \leq t \leq 1$. Therefore

$$\frac{||\mathbf{y} - [\mathbf{z} + t(\mathbf{x} - \mathbf{z})]||^2 - ||\mathbf{y} - \mathbf{z}||^2}{t} \geq 0,$$

if $0 < t \leq 1$, and hence

$$\left.\frac{d}{dt}||\mathbf{y} - [\mathbf{z} + t(\mathbf{x} - \mathbf{z})]||^2\right|_{t=0}$$

$$= \left.\frac{d}{dt}\left(||\mathbf{y} - [\mathbf{z} + t(\mathbf{x} - \mathbf{z})]||^2 - ||\mathbf{y} - \mathbf{z}||^2\right)\right|_{t=0}$$

$$= \lim_{t \to 0}\frac{||\mathbf{y} - [\mathbf{z} + t(\mathbf{x} - \mathbf{z})]||^2 - ||\mathbf{y} - \mathbf{z}||^2}{t} \geq 0,$$

b) If **x** belongs to C, then

$$||\mathbf{y} - [\mathbf{z} + t(\mathbf{x} - \mathbf{z})]||^2$$

$$= \{\mathbf{y} - [\mathbf{z} + t(\mathbf{x} - \mathbf{z})]\}.\{\mathbf{y} - [\mathbf{z} + t(\mathbf{x} - \mathbf{z})]\}$$

$$= \mathbf{y}.\mathbf{y} - 2t\mathbf{y}.\mathbf{z} - 2t\mathbf{y}.(\mathbf{x} - \mathbf{z}) + \mathbf{z}.\mathbf{z} + 2t\mathbf{z}.(\mathbf{x} - \mathbf{z}) + t^2(\mathbf{x} - \mathbf{z}).(\mathbf{x} - \mathbf{z}).$$

Therefore

$$0 \le \frac{d}{dt}||\mathbf{y} - [\mathbf{z} + t(\mathbf{x} - \mathbf{z})]||^2\Big|_{t=0}$$

$$= \left(-2\mathbf{y}.(\mathbf{x} - \mathbf{z}) + 2\mathbf{z}.(\mathbf{x} - \mathbf{z}) + 2t(\mathbf{x} - \mathbf{z}).(\mathbf{x} - \mathbf{z})\right)\Big|_{t=0}$$

$$= 2(\mathbf{z} - \mathbf{y}).(\mathbf{x} - \mathbf{z}).$$

It follows that

$$\mathbf{x}.(\mathbf{z} - \mathbf{y}) \ge \mathbf{z}.(\mathbf{z} - \mathbf{y})$$

and hence

$$(\mathbf{y} - \mathbf{z}).\mathbf{z} \ge (\mathbf{y} - \mathbf{z}).\mathbf{x}.$$

c) Since **y** does not belong to C, $\mathbf{y} \neq \mathbf{z}$. Therefore

$$(\mathbf{y} - \mathbf{z}).(\mathbf{y} - \mathbf{z}) > 0,$$

and hence

$$(\mathbf{y} - \mathbf{z}).\mathbf{y} > (\mathbf{y} - \mathbf{z}).\mathbf{z} \ge (\mathbf{y} - \mathbf{z}).\mathbf{x},$$

for all **x** in C, where the second inequality follows from part b.

Answer to Homework Problems for Chapter 4, Problem #1

Problem: 1) Solve

$$\max_{x_1 \geq 0,\, x_2 \geq 0} \left(\sqrt{x_1} + \sqrt{x_2}\right)^2$$

$$\text{s.t. } p_1 x_1 + p_2 x_2 = w.$$

Answer: The solution is not changed if we replace the objective function with the following monotone transformation of it

$$2\sqrt{x_1} + 2\sqrt{x_2},$$

so that the problem becomes

$$\max_{x_1 \geq 0,\, x_2 \geq 0} \left[2\sqrt{x_1} + 2\sqrt{x_2}\right]$$

$$\text{s.t. } p_1 x_1 + p_2 x_2 = w.$$

The Lagrangian for this problem is

$$\mathcal{L}(x_1, x_2, \lambda) = 2\sqrt{x_1} + 2\sqrt{x_2} - \lambda[p_1 x_1 + p_2 x_2].$$

From this, we see immediately that the first order conditions are

$$\frac{1}{\sqrt{x_1}} = \lambda p_1 \text{ and } \frac{1}{\sqrt{x_2}} = \lambda p_2.$$

Dividing the first of these equations by the second, we obtain

$$\frac{\sqrt{x_2}}{\sqrt{x_1}} = \frac{p_1}{p_2},$$

and hence

$$\frac{x_2}{x_1} = \frac{p_1^2}{p_2^2},$$

which is the same as

$$x_2 = \frac{p_1^2}{p_2^2} x_1 .$$

Substituting this equation into the budget equation, we obtain

$$p_1 x_1 + \frac{p_1^2}{p_2} x_1 = w,$$

so that

$$x_1 = \frac{wp_2}{p_1 p_2 + p_1^2} .$$

By symmetry,

$$x_2 = \frac{wp_1}{p_1 p_2 + p_2^2} .$$

Answer to Homework Problems for Chapter 4, Problem #2

Problem: 2) Calculate a consumer's demand for goods 1 and 2 as a function of p_1 and p_2, the prices of goods 1 and 2, respectively, when the consumer's utility function and initial endowment are as below. Draw the offer curve in each case.

a) $u(x_1, x_2) = x_1^5 x_2^2$, $\mathbf{e} = (10, 0)$,

b) $u(x_1, x_2) = \min(5x_1, 2x_2)$, $\mathbf{e} = (10, 0)$,

c) $u(x_1, x_2) = 5x_1 + 2x_2$, $\mathbf{e} = (10, 0)$,

d) $u(x_1, x_2) = \ln(x_1) + \ln(x_2)$, $\mathbf{e} = (1, 1)$.

Answer: a) Since the utility function is Cobb-Douglas,

$$p_1 x_1 = \frac{5}{7} w = \frac{5}{7}(10)\, p_1 = \frac{50}{7} p_1.$$

Therefore, if p_1 is positive, .

$$x_1 = \frac{50}{7}.$$

Similarly

$$p_2 x_2 = \frac{2}{7} 10 p_1 = \frac{20}{7} p_1,$$

so that

$$x_2 = \frac{20}{7} \frac{p_1}{p_2}.$$

If $p_1 = 0$, then demand is any point on the horizontal axis to the right of zero. If $p_2 = 0$, then demand is not defined.

The offer curve consists of the heavy lines in the diagram below.

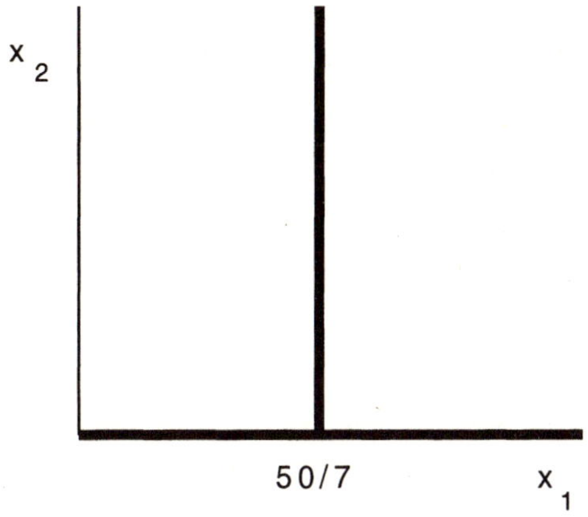

b) Since the utility function is Leontief, we need only solve the two simultaneous linear equations

$$p_1x_1 + p_2x_2 = 10p_1$$

and

$$x_2 = \frac{5}{2}x_1.$$

The solutions of these equations are

$$x_1 = \frac{20p_1}{2p_1 + 5p_2} \text{ and } x_2 = \frac{50p_1}{2p_1 + 5p_2}.$$

The offer curve is the heavy jagged line in the diagram below.

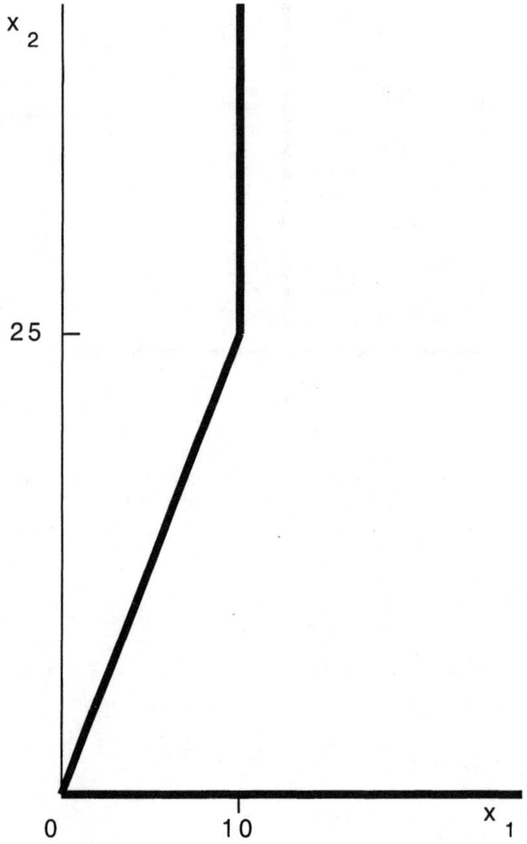

c) Suppose that both prices are positive.

If $\frac{p_2}{p_1} > \frac{2}{5}$, then $x_1 = 10$, $x_2 = 0$.

If $\frac{p_2}{p_1} = \frac{2}{5}$, demand is the set $\{(x_1, x_2) \in R^2_+ \mid 5x_1 + 2x_2 = 10\}$.

If $\frac{p_2}{p_1} < \frac{2}{5}$, $x_1 = 0$, $x_2 = \frac{10p_1}{p_2}$.

If either price is zero, demand is not defined.

The offer curve is the heavy jagged line below.

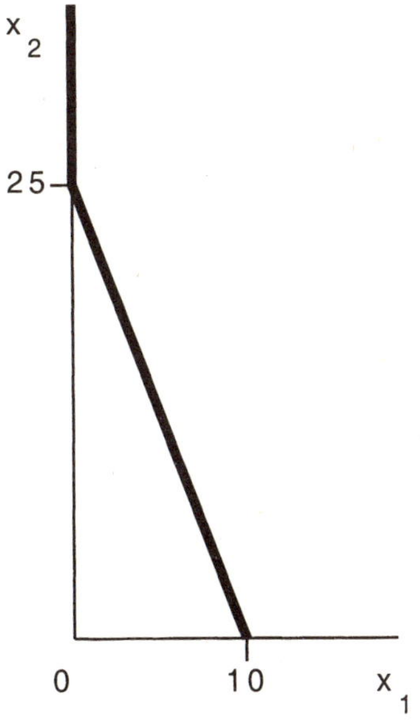

d) If either price is zero, then demand is undefined. So suppose that both prices are positive. Because the utility function is Cobb-Douglas, we know immediately that

$$x_1 = \frac{p_1 + p_2}{2p_1} \text{ and } x_2 = \frac{p_1 + p_2}{2p_2}.$$

We may normalize the price of commodity 1 to be 1. Substituting 1 for p_1 in the equations for x_1 and x_2, we see that

$$x_1 = \frac{1 + p_2}{2} \text{ and } x_2 = \frac{1 + p_2}{2p_2}.$$

Solving the first of these equations for p_2, we find that

$$p_2 = 2x_1 - 1 .$$

Subsituting this equation into that for x_2, we see that

$$x_2 = \frac{x_1}{2x_1 - 1}.$$

If we solve this equation for x_1, we obtain the expected symmetric expression

$$x_1 = \frac{x_2}{2x_2 - 1}.$$

Both of the last two equations express the offer curve. The curve goes through the point (1, 1) and has as asymptotes the vertical line $x_1 = 1/2$ and the horizontal line $x_2 = 1/2$. We can obtain a more easily recognized formula for the offer curve by calculating that

$$x_2 - \frac{1}{2} = \frac{x_1}{2x_1 - 1} - \frac{1}{2} = \frac{2x_1 - 2x_1 + 1}{4x_1 - 2} = \frac{1}{2}\frac{1}{2x_1 - 1}.$$

Since

$$x_1 - \frac{1}{2} = \frac{1}{2}(2x_1 - 1),$$

it follows that

$$\left(x_1 - \frac{1}{2}\right)\left(x_2 - \frac{1}{2}\right) = \frac{1}{4}.$$

That is, the offer curve is a hyperbola with origin at (1/2, 1/2). The curve looks roughly as in the diagram below.

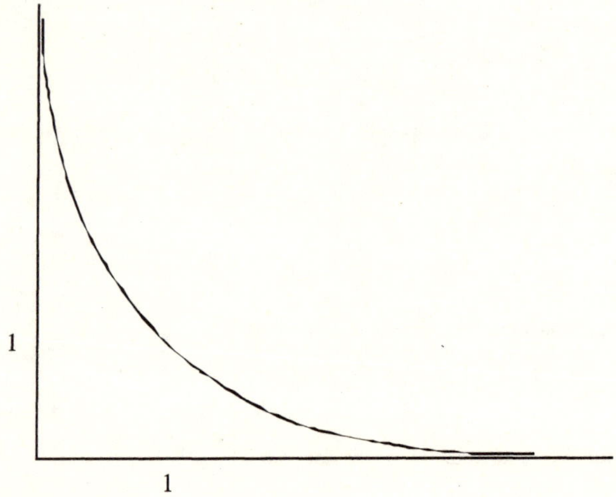

Answer to Homework Problems for Chapter 4, Problem #3

Problem: 3) Suppose that the production function for good 3 is

$$y_3 = \left(\sqrt{-y_1} + \sqrt{-y_2}\right)^2,$$

where commodities 1 and 2 are the inputs, $y_1 \le 0$, and $y_2 \le 0$. Let $\mathbf{p} = (p_1, p_2, p_3)$ be the vector of prices of the three commodities, where $\mathbf{p} >> \mathbf{0}$.

a) For what price vectors $\mathbf{p}$ is $\pi(\mathbf{p}) < \infty$, where $\pi(\mathbf{p})$ is the supremum of the possible profits?

b) Find $\pi(\mathbf{p})$ and $\eta(\mathbf{p})$, for all price vectors, where $\eta(\mathbf{p})$ is the set of profit maximizing input-output vectors.

Answer: If $y_2 < 0$, then the derivative of the objective or profit function approaches minus infinity as y_1 approaches zero. That is,

$$\lim_{y_1 \to 0} \frac{d}{dy_1}[p_3(\sqrt{-y_1} + \sqrt{-y_2})^2 + p_1y_1 + p_2y_2]$$

$$= -\lim_{y_1 \to 0}\left[p_3\left(1 + \frac{\sqrt{-y_2}}{\sqrt{-y_1}}\right)^2 + p_1\right] = -\infty,$$

so that the optimal value of y_1 must be negative. Symmetrically, if $y_1 < 0$, then $y_2 < 0$. Therefore either $(y_1, y_2) = 0$ or $(y_1, y_2) << 0$. Suppose that $(y_1, y_2) << 0$. Then the first order conditions of the profit maximization problem

$$\max_{y_1 \le 0,\, y_2 \le 0} \left[p_3(\sqrt{-y_1} + \sqrt{-y_2})^2 + p_1y_1 + p_2y_2\right]$$

are

$$-p_3\left(\frac{\sqrt{-y_1} + \sqrt{-y_2}}{\sqrt{-y_1}}\right) + p_1 = 0$$

and

$$-p_3\left(\frac{\sqrt{-y_1}+\sqrt{-y_2}}{\sqrt{-y_2}}\right)+p_2=0.$$

Hence

$$p_1\sqrt{-y_1}=p_3\left[\sqrt{-y_1}+\sqrt{-y_2}\right]$$

and

$$p_2\sqrt{-y_2}=p_3\left[\sqrt{-y_1}+\sqrt{-y_2}\right]$$

and

$$p_1\sqrt{-y_1}=p_2\sqrt{-y_2}.$$

That is,

$$\sqrt{-y_2}=\frac{p_1}{p_2}\sqrt{-y_1} \qquad \text{(A)}$$

and

$$y_2=\left(\frac{p_1}{p_2}\right)^2 y_1. \qquad \text{(B)}$$

Also

$$(p_1-p_3)\sqrt{-y_1}=p_3\sqrt{-y_2} \text{ and } (p_2-p_3)\sqrt{-y_2}=p_3\sqrt{-y_1},$$

and so

$$\frac{p_1-p_3}{p_3}=\sqrt{\frac{y_2}{y_1}}=\frac{p_3}{p_2-p_3}.$$

That is,

$$p_1p_2-p_1p_3-p_2p_3+p_3^2=p_3^2,$$

so that

$$p_3(p_1+p_2)=p_1p_2.$$

In conclusion,

$$p_3 = \frac{p_1 p_2}{p_1 + p_2}.$$

Substituting equations A and B into the profit function, we see that

$$p_3\left(\sqrt{-y_1} + \sqrt{-y_2}\right)^2 + p_1 y_1 + p_2 y_2$$

$$= p_3\left[\sqrt{-y_1}\left(1 + \frac{p_1}{p_2}\right)\right]^2 + p_1 y_1 + \frac{p_1^2}{p_2} y_1$$

$$= -p_3\left(\frac{p_1 + p_2}{p_2}\right)^2 y_1 + \frac{p_1(p_1 + p_2)}{p_2} y_1$$

$$= \left(\frac{p_1 + p_2}{p_2}\right)^2\left(-p_3 + \frac{p_1 p_2}{p_1 + p_2}\right) y_1 = 0,$$

since

$$p_3 = \frac{p_1 p_2}{p_1 + p_2},$$

and so maximum profit is zero.

Suppose that

$$p_3 > \frac{p_1 p_2}{p_1 + p_2}.$$

Fix output at some positive level v^2 and minimize the cost of producing that output. That is, solve the problem

$$\min_{y_1 \le 0,\, y_2 \le 0} (p_1 y_1 + p_2 y_2)$$

$$\text{s.t.} \ \sqrt{-y_1} + \sqrt{-y_2} \ge v.$$

The first order conditions of this problem are

$$p_1\sqrt{-y_1} = p_2\sqrt{-y_2}.$$

This condition implies equations A and B. After substituting these equations into the profit function, it becomes

$$p_3\left(\sqrt{-y_1} + \sqrt{-y_2}\right)^2 + p_1y_1 + p_2y_2$$

$$= \left(\frac{p_1 + p_2}{p_2}\right)^2\left(-p_3 + \frac{p_1p_2}{p_1 + p_2}\right)y_1,$$

as before. Since

$$p_3 > \frac{p_1p_2}{p_1 + p_2} \text{ and } y_1 < 0,$$

it follows that

$$\left(\frac{p_1 + p_2}{p_2}\right)^2\left(-p_3 + \frac{p_1p_2}{p_1 + p_2}\right)y_1 > 0,$$

and hence that profits are positive. Since the production function exhibits constant returns to scale, profits can be made arbitrarily large simply by multiplying y_1, y_2, and $y_3 = \left(\sqrt{-y_1} + \sqrt{-y_2}\right)^2$ by an arbitrarily large positive number t. Therefore $\pi(\mathbf{p}) = \infty$.

Suppose that

$$p_3 < \frac{p_1p_2}{p_1 + p_2}.$$

Again solve the problem

$$\min_{y_1 \le 0,\, y_2 \le 0} (p_1y_1 + p_2y_2)$$

$$\text{s.t. } \sqrt{-y_1} + \sqrt{-y_2} \ge v,$$

for some positive output level v, obtaining input levels $y_1 < 0$ and $y_2 < 0$. The first order conditions for this problem again imply that profit equals

$$\left(\frac{p_1 + p_2}{p_2}\right)^2\left(-p_3 + \frac{p_1 p_2}{p_1 + p_2}\right)y_1,$$

which is negative, since

$$p_3 < \frac{p_1 p_2}{p_1 + p_2} \text{ and } y_1 < 0.$$

Therefore the maximum profit is obtained by producing zero output from zero input. That is, $\pi(\mathbf{p}) = 0$.

We are now in a position to answer parts a and b of the problem.

Answer to a: $\pi(\mathbf{p})$ is finite if

$$p_3 \leq \frac{p_1 p_2}{p_1 + p_2}.$$

Answer to b:

$$\pi(\mathbf{p}) = \begin{cases} \infty, \text{ if } p_3 > \dfrac{p_1 p_2}{p_1 + p_2} \text{ and} \\ 0, \text{ if } p_3 \leq \dfrac{p_1 p_2}{p_1 + p_2}. \end{cases}$$

$$\eta(\mathbf{p}) = \begin{cases} \emptyset, \text{ if } p_3 > \dfrac{p_1 p_2}{p_1 + p_2}, \\ X, \text{ if } p_3 = \dfrac{p_1 p_2}{p_1 + p_2}, \\ \{(0, 0, 0)\}, \text{ if } p_3 < \dfrac{p_1 p_2}{p_1 + p_2}, \end{cases}$$

where $X = \left\{\left(-t, -t\left(\frac{p_1}{p_2}\right)^2, t\left(\frac{p_1 + p_2}{p_2}\right)^2\right) \middle| t \geq 0\right\}$. This formula for X is obtained by using equation

A to obtain expressions for y_2 and $y_3 = \left(\sqrt{-y_1} + \sqrt{-y_2}\right)^2$ in terms of y_1 and using the fact that $y_1 \leq 0$.

Answer to Homework Problems for Chapter 4, Problem #4

Problem: 4) In cases a and b below, find $\pi(\mathbf{p})$ and $\eta(\mathbf{p})$ for any vector $\mathbf{p}$ of appropriate dimension and such that $\mathbf{p} > 0$, where $\pi(\mathbf{p}) = \sup_{\mathbf{y} \in Y} \mathbf{p}.\mathbf{y}$ and $\eta(\mathbf{p}) = \{\mathbf{y} \in Y \mid \mathbf{p}.\mathbf{y} = \pi(\mathbf{p})\}$.

a) $Y = \{(y_1, y_2, y_3) \mid y_1 \leq 0, y_2 \leq 0, \text{ and } 0 \leq y_3 \leq (-y_1)^{1/4}(-y_2)^{1/2}\}$.

b) $Y = \{(y_1, y_2, y_3, y_4) \mid y_1 \geq 0, y_2 \geq 0, y_3 \leq 0, y_4 \leq 0, \text{ and } y_1^2 + y_2^2 \leq \sqrt{y_3 y_4}\}$.

Answer: a) If $p_3 = 0$, then $\pi(\mathbf{p}) = 0$ and $\eta(\mathbf{p}) = \{(0, 0, 0,)\}$, since output has no value. If $p_3 > 0$ and $p_1 = 0$ or $p_2 = 0$, then $\pi(\mathbf{p}) = \infty$ and $\eta(\mathbf{p}) = \emptyset$. So assume $\mathbf{p} \gg 0$.

The profit maximization problem is

$$\max_{y_1 \leq 0, y_2 \leq 0} [p_3(-y_1)^{1/4}(-y_2)^{1/2} + p_1 y_1 + p_2 y_2].$$

The first order conditions for this problem are

$$-\frac{1}{4}p_3(-y_1)^{-3/4}(-y_2)^{1/2} + p_1 = 0$$

and

$$-\frac{1}{2}p_3(-y_1)^{1/4}(-y_2)^{-1/2} + p_2 = 0 .$$

These may be rewritten as

$$4p_1 = p_3(-y_1)^{-3/4}(-y_2)^{1/2}$$

and

$$2p_2 = p_3(-y_1)^{1/4}(-y_2)^{-1/2}.$$

Dividing the second equation into the first, we obtain

$$\frac{2p_1}{p_2} = \frac{y_2}{y_1},$$

which is the same as

$$y_2 = \frac{2p_1 y_1}{p_2}.$$

If we substitute this equation into the profit maximization problem, we obtain

$$\max_{y_1 \le 0}\left[p_3\sqrt{\frac{2p_1}{p_2}}\,(-y_1)^{3/4} + 3p_1y_1\right].$$

This problem is of the form

$$\max_{x \ge 0}\,[ax^{3/4} - bx], \qquad \text{A)}$$

where

$$x = -y_1,\ a = p_3\sqrt{\frac{2p_1}{p_2}},\ \text{and } b = 3p_1.$$

Solving problem A, we find that

$$x = \left(\frac{3a}{4b}\right)^4,\ \text{output} = \frac{ax^{3/4}}{p_3} = \frac{1}{p_3}\left(\frac{3}{4}\right)^3\frac{a^4}{b^3},$$

and the maximum value of the objective function is

$$\pi = \frac{a}{4}\left(\frac{3a}{4b}\right)^3 = \frac{27}{256}\frac{a^3}{b^3}.$$

Substituting for a and b, we see that

$$y_1 = -\frac{p_3^4}{64p_1^2p_2^2},\ y_2 = -\frac{p_3^4}{32p_1p_2^3},\ y_3 = \frac{p_3^3}{16p_1p_2^2},\ \text{and profit} = \pi = \frac{1}{64}\frac{p_3^4}{p_1p_2^2}.$$

In summary,

$$\pi(\mathbf{p}) = \begin{cases} 0, \text{ if } p_3 = 0, \\ \dfrac{p_3^4}{64p_1p_2^2}, \text{ if } \mathbf{p} >> 0, \text{ and} \\ \infty, \text{ if } p_3 > 0 \text{ and } p_1 = 0 \text{ or } p_2 = 0, \end{cases}$$

and

$$\eta(\mathbf{p}) = \begin{cases} \{(0,\ 0,\ 0)\},\ \text{if } p_3 = 0 \\ \left\{\left(-\dfrac{p_3^4}{64p_1^2p_2^2},\ -\dfrac{p_3^4}{32p_1p_2^2},\ \dfrac{p_3^3}{16p_1p_2^2}\right)\right\},\ \text{if } \mathbf{p} >> 0, \text{ and} \\ \varnothing,\ \text{if } p_3 = 0 \text{ and } p_1 = 0 \text{ or } p_2 = 0. \end{cases}$$

<u>Answer</u>: b) If $p_1 = p_2 = 0$, then $\pi(\mathbf{p}) = 0$ and $\eta(\mathbf{p}) = \{(0,\ 0,\ 0)\}$. If $p_1 > 0$ or $p_2 > 0$ and $p_3 = 0$ or $p_4 = 0$, then $\pi(\mathbf{p}) = \infty$ and $\eta(\mathbf{p}) = \varnothing$. So assume that $p_1 > 0$ or $p_2 > 0$ and $p_3 > 0$ and $p_4 > 0$.

The profit maximization problem is

$$\max_{y_1 \geq 0,\, y_2 \geq 0,\, y_3 \leq 0,\, y_4 \leq 0} [p_1y_1 + p_2y_2 + p_3y_3 + p_4y_4]$$

$$\text{s.t. } y_1^2 + y_2^2 \leq \sqrt{y_3y_4}.$$

The Lagrangian of this problem is

$$\mathcal{L} = p_1y_1 + p_2y_2 + p_3y_3 + p_4y_4 - \lambda\left[y_1^2 + y_2^2 - \sqrt{y_3y_4}\right].$$

From this, we see immediately that the first order conditions are

$$p_1 - 2\lambda y_1 = 0,$$

$$p_2 - 2\lambda y_2 = 0,$$

$$p_3 - \frac{1}{2}\sqrt{\frac{y_4}{y_3}} = 0, \text{ and}$$

$$p_4 - \frac{1}{2}\sqrt{\frac{y_3}{y_4}} = 0.$$

The first two of these equations imply that

$$y_2 = \frac{p_2}{p_1}y_1. \qquad \text{B)}$$

The last two equations imply that

$$y_4 = \frac{p_3}{p_4} y_3. \qquad \text{C)}$$

If we substitute equations B and C into the profit maximization problem, it becomes

$$\max_{y_1 \geq 0,\, y_3 \leq 0} [p_1 y_1 + \frac{p_2^2}{p_1} y_1 + p_3 y_3 + p_3 y_3]$$

$$\text{s.t. } y_1^2 + \frac{p_2^2}{p_1^2} y_1^2 \leq \sqrt{y_3 \frac{p_3}{p_4} y_3},$$

which may be simplified to

$$\max_{y_1 \geq 0,\, y_3 \leq 0} \left[\left(\frac{p_1^2 + p_2^2}{p_1} \right) y_1 + 2 p_3 y_3 \right]$$

$$\text{s.t. } \left(\frac{p_1^2 + p_2^2}{p_1^2} \right) y_1^2 \leq -y_3 \sqrt{\frac{p_3}{p_4}}.$$

The constraint in this problem will be satisfied with equality, so that

$$y_1 = \left(\frac{p_1^2}{p_1^2 + p_2^2} \right)^{1/2} \left(\frac{p_3}{p_4} \right)^{1/4} \sqrt{-y_3}.$$

If we substitute this equation into the objective function of the maximization problem, it becomes the unconstrained problem

$$\max_{y_3 \leq 0} \left[\sqrt{p_1^2 + p_2^2} \left(\frac{p_3}{p_4} \right)^{1/4} \sqrt{-y_3} + 2 p_3 y_3 \right].$$

This problem is of the form

$$\max_{x \geq 0} [a\sqrt{x} - bx],$$

where

$$x = -y_3, \ a = \sqrt{p_1^2 + p_2^2}\left(\frac{p_3}{p_4}\right)^{1/4}, \text{ and } b = 2p_3.$$

The solution to this problem is

$$x = \left(\frac{a}{2b}\right)^2$$

and the maximum value of the objective function is

$$\pi = \frac{a^2}{4b}.$$

On substituting for x, a, and b in the formula for x, we find that

$$y_3 = -\left(\frac{a}{2b}\right)^2 = -(p_1^2 + p_2^2)\sqrt{\frac{p_3}{p_4}}\frac{1}{16p_3^2} = -\frac{1}{16}\frac{p_1^2 + p_2^2}{p_3^{3/2}p_4^{1/2}}.$$

Therefore

$$y_4 = \frac{p_3}{p_4}y_3 = -\frac{1}{16}\frac{p_1^2 + p_2^2}{p_3^{1/2}p_4^{3/2}}.$$

Similarly

$$y_1 = \left(\frac{p_1^2}{p_1^2 + p_2^2}\right)^{1/2}\left(\frac{p_3}{p_4}\right)^{1/4}\sqrt{-y_3} = \left(\frac{p_1^2}{p_1^2 + p_2^2}\right)^{1/2}\left(\frac{p_3}{p_4}\right)^{1/4}\frac{1}{4}\left(\frac{p_1^2 + p_2^2}{p_3^{3/2}p_4^{1/2}}\right)^{1/2} = \frac{1}{4}\frac{p_1}{\sqrt{p_3p_4}},$$

and

$$y_2 = \frac{p_2}{p_1}y_1 = \frac{1}{4}\frac{p_2}{\sqrt{p_3p_4}}.$$

Finally the maximum profit is

$$\pi = \frac{a^2}{4b} = \frac{1}{8}\frac{p_1^2 + p_2^2}{\sqrt{p_3p_4}}.$$

In summary,

$$\pi(\mathbf{p}) = \begin{cases} 0, \text{ if } p_1 = p_2 = 0, \\ \dfrac{1}{8}\dfrac{p_1^2 + p_2^2}{\sqrt{p_3 p_4}}, \text{ if } p_1 > 0 \text{ or } p_2 > 0 \text{ and } p_3 > 0 \text{ and } p_4 > 0, \text{ and} \\ \infty, \text{ if } p_1 > 0 \text{ or } p_2 > 0 \text{ and } p_3 = 0 \text{ or } p_4 = 0, \end{cases}$$

and

$$\eta(\mathbf{p}) = \begin{cases} \{(0, 0, 0, 0)\}, \text{ if } p_1 = p_2 = 0, \\ \left\{\left(\dfrac{1}{4}\dfrac{p_1}{\sqrt{p_3 p_4}}, \dfrac{1}{4}\dfrac{p_2}{\sqrt{p_3 p_4}}, -\dfrac{1}{16}\dfrac{p_1^2 + p_2^2}{p_3^{3/2} p_4^{1/2}}, -\dfrac{1}{16}\dfrac{p_1^2 + p_2^2}{p_3^{1/2} p_4^{3/2}}\right)\right\}, \\ \qquad \text{if } p_1 > 0 \text{ or } p_2 > 0, \text{ and } p_3 > 0 \text{ and } p_4 > 0 \\ \emptyset, \text{ if } p_1 > 0 \text{ or } p_2 > 0, \text{ and } p_3 = 0 \text{ or } p_4 = 0. \end{cases}$$

Answer to Homework Problems for Chapter 4, Problem #5

Problem: 5) Consider the Robinson Crusoe economy with utility function

$$u(x_1, x_2) = \ln(x_1) + 2\ln(x_2),$$

endowment vector $\mathbf{e} = (1, 0)$, and production function

$$y_2 = -2y_1,$$

where x_1 and x_2 are the consumptions of commodities 1 and 2, respectively, and (y_1, y_2) is the input-output vector of Robinson Crusoe's firm. Find all equilibria with the price of the first good equal to one.

Answer: An easy way to solve this problem is to notice that the equilibrium allocation maximizes Robinson Crusoe's utility and that by feasibility

$$x_2 = y_2 = -2y_1 = 2(1 - x_1).$$

Therefore the equilibrium allocation may be calculated by solving the problem

$$\max_{x_1 \geq 0} [\ln x_1 + 2\ln(2(1 - x_1))].$$

The first order conditions for this problem are

$$\frac{1}{x_1} = \frac{2}{1 - x_1},$$

so that

$$x_1 = 1/3.$$

It follows from feasibility that

$$y_1 = x_1 - 1 = -2/3, \text{ and } x_2 = y_2 = -2y_1 = 4/3.$$

The equilibrium price vector is the only one with $p_1 = 1$ that gives maximum profits equal to zero at $(y_1, y_2) = (-2/3, 4/3)$. That is, $\mathbf{p} = (1, 1/2)$. In summary, the equilibrium is $((x_1, x_2), (y_1, y_2), (p_1, p_2)) = ((1/3, 4/3), (-2/3, 4/3), (1, 1/2))$.

Answer to Homework Problems for Chapter 4, Problem #6

Problem: 6) a) Consider the Edgeworth box economy with utility functions

$u_A(x_1, x_2) = 3x_1 + x_2$ and

$u_B(x_1, x_2) = x_1 + 3x_2$

and endowment vectors $\mathbf{e}_A = (2, 0)$ and $\mathbf{e}_B = (0, 2)$. Find all equilibria with the price of the first good equal to one.

b) Consider the Edgeworth box economy with utility functions

$u_A(x_1, x_2) = x_1 + 3x_2$ and

$u_B(x_1, x_2) = 3x_1 + x_2$

and endowment vectors $\mathbf{e}_A = (2, 0)$ and $\mathbf{e}_B = (0, 2)$. Find all equilibria with the price of the first good equal to one.

Answer: a) An easy way to solve this problem is to draw the corresponding Edgeworth box, as below.

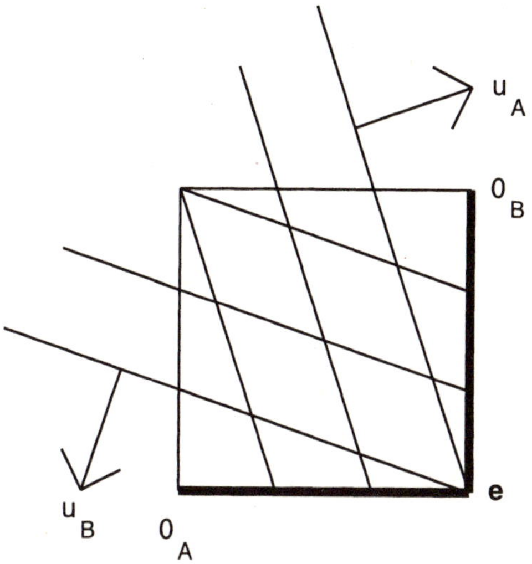

Three indifference curves for each of consumer A and B are drawn. Since the indifference curves of consumer A are steeper than those of consumer B, we see by maximizing the utility of one consumer along the indifference curve of the other that the Pareto optimal allocations are as indicated by the thick lines. The only one of these allocations that can have a budget line through it and the initial endowment point is the endowment itself. Therefore it is the only equilibrium allocation. The equilibrium prices must give a budget line through the endowment point that lies on or between the indifference curves of the two consumers through that point. That is, we must have

$$\frac{1}{3} \le \frac{p_2}{p_1} \le 3.$$

Since $p_1 = 1$, $1/3 \le p_2 \le 3$. Therefore the only equilibrium with the price of the first commodity equal to 1 is

$$\{((\mathbf{x}_A, \mathbf{x}_B), \mathbf{p}) = ((2, 0), (0, 2), (1, p_2)) \mid 1/3 \le p_2 \le 3\}.$$

Answer: b) The Edgeworth box for this economy is exactly like that of the previous part of the problem, except that the labels of the indifference curves are reversed, as in the diagram below.

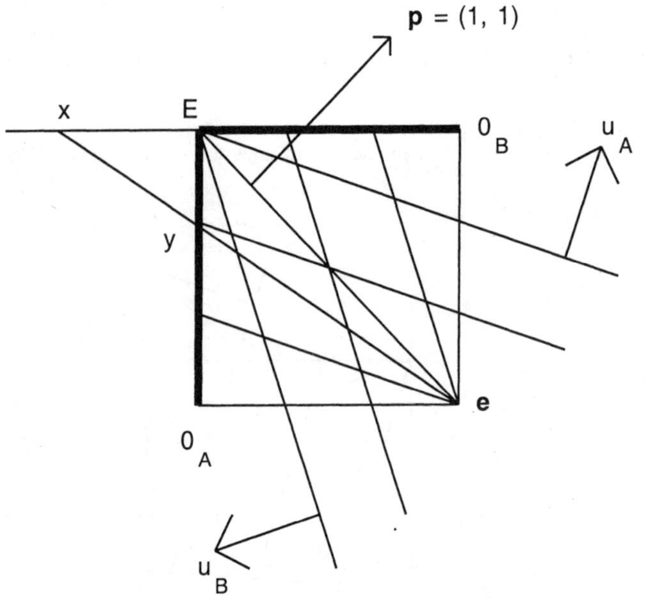

If we maximize the utility of one consumer over the indifference curve of the other, we see that the Pareto optimal allocations are the left and top edges of the box, as indicated by the thick lines. The only allocation among these that is an equilibrium is the upper left corner, indicated as E, and the price vector corresponding to this allocation is (1, 1). If we experimented with some other price vector, such as the one yielding the budget line **xe** for consumer B, then B would choose point x on that line and A would choose point y. Since these points do not coincide, this cannot be an equilibrium price vector. Therefore, the sole equilibrium with the price of the first commodity equal to 1 is

$$((\mathbf{x}_A, \mathbf{x}_B), \mathbf{p}) = ((0, 2), (2, 0), (1, 1)).$$

Answer to Homework Problems for Chapter 4, Problem #7

Problem: 7) Consider the Edgeworth box economy where

$$\mathbf{e}_A = (12, 0), \mathbf{e}_B = (0, 12) \text{ and}$$

$$u_A(x_1, x_2) = u_B(x_1, x_2) = x_1^{1/3}x_2^{2/3}.$$

a) Calculate and draw accurately the offer curves for each consumer.

b) Find all competitive equilibria with the price of the first good equal to one.

Answer: a) Because the utility functions are Cobb-Douglas and each consumer is endowed with only one commodity, we can calculate immediately that if x_A and x_B are demand vectors, then $x_{A1} = 12/3 = 4$ and $x_{B2} = (2/3)\,12 = 8$. Therefore the offer curves are as in the diagram below.

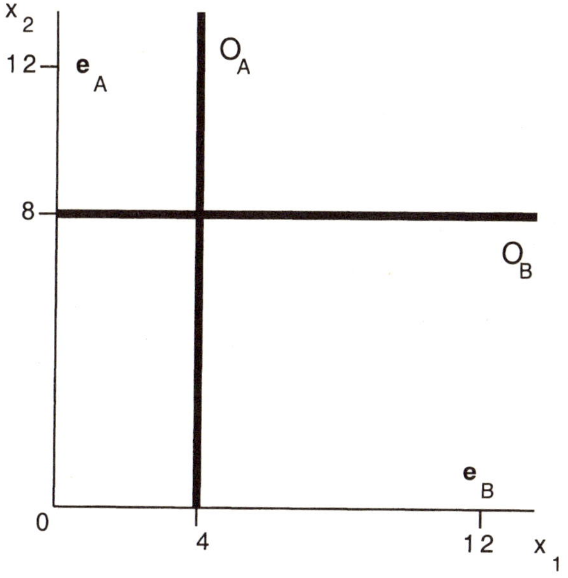

Answer b: Since $x_{A1} = 4$, feasibility implies that $x_{B1} = 8$. Since $x_{B2} = 8$, it follows that $x_{A2} = 4$. The price of commodity 2, p_2, is found by solving the budget equation for one of the consumers, say consumer A. That budget equation is

$$x_{A1} + p_2 x_{A2} = (1, p_2).\mathbf{e}_A,$$

which is

$$4 + 4p_2 = 12.$$

The solution of this equation is $p_2 = 2$. In summary the unique equilibrium is

$$(\mathbf{x}_A, \mathbf{x}_B, \mathbf{p}) = ((4, 4), (8, 8), (1, 2)).$$

Answer to Homework Problems for Chapter 4, Problem #8

Problem: 8) Consider the following Edgeworth box economy.

$$u_A(x_1, x_2) = \frac{1}{3}\ln(x_1) + \frac{2}{3}\ln(x_2), \quad \mathbf{e}_A = (18, 0),$$

$$u_B(x_1, x_2) = \frac{1}{2}\ln(x_1) + \frac{1}{2}\ln(x_2), \quad \mathbf{e}_B = (0, 20).$$

Find all competitive equilibria with prices that sum to one.

Answer: Because the utility functions are linear and each consumer is endowed with only one commodity, we can calculate immediately that $x_{A1} = 18/3 = 6$ and hence feasibility implies that $x_{B1} = 12$. Similarly $x_{B2} = 20/2 = 10$, and hence $x_{A2} = 10$. We may calculate the price p_1 from the budget equation of consumer A

$$x_{A1}p_1 + x_{A2}(1 - p_1) = (p_1, 1 - p_1).\mathbf{e}_A.$$

On substituting numbers for the allocation variables, we obtain the equation

$$6p_1 + 10(1 - p_1) = 18p_1.$$

The solution of this equation is $p_1 = 5/11$, so that $p_2 = 6/11$. In summary, the equilibrium is

$$(\mathbf{x}_A, \mathbf{x}_B, \mathbf{p}) = ((6, 10), (12, 10), (5/11, 6/11)).$$

Answer to Homework Problems for Chapter 4, Problem #9

Problem: 9) Consider an Edgeworth box economy with utility functions $u_A(x_1, x_2) = \min(3x_1, x_2)$ and $u_B(x_1, x_2) = \min(x_1, 3x_2)$.

a) Find the unique equilibrium when $\mathbf{e}_A = (4, 0)$ and $\mathbf{e}_B = (0, 4)$ and the price of good 1 equal to 1. Compute the utility of person A at the equilibrium.

b) Find the unique equilibrium when $\mathbf{e}_A = (6, 0)$ and $\mathbf{e}_B = (0, 4)$ and the price of good 1 equal to 1.

c) Compute the utility of person A at the equilibrium of part (b) and compare it with his utility in the equilibrium of part (a). Is there anything paradoxical about your finding? Can you explain intuitively why person A's utility level changes in the way that it does from part (a) to part (b)?

Answer: a) This problem may be solved algebraically as follows. Because of the nature of the utility functions,

$$x_{A2} = 3x_{A1} \text{ and } x_{B1} = 3x_{B2}.$$

Feasibility implies that

$$x_{A1} + x_{B1} = 4 \text{ and } x_{A2} + x_{B2} = 4.$$

The solution to these linear equations is

$$x_{A1} = x_{B2} = 1,\ x_{A2} = x_{B1} = 3.$$

In order to find the price of commodity 2, use the budget equation of person A

$$\mathbf{p}.\mathbf{x}_A = \mathbf{p}.\mathbf{e}_A,$$

which is

$$1 + 3p_2 = 4,$$

so that

$$p_2 = 1.$$

In summary, the equilibrium is

$$(\mathbf{x}_A, \mathbf{x}_B, \mathbf{p}) = ((1, 3), (3, 1), (1, 1)).$$

The utility of person A in this equilibrium is 3.

Answer: b) The relevant linear equations now become

$$x_{A2} = 3x_{A1},\ x_{B1} = 3x_{B2},\ x_{A1} + x_{B1} = 4, \text{ and } x_{A2} + x_{B2} = 6.$$

Proceeding as in part a, we find that the equilibrium is

$$(\mathbf{x}_A, \mathbf{x}_B, \mathbf{p}) = ((3/4, 9/4), (21/4, 7/4), (1, 7/3)).$$

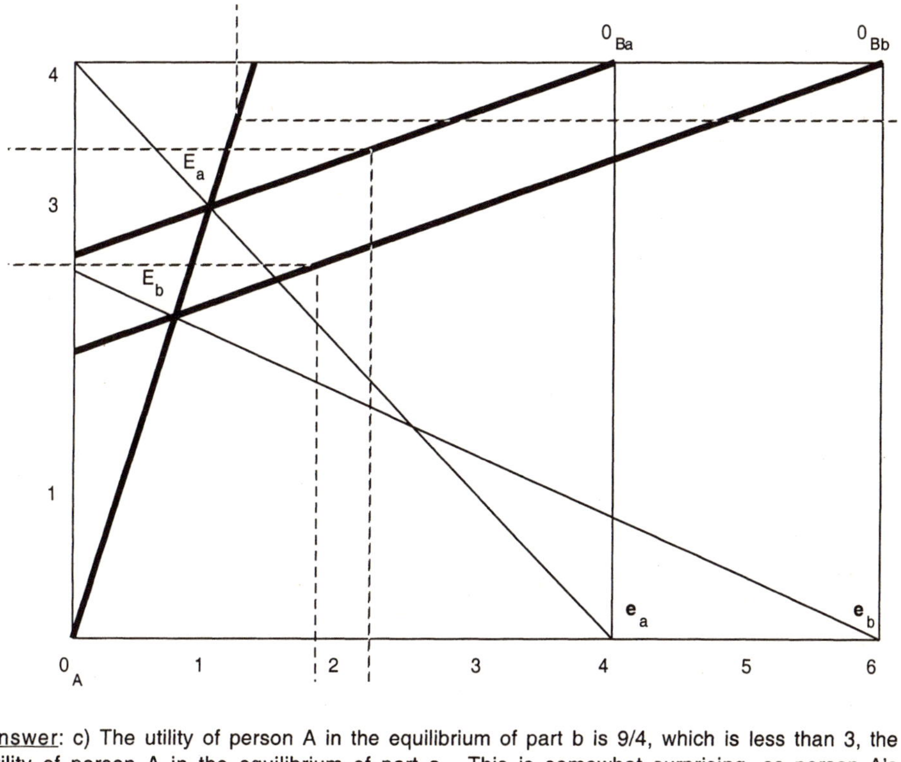

Answer: c) The utility of person A in the equilibrium of part b is 9/4, which is less than 3, the utility of person A in the equilibrium of part a. This is somewhat surprising, as person A's endowment is larger in part b than in part a. The explanation can be understood visually by considering the superposition of two Edgeworth boxes in the diagram above. The origins of person B in the models of parts a and b are labeled as 0_{Ba} and 0_{Bb}, respectively. The endowment points of the two models are indicated by $\mathbf{e}_a$ and $\mathbf{e}_b$, and the equilibrium allocations are indicated by E_a and E_b. The dashed lines are indifference curves. The heavy slanted lines are the locus of corners of the indifference curves of persons A and B and are the effective part of the offer curves of the two people. In the model of part b, the right-hand edge of the box is displaced to the right, and this movement brings the intersection of the offer curves downward along the offer curve of person A and therefore makes him or her worse off. This movement also increases the price of good 2, which is the commodity that person A must purchase. It is this increase in price that makes person A worse off. The increase in the supply of the commodity that person A provides turns the terms of trade against him or her. The change in terms of trade may be seen from the change in the slope of the budget lines in the two equilibria.

Answer to Homework Problems for Chapter 4, Problem #10

Problem: 10) Consider the following Edgeworth box economy.

$$u_A(x_1, x_2) = (\sqrt{x_1} + 2\sqrt{x_2})^2 = u_B(x_1, x_2).$$

$\mathbf{e}_A = (4, 1)$. $\mathbf{e}_B = (1, 4)$.

a) Find the set of Pareto optimal allocations and draw it in a box diagram. Indicate the endowment point.

b) Find the utility possibility frontier and draw it.

c) Find a competitive equilibrium with the price of good 1 equal to 1.

d) Find positive numbers a_A and a_B such that the competitive equilibrium allocation maximizes the welfare function $a_A u_A(x_{A1}, x_{A2}) + a_B u_B(x_{B1}, x_{B2})$ over the set of feasible allocations $(\mathbf{x}_A, \mathbf{x}_B)$.

Answer: a) Because the two consumers have the same utility function that is homogeneous of degree 1, the set of Pareto optimal allocations is the diagonal of the Edgeworth box, as indicated by the heavy line in the diagram below.

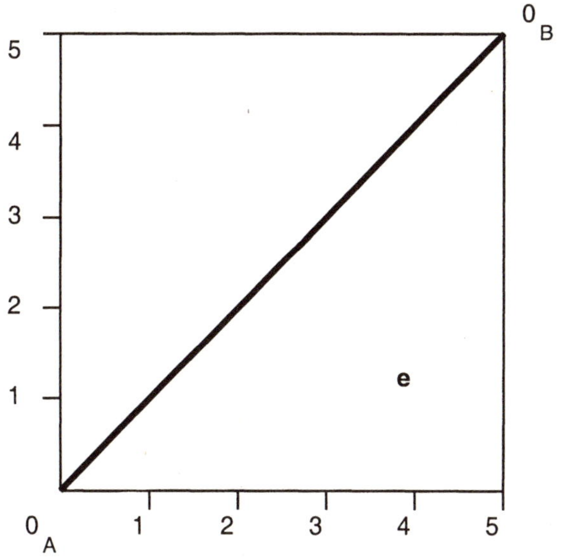

Answer: b) Because the utility functions are homogeneous of degree 1, the utility possibility frontier is a straight line, the heavy line shown in the diagram below.

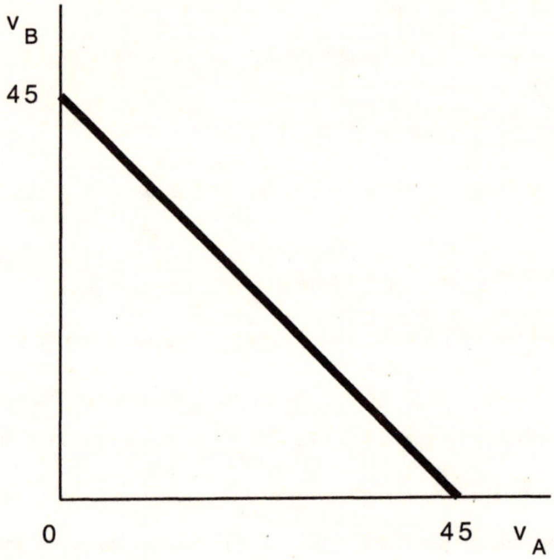

Answer: c) In order to find the ratio of the prices, use the equation

$$\frac{p_1}{p_2} = \frac{\partial u(x, x)/\partial x_1}{\partial u(x, x)/\partial x_2} = \frac{1/2\sqrt{x}}{1/\sqrt{x}} = \frac{1}{2}.$$

Since $p_1 = 1$, it follows that $p_2 = 2$. In order to find the allocation to person A, use that person's budget equation,

$$\mathbf{p}.\mathbf{x}_A = \mathbf{p}.\mathbf{e}_A.$$

If we let $\mathbf{x}_A = (x, x)$, this equation becomes

$$\mathbf{p}.(x, x) = \mathbf{p}.(4, 1),$$

that is

$$(1, 2).(x, x) = (1, 2).(4, 1).$$

Hence, $x = 2$, and the equilibrium is

$$(\mathbf{x}_A, \mathbf{x}_B, \mathbf{p}) = ((2, 2), (3, 3), (1, 2)).$$

Answer: d) From the drawing of the utility possibility frontier, we see that

$$a_A = a_B = 1.$$

Answer to Homework Problems for Chapter 4, Problem #11

Problem: 11) Consider the following Edgeworth box economy.

$u_A(x_1, x_2) = \min(4x_1, x_2)$. $\qquad$ $u_B(x_1, x_2) = 4x_1 + x_2$.

$\mathbf{e}_A = (0, 4)$. $\qquad$ $\mathbf{e}_B = (4, 0)$.

Do the following for this economy.

a) Show the set of Pareto optimal allocations in a box diagram.

b) Make a precise drawing of the utility possibility frontier.

c) Compute a general equilibrium such that the sum of the prices is one. Show the equilibrium allocation in a box diagram. Show the utility vector corresponding to the equilibrium allocation on a diagram of the utility possibility frontier.

d) Compute non-negative numbers a_A and a_B such that the equilibrium allocation maximizes the welfare function

$$a_A u_A(x_{A1}, x_{A2}) + a_B u_B(x_{B1}, x_{B2}).$$

Answer: a) The appropriate diagram is below. Sample indifference curves are dashed lines, and the set of Pareto optima is the heavy line.

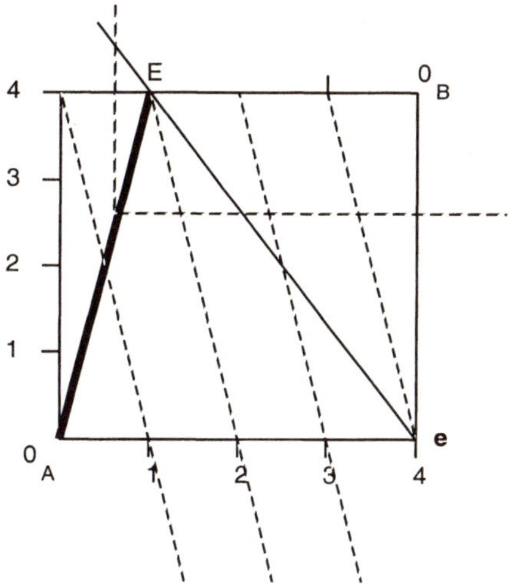

Answer: b) The appropriate diagram is below. The utility possibility frontier is shown with heavy lines.

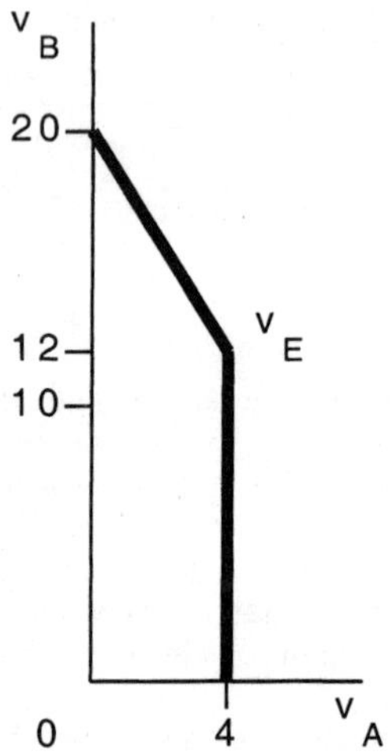

Answer: c) The unique general equilibrium with the price of commodity 1 equal to 1 is

$$(\mathbf{x}_A, \mathbf{x}_B, \mathbf{p}) = ((1, 4), (3, 0), (1, 3/4)).$$

The equilibrium allocation is shown as point E in the box diagram of part a. The budget line is the solid line going through points **e** and E. The utility vector corresponding to the equilibrium allocation is shown as point v_E in the diagram of the utility possibility frontier in part b.

Answer: d) Any vector (a_A, a_B) will do that satisfies the inequalities

$$2 \le \frac{a_A}{a_B} < \infty.$$

Answer to Homework Problems for Chapter 4, Problem #12

Problem: 12) Consider the following model with two consumers, A and B, and with two commodities, 1 and 2.

$u_A(x_1, x_2) = x_1 + \ln(x_2)$. $\qquad u_B(x_1, x_2) = x_1 + 2\ln(x_2)$.

$\mathbf{e}_A = (e_{A1}, e_{A2})$. $\qquad \mathbf{e}_B = (e_{B1}, e_{B2})$.

Assume that $e_{A1} > 10$, $e_{B1} > 10$, $e_{A2} > 0$, $e_{B2} > 0$, and $e_{A2} + e_{B2} \leq 1$.

a) Compute an equilibrium where the price of good 1 is 1. The equilibrium price of good 2 and the equilibrium allocations will be formulas in terms of the endowments. Hint: The endowments of good 1 are so large that each consumer consumes a positive amount of good 1 in equilibrium.

b) Show that the price of good 2 and the consumer's consumption of good 2 depend only on $e_{A2} + e_{B2}$.

Answer: a) The utility maximization problem of consumer A is

$$\max_{x_1 \geq 0,\, x_2 \geq 0} [x_1 + \ln x_2]$$

$$\text{s.t. } x_1 + p_2 x_2 = e_{A1} + p e_{A2}.$$

The Lagrangian of this problem is

$$\mathcal{L} = x_1 + \ln x_2 - \lambda(x_1 + p_2 x_2).$$

Assuming that both variables are positive, the first order conditions are

$$\lambda = 1$$

and

$$\frac{1}{x_2} = \lambda p.$$

It follows that

$$x_{A2} = \frac{1}{p_2}.$$

Similarly the utility maximization problem of consumer B is

$$\max_{x_1 \geq 0,\, x_2 \geq 0} [x_1 + 2\ln x_2]$$

$$\text{s.t. } x_1 + p_2 x_2 = e_{B1} + pe_{B2},$$

and its Lagrangian is

$$\mathcal{L} = x_1 + 2\ln x_2 - \lambda(x_1 + p_2 x_2).$$

It follows that

$$\lambda = 1$$

and

$$\frac{2}{x_2} = \lambda p,$$

so that

$$x_{B2} = \frac{2}{p_2}.$$

We can solve for p_2 by using the feasibility equation for commodity 2.

$$\frac{3}{p_2} = \frac{1}{p_2} + \frac{2}{p_2} = x_{A2} + x_{B2} = e_{A2} + e_{B2}.$$

Hence

$$p_2 = \frac{3}{e_{A2} + e_{B2}}.$$

The wealth of consumer A is

$$w_A = e_{A1} + p_2 e_{A2} = e_{A1} + \frac{3e_{A2}}{e_{A2} + e_{B2}}.$$

The expenditure of consumer A on commodity 2 is

$$p_2x_{A2} = p_2\frac{1}{p_2} = 1.$$

Since the price of commodity 1 is 1, it follows that

$$x_{A1} = w_A - p_2x_{A2} = e_{A1} + \frac{3e_{A2}}{e_{A2} + e_{B2}} - 1.$$

Since $e_{A1} > 10$, $x_{A1} > 0$. A similar reasoning implies that

$$x_{B1} = e_{B1} + \frac{3e_{B2}}{e_{A2} + e_{B2}} - 2,$$

which is positive, since $e_{B1} > 10$.

In summary, the equilibrium is

$$(\mathbf{x}_A, \mathbf{x}_B, \mathbf{p}) = \left(\left(e_{A1} + \frac{3e_{A2}}{e_{A2} + e_{B2}} - 1, \frac{e_{A2} + e_{B2}}{3}\right), \left(e_{B1} + \frac{3e_{B2}}{e_{A2} + e_{B2}} - 2, \frac{2(e_{A2} + e_{B2})}{3}\right), \left(1, \frac{3}{e_{A2} + e_{B2}}\right)\right).$$

Answer: b) It is evident from the formula just given for the equilibrium that the price of good 2 and the consumer's consumption of good 2 depend only on $e_{A2} + e_{B2}$.

Answer to Homework Problems for Chapter 4, Problem #13

Problem: 13) Compute an equilibrium for the following economy with labor, two produced goods, two consumers, A and B, and two firms, 1 and 2. In commodity vectors, the first component is labor-leisure time, the second component is the first produced good, and the third is the second produced good.

$$\mathbf{e}_A = (2, 0, 0),\ u_A(\ell, x_1, x_2) = \ell + x_1 + x_2,\ \theta_{A1} = 1,\ \theta_{A2} = 0,$$

$$\mathbf{e}_B = (2, 0, 0),\ u_B(\ell, x_1, x_2) = \ell x_1^2 x_2^3,\ \theta_{B1} = 0,\ \theta_{B2} = 1,$$

$$y_1 = 2\sqrt{L_1},\ y_2 = 2\sqrt{L_2},$$

where y_1 and y_2 are the outputs of produced goods 1 and 2, respectively, and L_1 and L_2 are the inputs of labor into the production of goods 1 and 2, respectively. Let the price of labor be one.

Hint: Use the fact that person A's utility function is linear to guess the equilibrium price vector.

Answer: If consumer A consumes a positive amount of every commodity, then the price of all commodities must be the same in equilibrium because of the nature of consumer A's utility function. So we may tentatively assume that all prices equal 1. In this case, the profit maximization problem for either firm is of the form

$$\max_{L \geq 0}\ [2\sqrt{L} - L].$$

The solution of this problem is $L = 1$, so that output is $y = 2$ and profit is $\pi = y - L = 1$. The wealth of consumer A is

$$w_A = \mathbf{p}.\mathbf{e}_A + \pi = (1, 1, 1).(2, 0, 0) + 1 = 3$$

Similarly the wealth of consumer B is

$$w_B = 3.$$

Because of the Cobb-Douglas form of consumer B's utility function, B's consumption of leisure is

$$\ell_B = \frac{1}{6} w_B = \frac{1}{6} 3 = \frac{1}{2}.$$

Similarly consumer B's consumption of commodities 1 and 2 are, respectively,

$$x_{B1} = \frac{2}{6}3 = 1 \text{ and } x_{B2} = \frac{3}{6}3 = \frac{3}{2}.$$

Feasibility implies that the consumption of leisure by consumer A is

$$\ell_A = e_{A0} + e_{B0} - \ell_B - L_1 - L_2 = 2 + 2 - \frac{1}{2} - 1 - 1 = \frac{3}{2}.$$

Similarly

$$x_{A1} = y_1 - x_{B1} = 2 - 1 = 1,$$

and

$$x_{A2} = y_2 - x_{B2} = 2 - \frac{3}{2} = \frac{1}{2}.$$

Since consumer A consumes a positive amount of every commodity, the tentative hypothesis made earlier about A's consumption is correct. In summary, the equilibrium is

$$((\ell_A, x_{A1}, x_{A2}), (\ell_B, x_{B1}, x_{B2}), (-L_1, y_1), (-L_2, y_2), \mathbf{p})$$

$$= ((3/2,\ 1,\ 1/2),\ (1/2,\ 1,\ 3/2),\ (-1,\ 2),\ (-1,\ 2),\ (1,\ 1,\ 1)).$$

Answer to Homework Problems for Chapter 4, Problem #14

Problem: 14) Compute an equilibrium for the following economy.

$$u_A(x_1, x_2) = x_1^{3/7} x_2^{4/7} = u_B(x_1, x_2).$$

$$\mathbf{e}_A = \mathbf{e}_B = \mathbf{0}.$$

$$Y_1 = \{(y_1, y_2) \mid y_1 \geq 0,\ 0 \leq y_2 \leq 3 - y_1\}.$$

$$Y_2 = \{(y_1, y_2) \mid y_1 \geq 0,\ 0 \leq y_2 \leq 4 - \frac{2y_1}{5}\}.$$

$$\theta_{A1} = 1,\ \theta_{A2} = 0,\ \theta_{B1} = 0,\ \theta_{B2} = 1.$$

Hint: Compute the total output possibility set. Use the fact that both consumers have the same Cobb-Douglas utility function.

Answer: The total input-output possibility set, $Y_1 + Y_2$, is as in the following diagram. The total output possibility set is shaded with dots and its frontier is the heavy line. The arrows perpendicular to the two straight line segments of the frontier are possible equilibrium price vectors.

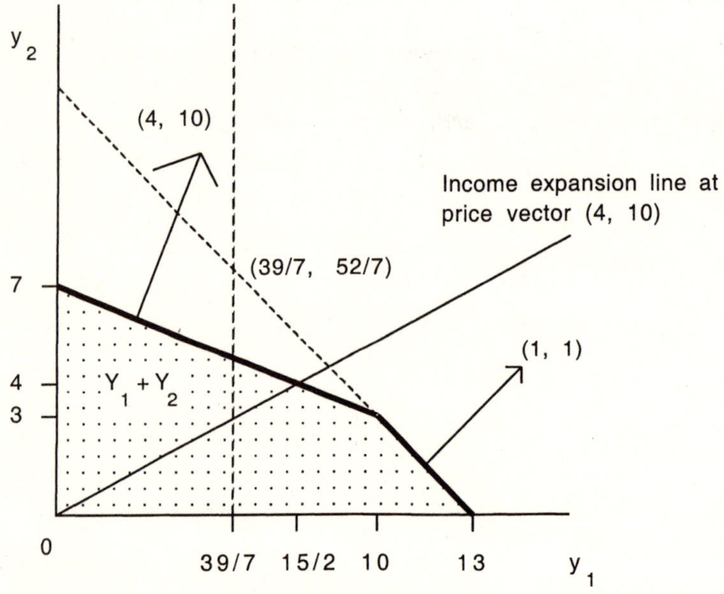

Let use suppose that the equilibrium price vector is (1, 1). Then the total wealth of the two consumers together is 13. That is, 13 is the maximum value of $(1, 1).\mathbf{y}$, for $\mathbf{y}$ in $Y_1 + Y_2$. Because the two consumers have the same Cobb-Douglas utility function with coefficients 3/7 and 4/7, the total consumption of commodity 1 is

$$x_1 = \frac{3}{7}(13) = \frac{39}{7}.$$

Similarly the total consumption of commodity 2 is

$$x_2 = \frac{4}{7}(13) = \frac{52}{7}.$$

The point $(y_1, y_2) = (39/7, 52/7)$ is not feasible, as is made clear in the above diagram. This point lies outside the production possibility frontier along a dashed line extending one of the straight line segments of the frontier.

Let us suppose that the equilibrium price vector is (4, 10). Then the total wealth of the two consumers is 70, and the total demand for commodity 1 satisfies the equation

$$4x_1 = \frac{3}{7}(70) = 30,$$

so that

$$x_1 = \frac{15}{2}.$$

Similarly the total demand for commodity 2 satisfies the equation

$$10x_2 = \frac{4}{7}(70) = 40,$$

so that

$$x_2 = 4.$$

The point $(y_1, y_2) = (15/2, 4)$ lies on the production possibility frontier. It is at the intersection of the frontier with the income expansion line for price vector (4, 10), as is shown in the diagram.

If the price vector is (4, 10) and the total production vector is (15/2, 4), then firm 1 maximizes profit by producing at the point $\mathbf{y}_1 = (0, 3)$, and firm 2's input-output possibility vector is $\mathbf{y}_2 = (15/2, 1)$, a vector that maximizes firm 2's profits at the price vector (4, 10). The maximum profits for firm 1 are

$$\pi_1 = (4, 10) . (0, 3) = 30.$$

Since consumer A owns all of firm 1 and none of firm 2, A's wealth is $w_A = \pi_1 = 30$. Consumer A's demand for commodity 1 satisfies the equation

$$4x_{A1} = \frac{3}{7}(30) = \frac{90}{7},$$

so that

$$x_{A1} = \frac{45}{14}.$$

Consumer A's consumption of commodity 2 satisfies the equation

$$10x_{A2} = \frac{4}{7}(30),$$

so that

$$x_{A2} = \frac{12}{7}.$$

From feasibility, we know that consumer B's demand for commodity 1 is

$$x_{B1} = \frac{15}{2} - \frac{45}{14} = \frac{30}{7}.$$

Similarly

$$x_{B2} = 4 - \frac{12}{7} = \frac{16}{7}.$$

In summary,

$$(\mathbf{x}_A, \mathbf{x}_B, \mathbf{y}_1, \mathbf{y}_2, \mathbf{p}) = \left(\left(\frac{45}{14}, \frac{12}{7}\right), \left(\frac{30}{7}, \frac{16}{7}\right), (0, 3), \left(\frac{15}{2}, 1\right), (4, 10)\right).$$

Answer to Homework Problems for Chapter 4, Problem #15

Problem: 15) Suppose that there is one input, labor (L), and that there are two outputs, goods 1 and 2. The production function for good 1 is $y_1 = f_1(L)$ and the production function for good 2 is $y_2 = f_2(L)$. There is one unit of labor available for use in the production of goods 1 or 2. Calculate a formula for the total ouput possibility set for goods 1 and 2 and draw it when

a) $f_1(L) = L$ and $f_2(L) = 2L$;

b) $f_1(L) = \sqrt{L}$ and $f_2(L) = 2\sqrt{L}$.

Answer: a) Let L_1 and L_2 be the quantities of labor used to produce goods 1 and 2, respectively. Then the equations describing the production possibility frontier are

$$L_1 + L_2 = 1,$$

$$y_1 = L_1,$$

and

$$y_2 = 2L_2.$$

It follows that

$$y_2 = 2(1 - L_1) = 2 - 2L_1 = 2 - 2y_1.$$

The output possibility set for goods 1 and 2 is

$$Y = \{(y_1, y_2) \in R^2_+ \mid y_2 \leq 2 - 2y_1\}.$$

This set is portrayed in the diagram below.

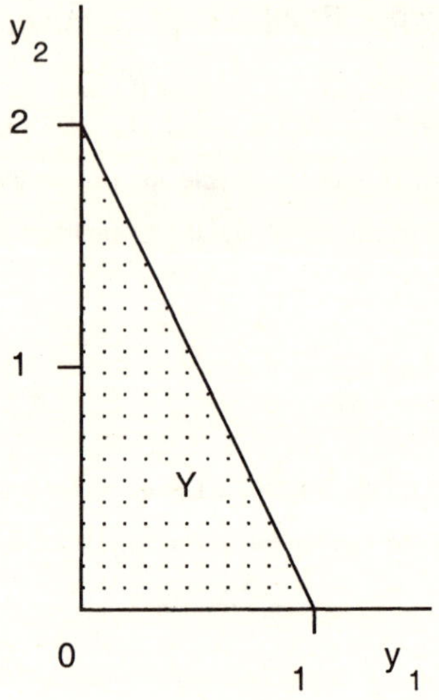

Answer: b) Now the relevant equations describing the production possibility frontier become

$$L_1 + L_2 = 1,$$

$$y_1 = \sqrt{L_1},$$

and

$$y_2 = 2\sqrt{L_2},$$

so that

$$L_1 = y_1^2,$$

and

$$y_2 = 2\sqrt{1 - L_1} = 2\sqrt{1 - y_1^2}.$$

This equation implies that

$$4y_1^2 + y_2^2 = 4,$$

which is the equation for an ellipse. The output possibility set for goods 1 and 2 is

$$Y = \left\{ (y_1, y_2) \in R^2_+ \;\middle|\; y_2 \le 2\sqrt{1 - y_1^2} \right\}.$$

This set is pictured below.

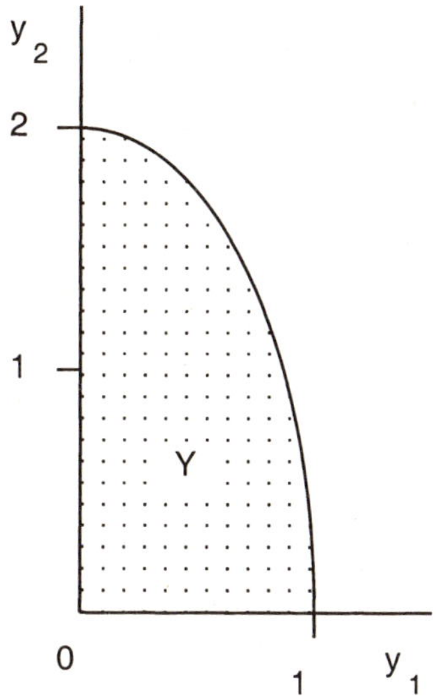

Answer to Homework Problems for Chapter 4, Problem #16

Problem: 16) There are two primary inputs, labor (L) and land (T), and two outputs, goods 1 and 2. The production function of good 1 is

$$y_1 = L^{1/4}T^{3/4},$$

and the production function for good 2 is

$$y_2 = L^{3/4}T^{1/4}.$$

There is one unit of labor and one unit of land available for the production of goods 1 and 2.

a) Compute a formula for and sketch in the box diagram the set of efficient allocations of land and labor to the production of goods 1 and 2.

b) Sketch the total output possibility set for goods 1 and 2.

c) What allocation of labor and land to the production of the two outputs maximizes the sum of the two outputs, $y_1 + y_2$?

Answer: a) The set of efficient allocations may be computed as follows. Let

$$f_1(L, T) = L^{1/4}T^{3/4}$$

and let

$$f_2(L, T) = L^{3/4}T^{1/4}.$$

Let L and T be the inputs of labor and land, respectively, into the production of good 1. The efficiency locus is determined by the equation

$$\frac{\dfrac{\partial f_1(L, T)}{\partial L}}{\dfrac{\partial f_1(L, T)}{\partial T}} = \frac{\dfrac{\partial f_2(1-L, 1-T)}{\partial L}}{\dfrac{\partial f_2(1-L, 1-T)}{\partial T}}.$$

After substituting the formulas for f_1 and f_2, this equation becomes

$$\frac{\frac{1}{4}\left(\frac{T}{L}\right)^{3/4}}{\frac{3}{4}\left(\frac{L}{T}\right)^{1/4}} = \frac{\frac{3}{4}\left(\frac{1-T}{1-L}\right)^{1/4}}{\frac{1}{4}\left(\frac{1-L}{1-T}\right)^{3/4}}.$$

After simplification, this equation becomes

$$\frac{1}{3}\frac{T}{L} = 3\frac{1-T}{1-L},$$

so that

$$T - TL = 9L - 9TL$$

and hence

$$T(1 + 8L) = 9L.$$

That is,

$$T = \frac{9L}{1 + 8L}. \qquad \text{(A)}$$

This last equation can be rewritten as

$$1 - L = \frac{9(1 - T)}{1 + 8(1 - L)}.$$

Hence the locus of efficient points looks the same from the point of view of person B as it does from the point of view of person A, with the axes reversed. That is, if (L, T) = (a, b) belongs to the locus, so does the point (1 − L, 1 − T) = (b, a) seen from consumer B's origin in the box diagram. Hence, (L, T) = (1 − b, 1 − a) also belongs to the efficiency locus, seen from A's origin. This means that the locus is symmetric about the diagonal going from the northwest to

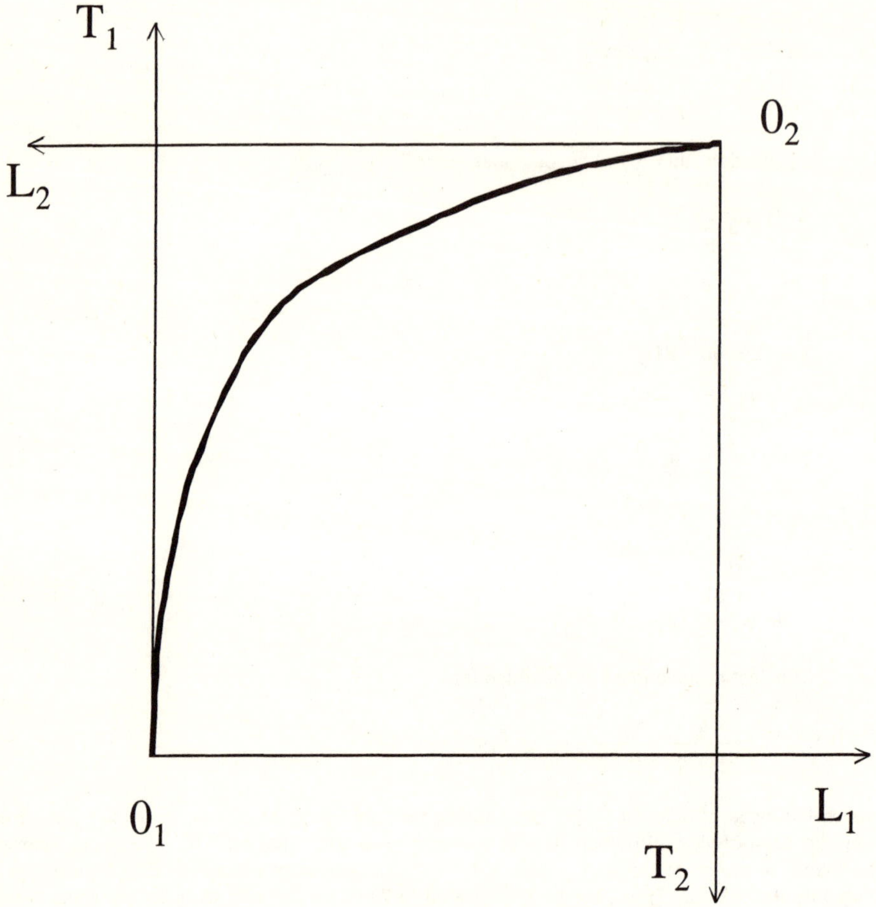

the southeast corner of the box. That is, if the box were folded along this diagonal, the two halves of the locus would coincide. This insight reduces the work of finding enough points on the locus to draw it. From equation A, we see that the points (0, 0), (1/4, 3/4), (1/2, 9/10), (3/4, 27/28), and (1, 1) belong to the locus. By the symmetry, the points (1/10, 1/2) and (1/28, 1/4) belong to it as well. The sketch above of the efficiency was obtained by running a smooth curve through these seven points.

Answer: b) Because of the symmetry of the problem, it should be clear that the point $(y_1, y_2) = (a, b)$ belongs to the output possibility set if and only if the point $(y_1, y_2) = (b, a)$ belongs to it. This symmetry economizes on the number of calculations one must make to find a few points on the frontier of the set. Such points are listed below.

$$(L, T) = (0, 0),\ y_1 = (0)^{1/4}(0)^{3/4} = 0,\ y_2 = (1)^{3/4}(1)^{1/4} = 1,$$

$$y_1 = 0.1537,\ y_2 = 0.9056,$$

$$(L, T) = \left(\frac{1}{16}, \frac{3}{8}\right),\ y_1 = \left(\frac{1}{16}\right)^{1/4}\left(\frac{3}{8}\right)^{3/4} \cong 0.2396,\ y_2 = \left(\frac{15}{16}\right)^{3/4}\left(\frac{5}{8}\right)^{1/4} \cong 0.8471,$$

$$y_1 = 0.3344,\ y_2 = 0.7770,$$

$$(L, T) = \left(\frac{1}{4}, \frac{3}{4}\right),\ y_1 = \left(\frac{1}{4}\right)^{1/4}\left(\frac{3}{4}\right)^{3/4} \cong 0.5699,\ y_2 = \left(\frac{3}{4}\right)^{3/4}\left(\frac{1}{4}\right)^{1/4} \cong 0.5699,$$

$$(L, T) = \left(\frac{1}{2}, \frac{9}{10}\right),\ y_1 = \left(\frac{1}{2}\right)^{1/4}\left(\frac{9}{10}\right)^{3/4} \cong 0.7770,\ y_2 = \left(\frac{1}{2}\right)^{3/4}\left(\frac{1}{10}\right)^{1/4} \cong 0.3344,$$

$$y_1 = 0.8471,\ y_2 = 0.2396,$$

$$(L, T) = \left(\frac{3}{4}, \frac{27}{28}\right),\ y_1 = \left(\frac{3}{4}\right)^{1/4}\left(\frac{27}{28}\right)^{3/4} \cong 0.9056,\ y_2 = \left(\frac{1}{4}\right)^{3/4}\left(\frac{1}{28}\right)^{1/4} \cong 0.1537.$$

$$(L, T) = (1, 1),\ y_1 = (1)^{1/4}(1)^{3/4} = 1,\ y_2 = (0)^{3/4}(0)^{1/4} = 0.$$

The sketch below is a smooth curve going through these nine points.

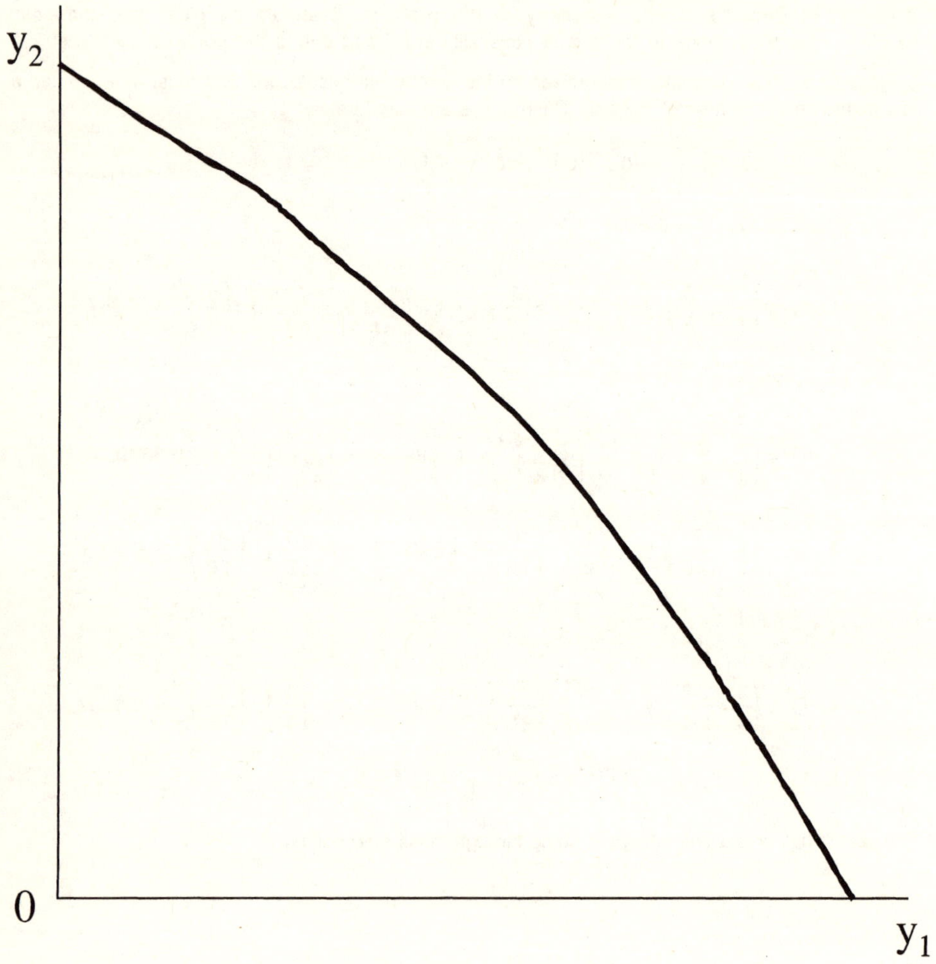
y2
0
y1

Answer: c) We are asked to solve the problem

$$\max_{L \geq 0,\, T \geq 0} \left[L^{1/4}T^{3/4} + (1 - L)^{3/4}(1 - T)^{1/4}\right].$$

Since the solution will lie on the efficiency locus, we know from part a that

$$T = \frac{9L}{1 + 8L} \qquad (B)$$

and hence

$$1 - T = \frac{1 - L}{1 + 8L}. \qquad (C)$$

If we set equal to zero the partial derivative of the objective function with respect to L, we obtain

$$\frac{1}{4}\left(\frac{T}{L}\right)^{3/4} - \frac{3}{4}\left(\frac{1 - T}{1 - L}\right)^{1/4},$$

so that

$$\left(\frac{T}{L}\right)^{3/4} = 3\left(\frac{1 - T}{1 - L}\right)^{1/4}.$$

On substituting the equations B and C for T and 1 – T, we obtain

$$\left(\frac{9}{1 + 8L}\right)^{3/4} = 3\left(\frac{1}{1 + 8L}\right)^{1/4}.$$

This equation simplifies to

$$\left(\frac{1}{1 + 8L}\right)^{1/2} = \left(\frac{1}{3}\right)^{1/2},$$

so that

$$1 + 8L = 3$$

and hence $L = 1/4$. It follows from equation B that $T = 3/4$. In summary, the allocation of labor and land to the production of good 1 is

$$(L_1, T_1) = (1/4, 3/4),$$

and the allocation of labor and land to the production of good 2 is

$$(L_2, T_2) = (3/4, 1/4).$$

Answer to Homework Problems for Chapter 4, Problem #17

Problem: 17) There is one primary good, labor, and there are two outputs, goods 1 and 2. Good 1 is used as an input in the production of good 2 and good 2 is used as an input in the production of good 1. The production function for good 1 is $y_1 = f_1(y_{12}, L)$, where y_{12} is the amount of good 2 used as an input in the production of good 1. The production function for good 2 is $y_2 = f_2(y_{21}, L)$, where y_{21} is the amount of good 1 used in the production of good 2. There is one unit of labor to use in the production of goods 1 or 2.

a) Compute a formula for the total output possibility set for goods 1 and 2 and draw it when

$$f_1(y_{12}, L) = \min(2y_{12}, L) \text{ and}$$

$$f_2(y_{21}, L) = \min(3y_{21}, L).$$

b) Suppose that the price of labor is 1. What are the prices of goods 1 and 2 such that if, when each production process is operated so as to maximize profits at these prices, the two processes together can produce a positive total amount of each of goods 1 and 2 while using the one unit of labor available?

Answer: a) If the entire one unit of labor is used in the production of good 1, then the production function for good 1 is

$$y_1 = \min(2y_{12}, 1).$$

If we think of the input of good 2 as negative, then the input-output possibility set for the production of good 1 from good 2 is

$$Y_1 = \{(y_1, y_2) \mid y_2 \leq 0 \text{ and } y_1 \leq \min(-2y_2, 1)\}.$$

This set is portrayed in the fourth quadrant of the figure below.

If the entire one unit of labor is used in the production of good 2, then the production function for good 2 is

$$y_2 = \min(3y_{21}, 1).$$

If we think of the input of good 1 as negative, then the input-output possibility set for the production of good 2 from good 1 is

$$Y_2 = \{(y_1, y_2) \mid y_1 \leq 0 \text{ and } y_2 \leq \min(-3y_1, 1)\}.$$

This set is portrayed in the second quadrant of the figure below.

Let

$$\overline{Y}_1 = \{t(y_1, y_2, -1) \mid t \geq 0 \text{ and } (y_1, y_2) \in Y_1\}.$$

Then $\overline{Y}_1$ is the input-output possibility set for the production of good 1 from labor and good 2. Similarly $\overline{Y}_2$ is the input-output possibility set for the production of good 2 from labor and good 1, where

$$\overline{Y}_2 = \{t(y_1, y_2, -1) \mid t \geq 0 \text{ and } (y_1, y_2) \in Y_2\}.$$

The total input–output possibility set is $\overline{Y}_1 + \overline{Y}_2$.

The total input-output possibility set may be used to see that any convex combination of a point in Y_1 and a point in Y_2 may be produced using one unit of labor. Let $y_1 \in Y_1$ and $y_2 \in Y_2$ and let α be such that $0 < \alpha < 1$. Then $(\alpha y_1, -\alpha) \in \overline{Y}_1$, and $((1-\alpha) y_2, -(1-\alpha)) \in \overline{Y}_2$, so that

$$(\alpha y_1, -\alpha) + ((1-\alpha) y_2, -(1-\alpha)) = (\alpha y_1 + (1-\alpha) y_2, -1) \in \overline{Y}_1 + \overline{Y}_2,$$

which is the same as saying that $\alpha y_1 + (1-\alpha) y_2$ may be produced using one unit of labor. Therefore the output possibility frontier for goods 1 and 2 is, in the figure, the part of the line segment from the point (–1/3, 1) to the point (1, –1/2) that lies in the non-negative quadrant. This line is

$$y_2 = \frac{5}{8} - \frac{9}{8} y_1.$$

This line segment intersects the vertical axis at the point (0, 5/8) and horizontal axis at the point (5/9, 0). That is, 5/8 is the maximum amount of good 2 that can be produced if the net output of good 1 is zero, and 5/9 is the maximum amount of good 1 that can be produced if the net output of good 2 is zero. The output possibility set for goods 1 and 2 is the heavily shaded triangle Y with vertices (0, 0), (5/9, 0), and (0, 5/8).

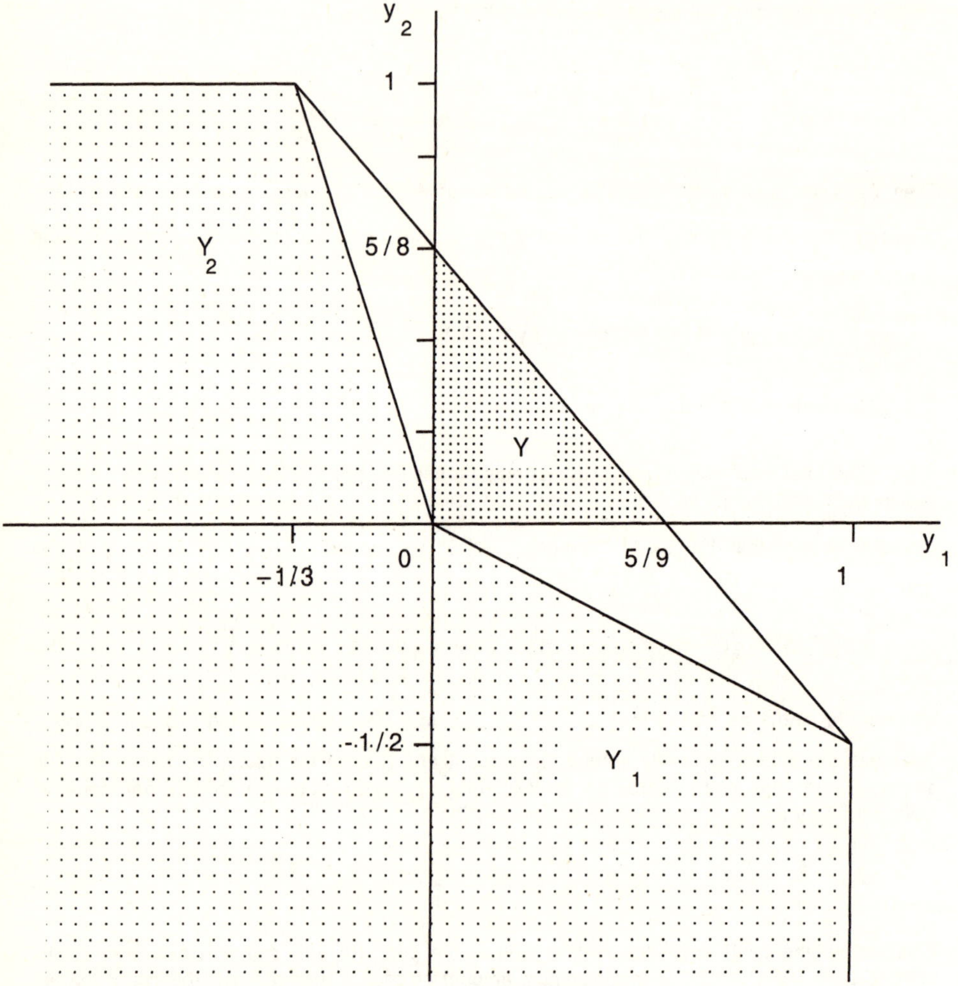

<u>Answer</u>: b) Let **p** be the price vector in question. Since $\overline{Y}_1$ and $\overline{Y}_2$ are cones, the maximum profits earned in each production process must be zero. Let $\mathbf{y} \in \overline{Y}_1 + \overline{Y}_2$ be the total input-output vector that produces a positive amount of each of goods 1 and 2. That is, $\mathbf{y} = (y_1, y_2, -1)$, where $y_1 > 0$ and $y_2 > 0$. Since $\mathbf{y} \in \overline{Y}_1 + \overline{Y}_2$, $\mathbf{y}$ may be written as $\mathbf{y} = \mathbf{y}^1 + \mathbf{y}^2$, where $\mathbf{y}^1 \in \overline{Y}_1$ and $\mathbf{y}^2 \in \overline{Y}_2$. Since maximum profits are earned in each

production process, it must be that $\mathbf{p}.\mathbf{y}^1 = 0 = \mathbf{p}.\mathbf{y}^2$ and hence $\mathbf{p}.\mathbf{y} = 0$. Since (y_1, y_2) lies in the output possibility set, there is an α such that $0 < \alpha < 1$ and

$$(y_1, y_2) \leq \alpha(5/9, 0) + (1 - \alpha)(0, 5/8).$$

Therefore

$$\mathbf{y} = (y_1, y_2, -1) \leq \alpha(5/9, 0, -1) + (1 - \alpha)(0, 5/8, -1),$$

and so

$$0 = \mathbf{p}.\mathbf{y} = \mathbf{p}.(y_1, y_2, -1) \leq \alpha\mathbf{p}.(5/9, 0, -1) + (1 - \alpha)\mathbf{p}.(0, 5/8, -1) \leq 0 + 0 = 0,$$

where the second inequality follows because (5/9, 0, −1) and (0, 5/8, −1) belong to the total input-output possibility set $\bar{Y}_1 + \bar{Y}_2$, and we know that the maximum profits to be earned in this cone are zero. Since these vectors earn at most zero profits, the above inequality implies that

$$\mathbf{p}.(5/9, 0, -1) = 0$$

and

$$\mathbf{p}.(0, 5/8, -1) = 0.$$

Since the third component of $\mathbf{p}$, the price of labor, is 1, these two equations imply, in turn, that

$$p_1 = \frac{9}{5},$$

and

$$p_2 = \frac{8}{5}.$$

That is, $\mathbf{p} = (9/5, 8/5, 1)$.

Answer to Homework Problems for Chapter 4, Problem #18

Problem: 18) An economy with two produced commodities and labor has linear production processes represented by activity vectors (-1, -1, 3) and (-1, 2, -1), where the first commodity is labor. If the price of labor is one, what are the prices of the other two commodities in a competitive equilibrium in which positive amounts of both the second and third goods are consumed?

Answer: Because the model is linear, it has constant returns to scale, so that maximum profits are zero in a competitive equilibrium. Since positive amounts of both outputs are produced, both processes are used and both must earn zero profits. Therefore, the desired price vector **p** is of the form $(1, p_2, p_3)$ and must satisfy the equations

$$(1, p_2, p_3).(-1, -1, 3) = 0$$

and

$$(1, p_2, p_3).(-1, 2, -1) = 0.$$

These equations may be written as

$$-1 - p_2 + 3p_3 = 0$$

and

$$-1 + 2p_2 - p_3 = 0.$$

The solution of these equations is $p_2 = 4/5$ and $p_3 = 3/5$, so that the desired price vector is **p** = $(-1,\ 4/5,\ 3/5)$.

Answer to Homework Problems for Chapter 4, Problem #19

Problem: 19) There are two primary goods, goods 1 and 2, and there are two produced goods, goods 3 and 4. There is an endowment of one unit of each of the primary goods. The production functions for goods 3 and 4 are, respectively,

$$f_3(y_1, y_2) = \min(2y_1, y_2) \text{ and } f_4(y_1, y_2) = \min(y_1, 2y_2).$$

a) In a box diagram, indicate the set of efficient allocations of goods 1 and 2 to the production of goods 3 and 4.

b) Draw the output possibility set for goods 3 and 4.

c) Suppose that equal positive quantities of goods 3 and 4 are produced at a point, $\underline{z}$, on the output possibility frontier for goods 3 and 4. If the price of good 4 is one, what are the possible prices of goods 1, 2, and 3, such that the point $\underline{z}$ would be produced if both production processes were operated so as to maximize profits at these prices and if no more than the endowments of goods 1 and 2 were used in production?

Answer: a) The efficient allocations are shaded in the diagram below.

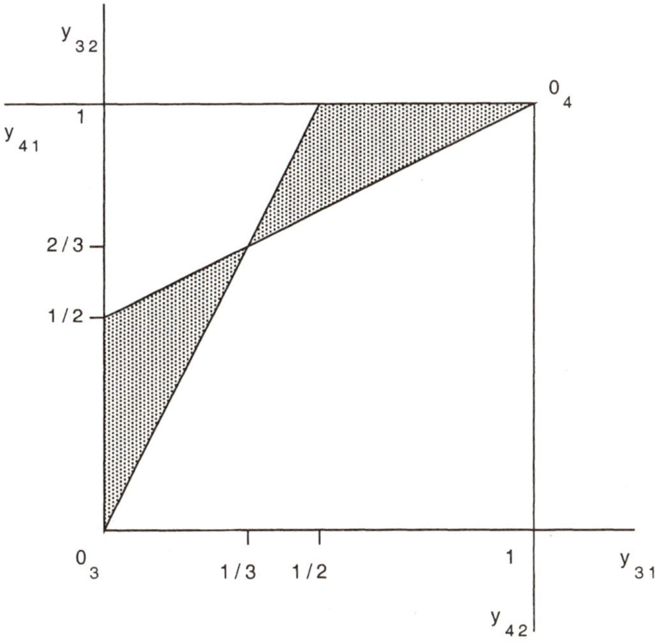

Answer: b) The output possibility set is the shaded region in the diagram below.

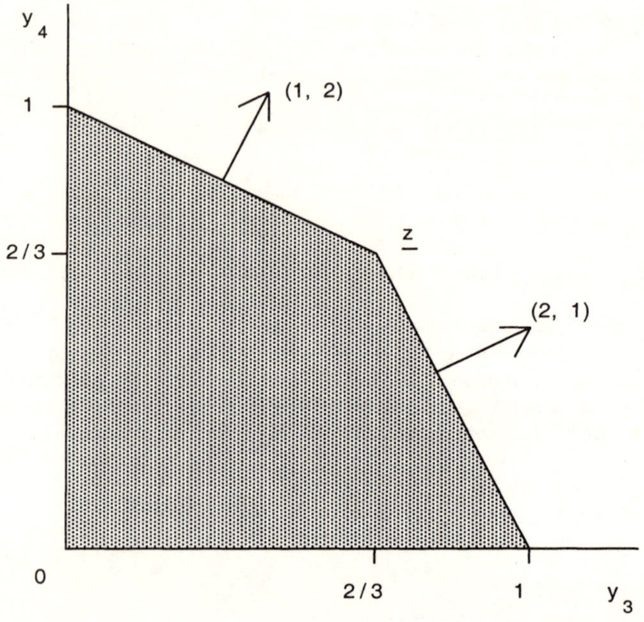

Answer: c) The point (2/3, 2/3) is the point $\underline{z}$ on the output possibility frontier where equal quantities of the two goods are produced. Let p_n be the price of good n, for each n. The vectors (1, 2) and (2, 1) are vectors of prices for the third and fourth goods that are perpendicular to the two faces of the output possibility frontier. The vector (p_3, p_4) must be between these vectors in direction, if it is to be perpendicular to the output possibility frontier at the point $\underline{z}$ = (2/3, 2/3). This means that

$$\frac{1}{2} \leq \frac{p_3}{p_4} \leq 2.$$

Since $p_4 = 1$, we have that

$$\frac{1}{2} \leq p_3 \leq 2.$$

Because the production processes have constant returns to scale, maximum profits are zero for each. Since twice as much of good 2 as good 1 is used to produce good 3, profits are zero in the production of good 3 if and only if

$$p_1 + 2p_2 = p_3.$$

Similarly since twice as much of good 1 as good is used to produce good 4, profits are zero in the production of good 4 if and only if

$$2p_1 + p_2 = p_4 = 1.$$

In summary, the set of possible prices for goods 1, 2, and 3 if $\underline{z}$ is produced and profits are maximized is

$$\{(p_1, p_2, p_3) \mid 1/2 \leq p_3 \leq 2,\ p_1 + 2p_2 = p_3,\ 2p_1 + p_2 = 1\}.$$

Answer to Homework Problems for Chapter 4, Problem #20

Problem: 20) Think of a society with three commodities, labor, food, and wood. It has four linear activities, described by the following matrix.

	activity 1	activity 2	activity 3	activity 4
food	5	7	−5	−3
wood	−2	−6	12	10
labor	−1	−1	−1	−1

The society has one unit of labor available.

a) Plot the society's output possibility frontier for food and wood.

b) Suppose the society consumes both food and wood and that all commodities are priced so that activities are operated so as to maximize profits at those prices. If production is organized efficiently, what must the prices of food and wood be in terms of labor?

Answer: a) The output possibility frontier is found by plotting the top two coefficients for each activity. The non-labor components of each activity are indicated by crosses. The cross for activity k is labeled $\mathbf{a}_k$. The output possibility frontier is the thick line part of the line segment from $\mathbf{a}_4$ to $\mathbf{a}_1$ that is in the non-negative quadrant. It intercepts the vertical axis at 11/2 and the horizontal axis at 11/3. The vector (3, 2) is orthogonal to the frontier and may be thought of as a price vector for food and wood, respectively. A way to check that the third and second activities are not used in defining the frontier is to check the profit earned by each activity at these prices. The cost of labor may be ignored in this calculation, since one unit of labor is used in each activity vector. Thus

$$(3, 2).\mathbf{a}_1 = (3, 2).(5, -2) = 11.$$

$$(3, 2).\mathbf{a}_2 = (3, 2).(7, -6) = 9.$$

$$(3, 2).\mathbf{a}_3 = (3, 2).(-5, 12) = 9.$$

$$(3, 2).\mathbf{a}_4 = (3, 2).(-3, 10) = 11.$$

The activities used are the ones earning the most profit, and the equation defining the frontier is

$$(3, 2).(y_1, y_2) = 11,$$

where y_1 and y_2 are the quantities of food and wood, respectively.

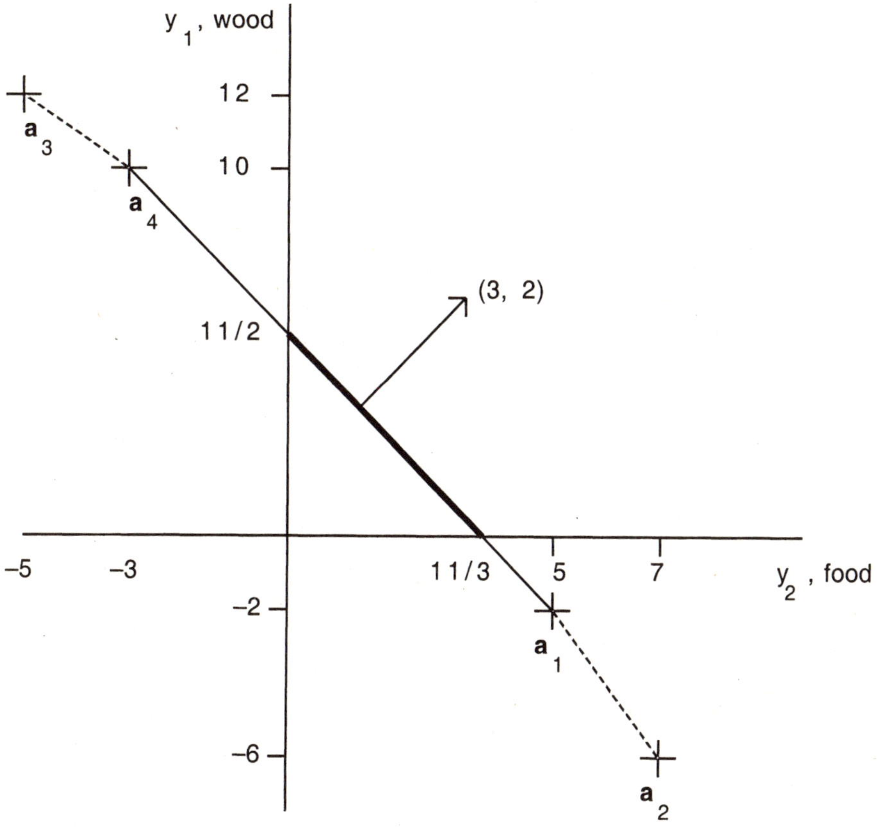

Answer: b) Since the first and fourth activities must earn zero profit, the price vector $(p_1, p_2, 1)$ satisfies the equations

$$(p_1, p_2, 1).(5, -2, -1) = 0$$

$$(p_1, p_2, 1).(-3, 10, -1) = 0.$$

These may be written as

$$5p_1 - 2p_2 = 1$$

$$-3p_1 + 10p_2 = 1.$$

The solution of these equations is $p_1 = 3/11$ and $p_2 = 2/11$, so that the entire price vector is $(p_1, p_2, 1) = (3/11, 2/11, 1)$.

Answer to Homework Problems for Chapter 4, Problem #21

Problem: 21) Consider the following linear activity model. There are two produced goods, food and wood, and two primary inputs, labor and land. One unit of each of labor and land are available. There are three activities, with coefficient vectors given in the following table.

	activity 1	activity 2	activity 3
food	6	6	- 1
wood	- 1	- 1	6
labor	- 2	- 1	- 2
land	- 1	- 2	- 1

a) Find the production possibility frontier between food and wood.
b) Draw the frontier.
c) What are the prices of food, wood, and land in terms of labor if prices are such that profits are maximized and twice as much food is produced as wood?

Answer: a, b) I find the output possibility frontier by defining finitely many points on it such that all the other points are convex combinations of these points. These points may be found by considering the set of all possible feasible vectors of activity levels. A vector of activity levels is of the form $\mathbf{x} = (x_1, x_2, x_3)$, where x_k is the level at which activity k is operated, for k = 1, 2, 3. That is, if the activity level vector is $\mathbf{x}$, then the total input-output vector is

$$x_1\begin{pmatrix}6\\-1\\-2\\-1\end{pmatrix} + x_2\begin{pmatrix}6\\-1\\-1\\-2\end{pmatrix} + x_3\begin{pmatrix}-1\\6\\-2\\-1\end{pmatrix}.$$

The vector $\mathbf{x}$ is feasible if the total input-output vector consumes no more than the available resources. That is, $\mathbf{x}$ is feasible if $\mathbf{x} \geq 0$ and

$$2x_1 + x_2 + 2x_3 \leq 1$$

and

$$x_1 + 2x_2 + x_3 \leq 1.$$

This set is pictured in the next diagram. The upper surfaces of the set are shaded. The dashed lines are the intersections of the planes $2x_1 + x_2 + 2x_3 = 1$ or $x_1 + 2x_2 + x_3 = 1$ with the planes $x_1 = 0$, $x_2 = 0$, or $x_3 = 0$. The second coordinate axis going into the paper is stretched for clarity. One may see from the diagram that every point in this set is a convex combination

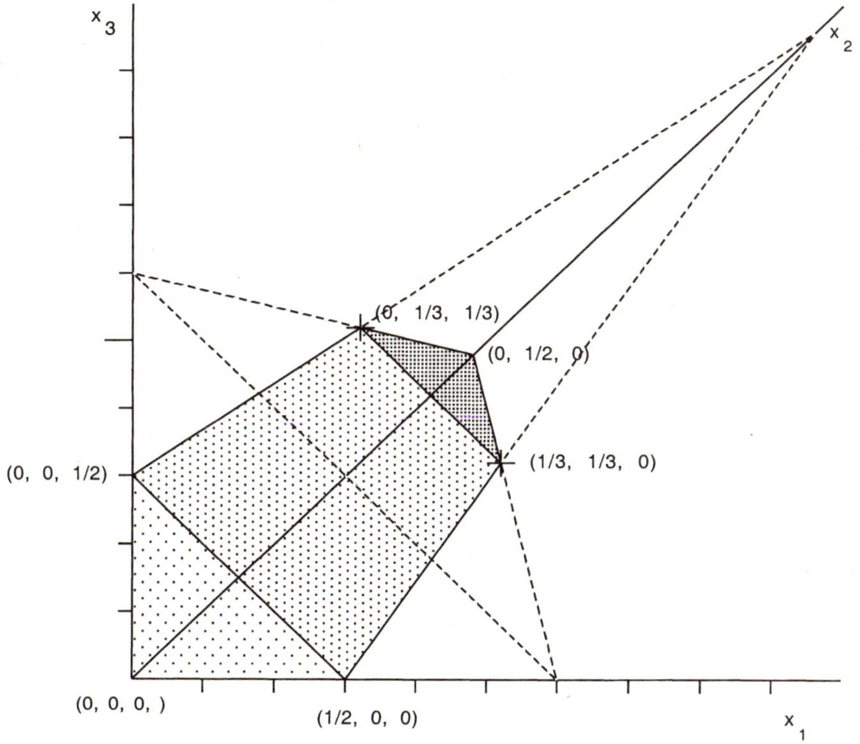

of six vertices or corners of the set. These vertices are (0, 0, 0), (1/2, 0, 0), (1/3, 1/3, 0), (0, 1/2, 0), (0, 1/3, 1/3), and (0, 0, 1/2). It follows that every feasible output vector is a convex combination of the output vectors obtained from these six activity level vectors. The following table presents these output vectors (y_1, y_2).

$\mathbf{x}$ = (0, 0, 0)	(y_1, y_2) = (0, 0)
$\mathbf{x}$ = (1/2, 0, 0)	(y_1, y_2) = (3, −1/2)
$\mathbf{x}$ = (1/3, 1/3, 0)	(y_1, y_2) = (4, −2/3)
$\mathbf{x}$ = (0, 1/2, 0)	(y_1, y_2) = (3, −1/2)
$\mathbf{x}$ = (0, 1/3, 1/3)	(y_1, y_2) = (5/3, 5/3)
$\mathbf{x}$ = (0, 0, 1/2)	(y_1, y_2) = (−1/2, 3)

The points (3, −1/2), (4, −2/3), (5/3, 5/3), and (−1/2, 3) appear as crosses in the next diagram. The output possibility frontier is the outer edge of the set of convex combinations of these vectors. The set of convex combinations is shaded with dots and the frontier is the heavy line. It goes from the point (0, 105/39) to (5/3, 5/3) to (10/3, 0).

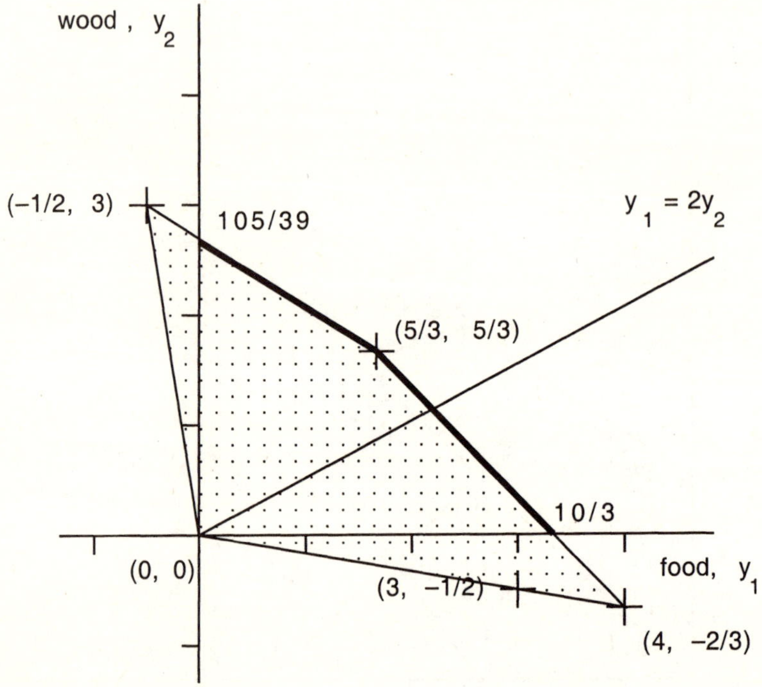

Answer: c) The line $y_1 = 2y_2$ is shown in the above figure. It intersects the frontier at a point between the points (5/3, 5/3) and (4, −2/3). (The intersection point is at (20/9, 10/9).) The output vector (5/3, 5/3) is produced using activities 2 and 3. The net output vector (4, −2/3) is produced using activities 1 and 2. Therefore all three activities are used. These activities must earn zero profits, since profits are maximized and linear models have constant returns to scale. Since all prices are in terms of labor, its price is 1, and the price vector has the form $\mathbf{p} = (p_1, p_2, 1, p_4)$. Since all three activities earn zero profits, this price vector satisfies the equations

$$(p_1, p_2, 1, p_4).(6, -1, -2, -1) = 0$$

$$(p_1, p_2, 1, p_4).(6, -1, -1, -2) = 0$$

$$(p_1, p_2, 1, p_4).(-1, 6, -2, -1) = 0.$$

These may be written as

$$6p_1 - p_2 - p_4 = 2$$

$$6p_1 - p_2 - 2p_4 = 1$$

$$-p_1 + 6p_2 - p_4 = 2.$$

The solution to these equations is

$$\mathbf{p} = (p_1, p_2, 1, p_4) = (3/5, 3/5, 1, 1).$$

Answer to Homework Problems for Chapter 4, Problem #22

Problem: 22) Suppose that steel (S) is produced from coal (C) and labor (L) according to the production function $S = 2\sqrt{CL}$, and coal is produced from steel and labor according to the production function $C = \sqrt{SL}$. There is one unit of labor available for coal and steel production. Find the production possibility frontier for coal and steel.

Answer: The input-output set Y is pictured in the next diagram. The production possibility frontier is the heavy line. The first task is to find a precise formula for the frontier. Let S_1 be

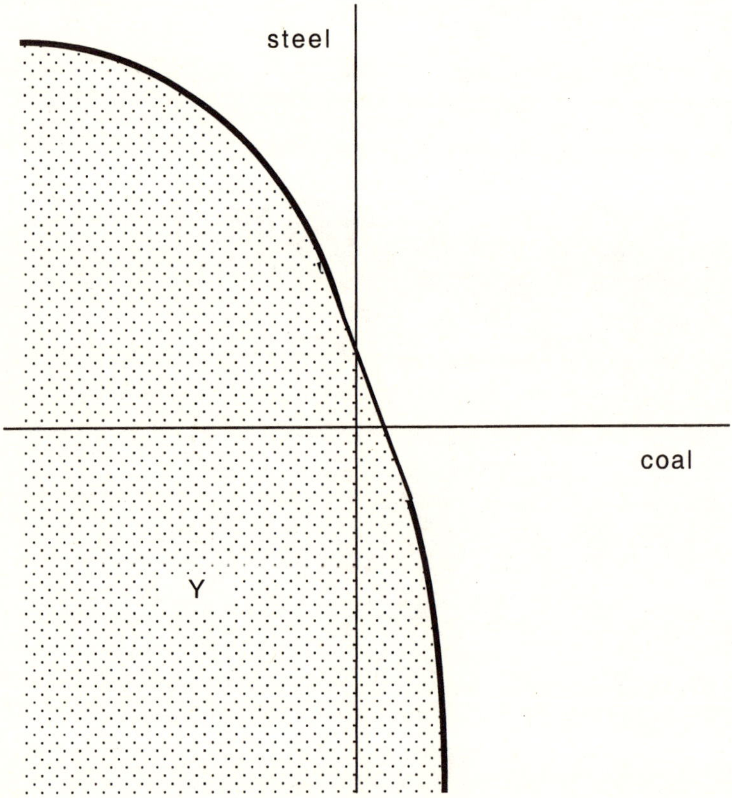

steel output and let C_1 be coal input used to produce steel, where $C_1 < 0$. Steel output and coal input are related by the equation

$$S_1 = 2\sqrt{-C_1}.$$

The tangent line to this production function is

$$S = 2\sqrt{-C_1} + \left(-\frac{1}{\sqrt{-C_1}}\right)(C - C_1) = \sqrt{-C_1} - \frac{C}{\sqrt{-C_1}},$$

where C and S are the net outputs of coal and steel, respectively. Let C_2 be coal output and let S_2 be the input of steel used to produce coal, where $S_2 < 0$. Coal output and steel input are related by the equation

$$C_2 = \sqrt{-S_2},$$

which is the same as

$$S_2 = -C_2^2.$$

The tangent line to this last function is

$$S = -C_2^2 (-2C_2)(C - C_2) = C_2^2 - 2C_2 C.$$

The straight segment of the production possibility frontier is part of both of these tangent lines, so that the two lines must coincide. If the tangent lines coincide, they have the same coefficients, which implies the two equations

$$\sqrt{-C_1} = C_2^2$$

and

$$\frac{1}{\sqrt{-C_1}} = 2C_2.$$

These equations imply that

$$C_2^2 = \frac{1}{2C_2},$$

so that

$$C_2 = \left(\frac{1}{2}\right)^{1/3}.$$

Therefore the tangent line is

$$S = \left(\frac{1}{2}\right)^{2/3} - 2^{2/3}C.$$

That is, if the net output of coal is zero, $2^{-2/3}$ units of steel are produced and if the net output of steel is zero, the net output of coal is $2^{-4/3}$. The straight segment of the production possibility frontier is defined by the function $S = \left(\frac{1}{2}\right)^{2/3} - 2^{2/3}C$ with C varying from $C_1 = -2^{-4/3}$ to $C_2 = 2^{-1/3}$. The curved segments of the production possibility frontiers are defined by the production functions $S = 2\sqrt{-C}$ in the second quadrant and $C = \sqrt{-S}$ in the fourth quadrant.

Answer to Homework Problems for Chapter 4, Problem #23

Problem: 23) Two people live on separate islands, Houtt and Coutt. Each person is endowed with one unit of labor. There are two produced goods, cloth and food. The utility function of each person is

$$u(x_F, x_C) = \frac{\ln(x_F)}{4} + \frac{3\ln(x_C)}{4},$$

where the notation should be obvious. On Houtt Island, the production functions for food and cloth are

$$y_F = 20L \text{ and } y_C = 10L,$$

respectively, where again the notation should be obvious. On Coutt Island, the production functions for food and cloth are

$$y_F = 10L \text{ and } y_C = 20L.$$

The two people cannot trade in food, cloth, or labor.

a) Compute the output possibility frontiers for food and cloth for the two islands separately, assuming that each island can use only the labor of the person on that island.

b) Compute an equilibrium for each island separately with the price of labor equal to one on both islands.

c) Compute the utility of Houtt and Coutt in the equilibrium. (This is the maximum each can obtain without trade.)

Now suppose that Houtt and Coutt can trade cloth and food freely, but still cannot trade labor. That is, neither can go work on the other's island.

d) What is the output possibility frontier for food and cloth now?

e) Compute a competitive equilibrium with free trade. Be sure to specify the production of Houtt and Coutt of each good. Let the price of Houtt's labor be one. Be sure to specify all prices, including the price of Coutt's labor.

f) What are the utility levels of Houtt and Coutt in the equilibrium with trade? Compare these utility levels with those from part (c).

Answer: a) Houtt's production possibility frontier is shown in the next diagram as a heavy line. Given the production functions and the fact that only one unit of labor is available, Houtt's output possibility frontier is

$$\{(y_F, y_C) = (20L, 10(1 - L)) \mid 0 \le L \le 1\} = \{(y_F, y_C) \in R^2_+ \mid y_C = 10 - \frac{1}{2}y_F\}.$$

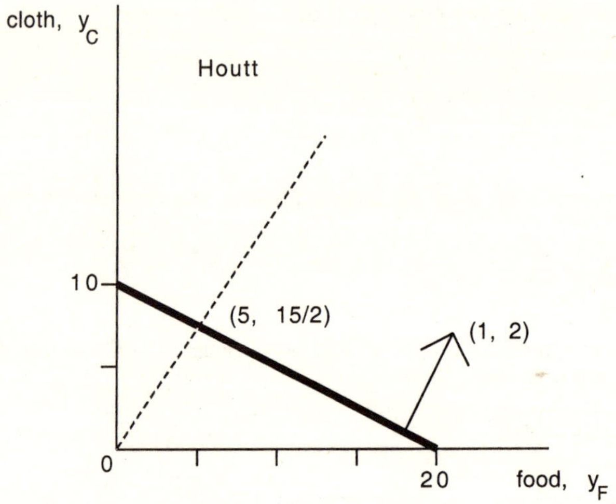

Similarly Coutt's production possibility frontier is

$$\{(y_F, y_C) = (10L, 20(1 - L)) \mid 0 \le L \le 1\} = \{(y_F, y_C) \in R^2_+ \mid y_C = 20 - 2y_F\}.$$

Coutt's output possibility frontier is shown as a heavy line in the next diagram.

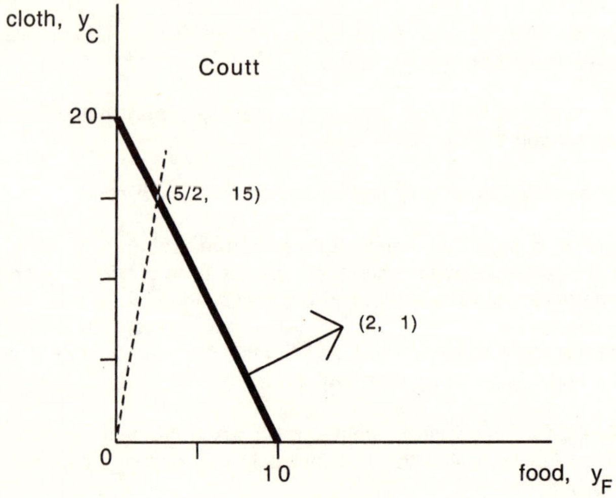

Answer: b) Since the utility function is Cobb-Douglas, Houtt will consume a positive amount of each output. Therefore the fact that the slope of Houtt's output possibility frontier is −1/2 implies that the price of cloth will be twice that of food. Provisionally let the price of food be 1 and that of cloth be 2, as shown in the first diagram above. Then Houtt's wealth is 20 and the demand for food satisfies the equation

$$x_F = \frac{1}{4}20 = 5.$$

Similarly the demand for cloth satisfies the equation

$$2x_C = \frac{3}{4}20,$$

so that

$$x_C = 15/2.$$

Notice that the dashed line in the first diagram is Houtt's income expansion line when the price of cloth is twice that of the price of food. The equilibrium allocation is at the intersection of the income expansion line and the production possibility frontier.

Since production satisfies constant returns to scale, profits are zero and so the price of labor is 20 when the price of food is 1 and the price of cloth is 2. If we normalize prices so that the price of labor is 1, then the price of food is 1/20 and the price of cloth is 1/10. In summary, the equilibrium on Houtt's island is

$$((p_L, p_F, p_C), (\overline{x}_F, \overline{x}_C), (-\overline{L}_F, \overline{y}_F), (-\overline{L}_C, \overline{y}_C))$$

$$= ((1, 1/20, 1/10), (5, 15/2), (-1/4, 5), (-3/4, 15/2)).$$

Using the same method, we see that the equilibrium on Coutt's island is

$$((p_L, p_F, p_C), (\overline{x}_F, \overline{x}_C), (-\overline{L}_F, \overline{y}_F), (-\overline{L}_C, \overline{y}_C))$$

$$= ((1, 1/10, 1/20), (5/2, 15), (-1/4, 5/2), (-3/4, 15)).$$

Answer: c) Houtt's utility from the equilibrium allocation is

$$v_H = \frac{1}{4}\ln 5 + \frac{3}{4}\ln \frac{15}{2}.$$

Coutt's utility from the equilibrium allocation is

$$v_C = \frac{1}{4}\ln\frac{5}{2} + \frac{3}{4}\ln 15.$$

Answer: d) The output possibility frontier is the heavy line in the next diagram. It is obtained by taking the northeast frontier of the sum of the output possibility sets for Houtt and Coutt when their islands produce in isolation.

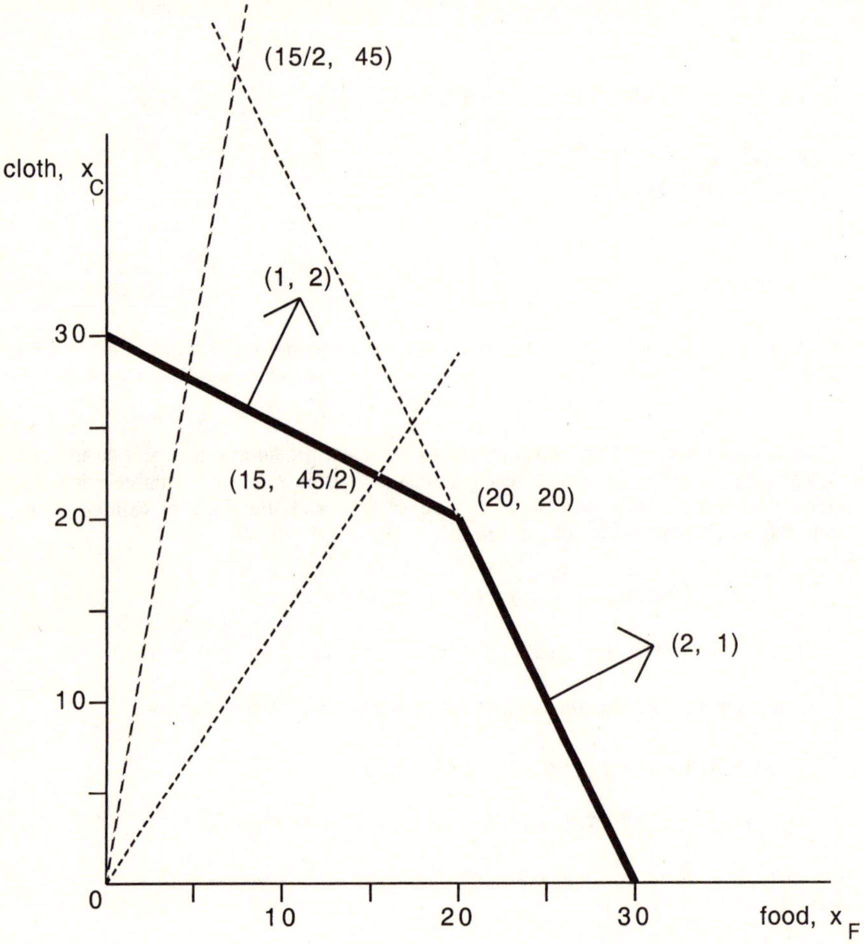

Answer: e) Let us assume that the vector of total outputs will be inside one of the two faces of the total output frontier. If it is on the lower face, the price of food is twice that of cloth. At these relative prices for food and cloth, the income expansion line for both consumers is the steeper of the positively sloped dashed lines. The equation for this line is $x_C = 6x_F$. This line does not intersect the lower face of the output possibility frontier, so that the price of food cannot be twice that of cloth in equilibrium.

If the total output is inside the upper face, then cloth is twice as expensive as food and the income expansion line for both consumers is the flatter positively sloped dashed line, $x_C = (3/2)x_F$. This line intersects the upper face at the point $(y_F, y_C) = (15, 15/2)$, which is interior to the face. This is the vector of total outputs or consumptions in equilibrium.

If the price of cloth is twice that of food, Coutt maximizes profits by producing 20 units of cloth and no food, so that, using obvious notation, $\mathbf{y}_C = (y_{CF}, y_{CC}) = (0, 20)$. Houtt maximizes profits by producing anywhere along the Houtt island output possibility frontier. To achieve a total output (15, 45/2), Houtt produces 15 units of food and 5/2 units of cloth. That is, $\mathbf{y}_H = (y_{HF}, y_{HC}) = (15, 5/2)$.

If the price of food is 1 and that of cloth is 2, then Houtt's wealth is 20, so that her or his consumption of food satisfies the equation

$$x_{HF} = \frac{1}{4}20 = 5,$$

and her or his consumption of cloth satisfies the equation

$$2x_{HF} = \frac{3}{4}20 = 15.$$

That is,

$$x_{HF} = \frac{15}{2}.$$

By feasibility, we know that Coutt's consumptions are

$$x_{CF} = 15 - 5 = 10$$

and

$$x_{cc} = \frac{45}{2} - \frac{15}{2} = 15.$$

If the price of food is 1 and the price of cloth is 2, then Houtt's revenue from production is 20, so that the price of her or his labor is 20. If we normalize prices so that Houtt's wage is 1, then the price of food is 1/20 and that of cloth is 1/10. At these prices, Coutt's revenue from production is 20/10 = 2, which must be the value of her or his labor, since profits are zero.

In summary, the equilibrium is, using obvious notation,

$$((p_{HL}, p_{CL}, p_F, p_C), (\overline{x}_{HF}, \overline{x}_{HC}), (\overline{x}_{CF}, \overline{x}_{CC}), (-\overline{L}_{HF}, \overline{y}_{HF}), (-\overline{L}_{HC}, \overline{y}_{HC}),$$

$$(-\overline{L}_{CF}, \overline{y}_{CF}), (-\overline{L}_{CC}, \overline{y}_{CC}))$$

$$= ((1, 2, 1/20, 1/10), (5, 15/2), (10, 15), (-3/4, 15), (-1/4, 5/2),$$

$$(0, 0), (-1, 20)).$$

Answer: f) Houtt's utility with trade is

$$v_H = \frac{1}{4}\ln 5 + \frac{3}{4}\ln \frac{15}{2},$$

which is the same as her or his utility before trade. In fact, Houtt has the same consumption in both situations.

Coutt's utility with trade is

$$v_C = \frac{1}{4}\ln 10 + \frac{3}{4}\ln 15,$$

which exceeds her or his utility before trade of

$$v_C = \frac{1}{4}\ln \frac{5}{2} + \frac{3}{4}\ln 15.$$

Coutt does better with trade because her or his consumption of food increases from 5/2 to 10 while the consumption of cloth stays constant at 15.

Answer to Homework Problems for Chapter 4, Problem #24

Problem: 24) Robinson Crusoe and Friday live on separate islands and produce two goods, food and cloth using two factors of production, labor (L) and land (T). The utility functions of both Crusoe and Friday are

$$u(x_F, x_C) = x_F x_C,$$

where the notation should be obvious. The production function for food is

$$y_F = 4L^{3/4}T^{1/4}.$$

The production function for cloth is

$$y_C = 4L^{1/4}T^{3/4}.$$

Crusoe is endowed with two units of labor and one of land. Friday is endowed with one unit of labor and two of land.

a) Suppose there is no trade between the islands. Compute separate equilibria for Crusoe and Friday, letting the labor of each be the unit of account on his own island.

b) Suppose there is free trade between the islands in cloth and food, but no trade in labor and land. Compute the equilibrium for the two islands together with the labor of Crusoe as unit of account. (Hint: Use the symmetry of the problem.)

Answer: Before proceeding with the solution, it is important to notice the symmetry of the problem. Land plays the same role on Crusoe's island as labor does on Friday's, and labor plays the same role for Crusoe as does land for Friday. Similarly the roles of food and cloth are interchanged when going from Crusoe's to Friday's island.

The equilibria will not be changed if we replace the utility function by a monotone transformation of it, so I replace the utility function with the natural logarithm of it,

$$\ln u(x_F, x_C) = \ln x_F + \ln x_C.$$

This replacemen makes calculations easier.

In order to keep track of variables, I use two subscripts. For allocation variables, the first subscript is C or F, which stand for Crusoe and Friday, respectively. The second is again C or F, which stand for cloth and food, respectively. Thus, L_{CF} stands for labor used on Crusoe's island in food production, T_{FC} stands for land used on Friday's island in cloth production, y_{CC} stands for Crusoe's production of cloth, and x_{FF} stands for Friday's food consumption. For prices the first subscript is C or F, which stand for Crusoe and Friday, and the second subscript is F, C, L, or T, which stand, respectively, for food, cloth, labor, and land. When there is free trade, the prices for food and cloth cannot vary with the island, so that their prices are p_F and p_C, respectively.

a) I find the solution for Crusoe's island. The solution for Friday's island may then be found by using the symmetry just described. In the calculation that immediately follows, I let $L = L_{CF}$ and $T = T_{CF}$. Equilibrium allocations in one consumer economies maximize the utility of the consumer over feasible allocations. Therefore we may find the equilibrium allocation simply by maximizing Crusoe's utility. If we substitute the production functions into Crusoe's utility function and maximize it over feasible allocations of Crusoe's labor and land, we obtain the problem

$$\max_{L \geq 0,\, T \geq 0} \left[\ln L^{3/4}T^{1/4} + \ln (2 - L)^{1/4}(1 - T)^{3/4}\right].$$

If we multiple the objective function by 4, this problem may be rewritten as

$$\max_{L \geq 0,\, T \geq 0} \left[3\ln L + \ln T + \ln (2 - L) + 3\ln (1 - T)\right].$$

If we set the derivative of the objective function with respect to L equal to zero, we obtain the equation

$$\frac{3}{L} = \frac{1}{2 - L},$$

which implies that

$$L = 3/2.$$

If we set the derivative of the objective function with respect to T equal to zero, we obtain the equation

$$\frac{1}{T} = \frac{3}{1 - T},$$

which implies that

$$T = 1/4.$$

That is, $L_{CF} = 3/2$, and $T_{CF} = 1/4$. By feasibility, $L_{CC} = 2 - L_{CF} = 1/2$, and $T_{CC} = 1 - T_{CF} = 3/4$. It follows that

$$x_{CF} = y_{CF} = 4L_{CF}^{3/4}T_{CF}^{1/4} = 4\left(\frac{3}{2}\right)^{3/4}\left(\frac{1}{4}\right)^{1/4} = 2^{3/4}3^{3/4},$$

and

$$x_{CC} = y_{CC} = 4L_{CC}^{1/4}T_{CC}^{3/4} = 4\left(\frac{1}{2}\right)^{1/4}\left(\frac{3}{4}\right)^{3/4} = 2^{1/4}3^{3/4}.$$

These equations determine the allocation for the equilibrium on Crusoe's island, when it operates in isolation. In order to obtain the equilibrium prices, we may consider the profit maximization problems for the production of food and cloth. The profit maximization problem for food is

$$\max_{L \geq 0,\, T \geq 0} [p_{CF} 4L^{3/4}T^{1/4} - L - p_{CT} T],$$

where L and T again stand for L_{CF} and T_{CF}, respectively. No symbol for the price of labor appears here, because it is assumed to be 1. If we set the derivative of the objective function with respect to L equal to zero, we obtain the equation

$$3p_{CF}\left(\frac{T}{L}\right)^{1/4} = 1,$$

so that

$$p_{CF} = \frac{1}{3}\left(\frac{L_{CF}}{T_{CF}}\right)^{1/4} = \frac{1}{3}\left(\frac{3/2}{1/4}\right)^{1/4} = \frac{2^{1/4}}{3^{3/4}}. \qquad \text{(A)}$$

If we set the derivative of the objective function with respect to T equal to zero, we obtain the equation

$$p_{CF}\left(\frac{L}{T}\right)^{3/4} = p_{CT},$$

so that

$$p_{CT} = p_{CF}\left(\frac{L_{CF}}{T_{CF}}\right)^{3/4} = \frac{2^{1/4}}{3^{3/4}}\left(\frac{3/2}{1/4}\right)^{3/4} = 2. \qquad \text{(B)}$$

The profit maximization problem for cloth is

$$\max_{L \geq 0,\, T \geq 0} [p_{CC} 4L^{1/4}T^{3/4} - L - p_{CT} T],$$

where L and T now stand for L_{CC} and T_{CC}, respectively. If we set the derivative of the objective function with respect to L equal to zero, we obtain the equation

$$p_{CC}\left(\frac{T}{L}\right)^{3/4} = 1,$$

so that

$$p_{CC} = \left(\frac{L_{CC}}{T_{CC}}\right)^{3/4} = \left(\frac{1/2}{3/4}\right)^{3/4} = \left(\frac{2}{3}\right)^{3/4}.$$

In summary, the equilibrium on Crusoe's island is described by the equations

$$x_{CF} = y_{CF} = 2^{3/4}3^{3/4},\ x_{CC} = y_{CC} = 2^{1/4}3^{3/4},$$

$$L_{CF} = 3/2,\ T_{CF} = 1/4,\ L_{CC} = 1/2,\ T_{CC} = 3/4,$$

$$p_{CF} = 2^{1/4}3^{-3/4},\ p_{CC} = 2^{3/4}3^{-3/4},\ p_{CL} = 1,\ p_{CT} = 2.$$

I now find the equilibrium for <u>Friday's island</u>. This may be read off simply by taking advantage of the symmetry between the two islands. In calculating prices, we must remember that the price of Friday's labor must be 1, so that we have to divide all prices by the price for labor that we obtain from symmetry. This latter price is $p_{FL} = p_{CT} = 2$, so that all prices obtained through the symmetry must be divided by 2. The equilibrium on Friday's island is described by the equations

$$x_{FF} = y_{FF} = y_{CC} = 2^{1/4}3^{3/4},\ x_{FC} = y_{FC} = y_{CF} = 2^{3/4}3^{3/4},$$

$$L_{FF} = T_{CC} = 3/4,\ L_{FC} = T_{CF} = 1/4,\ T_{FF} = L_{CC} = 1/2,\ T_{FC} = L_{CF} = 3/2,$$

$$p_{FF} = p_{CC} = 2^{3/4}3^{-3/4}2^{-1} = 2^{-1/4}3^{-3/4},\ p_{FC} = p_{CF} = 2^{1/4}3^{-3/4}2^{-1} = 2^{-3/4}3^{-3/4},$$

$$p_{FL} = p_{CT}/2 = 2/2 = 1,\ p_{FT} = p_{CL}/2 = 1/2.$$

<u>Answer</u>: b) In this part, the symmetry of the problem helps a great deal. The total output possibility set is symmetric about the diagonal. To see why this is so, let (y_F, y_C) be a point in the output possibility set, where y_F and y_C are the outputs of food and cloth, respectively. This point is realized by a production allocation of labor and land $(L_{CF}, L_{CC}, T_{CF}, T_{CC}, L_{FF}, L_{FC}, T_{FF}, T_{FC})$

that leads to outputs by Crusoe of Friday of $y_{CF}, y_{CC}, y_{FF}, y_{FC}$, where $y_F = y_{CF} + y_{FF}$ and $y_C = y_{CC} + y_{FC}$. We may obtain a new production allocation by having Crusoe and Friday exchange input allocations while switching the roles of labor and land. Let the new allocation by underscored, so that $\underline{L}_{CF} = T_{FC}$, $\underline{L}_{CC} = T_{FF}$, and so on. This new allocation results in new outputs, $\underline{y}_{CF}, \underline{y}_{CC}, \underline{y}_{FF}, \underline{y}_{FC}$, where $\underline{y}_{CF} = y_{FC}$, $\underline{y}_{CC} = y_{FF}$, and so on. The resulting new point on the total output possibility set is $(\underline{y}_F, \underline{y}_C) = (y_C, y_F)$. That is, the total output possibility set is symmetric about the line of slope 1 through the origin. Hence if the price of food and cloth were the same, revenues would be maximized by producing the same amounts of both outputs.

Another important observation is that since the total inputs of labor and land are fixed, the total cost of inputs does not depend on the allocation, as long as the allocation is feasible. Therefore if a production allocation maximizes profits and is feasible, it maximizes revenue among feasible allocations. Since an equilibrium allocation maximizes profits and is feasible, it maximizes revenue from output, and so produces the same amount of both outputs, if the prices of the two outputs are the same.

The utility function of both Crusoe and Friday is also symmetric about the diagonal, so that if the price of food and cloth are the same, both consumers consume the same amounts of both commodities. We see therefore that we can achieve an equilibrium by having the price of food and cloth be the same.

Let us provisionally let the price of food and cloth be 1 and maximize the revenue from Crusoe's production. This calculation will give us Crusoe's allocation of labor and land and his output of food and cloth. We can then use symmetry to obtain Friday's input and output allocation. Symmetry will then give us Crusoe's and Friday's consumption of food and cloth. We can then let the price of Crusoe's labor be 1 and use the first order conditions of Crusoe's profit maximization problem to obtain the prices of food and cloth and the price of Crusoe's land. Symmetry then gives us the prices of Friday's labor and land.

Crusoe's revenue maximization problem is

$$\max_{L \geq 0,\, T \geq 0} \left[4L^{3/4}T^{1/4} + 4(2 - L)^{1/4}(1 - T)^{3/4}\right],$$

where L stands for L_{CF} and T stands for T_{CF}. If we set the derivative of the objective function with respect to L equal to zero, we obtain

$$3\left(\frac{T}{L}\right)^{1/4} = \left(\frac{1 - T}{2 - L}\right)^{3/4}. \qquad \text{(C)}$$

If we set the derivative of the objective function with respect to T equal to zero, we find that

$$\left(\frac{L}{T}\right)^{3/4} = 3\left(\frac{2-L}{1-T}\right)^{1/4}. \tag{D}$$

If we invert both sides of equation D, we have

$$3\left(\frac{T}{L}\right)^{3/4} = \left(\frac{1-T}{2-L}\right)^{1/4}. \tag{E}$$

If we multiply equations C and E, we arrive at

$$9\left(\frac{T}{L}\right) = \frac{1-T}{2-L}.$$

A little algebra shows that this equation implies that

$$L = \frac{18T}{1+8T}. \tag{F}$$

Hence

$$2 - L = \frac{2(1-T)}{1+8T}. \tag{G}$$

If we substitute equations F and G into equation E, we find that

$$3\left(\frac{T(1+8T)}{18T}\right)^{1/4} = \left(\frac{(1-T)(1+8T)}{2(1-T)}\right)^{3/4}.$$

A little more algebra then reveals that L = 15/8 and T = 5/8. That is, $L_{CF} = 15/8$, $L_{CC} = 1/8$, $T_{CF} = 5/8$, and $T_{CC} = 3/8$. It follows that

$$y_{CF} = 4(L_{CF})^{3/4}(T_{CF})^{1/4} = 4\left(\frac{15}{8}\right)^{3/4}\left(\frac{5}{8}\right)^{1/4} = \frac{5}{2}3^{3/4}$$

$$y_{CC} = 4(L_{CC})^{1/4}(T_{CC})^{3/4} = 4\left(\frac{1}{8}\right)^{1/4}\left(\frac{3}{8}\right)^{3/4} = \frac{1}{2}3^{3/4}.$$

I now show that

$$x_{CF} = x_{CC} = \frac{y_{CF} + y_{CC}}{2} = \frac{3}{2}3^{3/4}. \tag{H}$$

It has already been argued that the consumers consume the same amount of the two produced goods, so that $x_{CF} = x_{CC}$. The symmetry of the problem implies that $x_{CC} = x_{FF}$. That is, Crusoe consumes the as much cloth as Friday does food. It follows that $x_{CF} = x_{FF}$. That is, Crusoe and Friday consume the same amount of food, which must therefore equal the average amount of food produced. That is, $x_{CF} = (y_{CF} + y_{FF})/2$. By symmetry again, $y_{FF} = y_{CC}$, so that $x_{CF} = (y_{CF} + y_{CC})/2$. The second equation in H follows by substituting the values for y_{CF} and y_{CC}.

Friday's allocation can now be obtained from symmetry. Thus,

$$L_{FF} = T_{CC} = 3/8$$

so that

$$L_{FC} = 1 - L_{FF} = 5/8.$$

Also

$$T_{FF} = L_{CC} = 1/8,$$

so that

$$T_{FC} = 2 - T_{FF} = 1\,5/8.$$

Also

$$y_{FF} = y_{CC} = \frac{1}{2}3^{3/4}$$

$$y_{FC} = y_{CF} = \frac{5}{2}3^{3/4}$$

$$x_{FF} = x_{FC} = x_{CF} = \frac{3}{2}3^{3/4}.$$

Let us now drop the assumption that the price of food and cloth are 1 and adopt the normalization that the price of Crusoe's labor is 1. The renormalization of prices does not change the allocation that has just been calculated. I now calculate the equilibrium prices. Since $p_{CL} = 1$, it follows that $p_{FT} = p_{CL} = 1$.

Let us now drop the assumption that the prices of food and cloth are 1. Changing these prices does not change the allocation variables that have already been

The first equation of equations A still applies, so that

$$p_F = p_{CF} = \frac{1}{3}\left(\frac{L_{CF}}{T_{CF}}\right)^{1/4} = \frac{1}{3}\left(\frac{15/8}{5/8}\right)^{1/4} = \left(\frac{1}{3}\right)^{3/4}. \qquad (I)$$

Since the price of food and cloth are the same,

$$p_C = p_F = \left(\frac{1}{3}\right)^{3/4}.$$

The first equation of equations B still applies, so that

$$p_{CT} = p_F\left(\frac{L_{CF}}{T_{CF}}\right)^{3/4} = \frac{1}{3}\left(\frac{L_{CF}}{T_{CF}}\right)^{1/4}\left(\frac{L_{CF}}{T_{CF}}\right)^{3/4} = \frac{1}{3}\frac{L_{CF}}{T_{CF}} = \frac{1}{3}\frac{15/8}{5/8} = 1,$$

where the second equation follows by substituting equation I. Symmetry now implies that

$$p_{FL} = p_{CT} = 1.$$

In summary, the equilibrium is described by the equations

$$x_{CF} = x_{CC} = x_{FF} = x_{FC} = \frac{3}{2}3^{3/4}$$

$$y_{CF} = \frac{5}{2}3^{3/4} = y_{FC}$$

$$y_{CC} = \frac{1}{2}3^{3/4} = y_{FF}$$

$$L_{CF} = \frac{15}{8} = T_{FC}$$

$$L_{CC} = \frac{1}{8} = T_{FF}$$

$$T_{CF} = \frac{5}{8} = L_{FC}$$

$$T_{CC} = \frac{3}{8} = L_{FF}$$

$$p_F = p_C = \left(\frac{1}{3}\right)^{3/4}$$

$$p_{CL} = p_{CT} = p_{FL} = p_{FT} = 1.$$

Answer to Homework Problems for Chapter 4, Problem #25

Problem: 25) Consider an Edgeworth box economy with endowments $\mathbf{e}_A = (1, 0)$ and $\mathbf{e}_B = (0, 1)$ and utility functions $u_A(x_1, x_2)$ and $u_B(x_1, x_2)$.

a) Can an equilibrium exist if both utility functions are everywhere strictly decreasing with respect to x_1 and x_2?

b) Does an equilibrium necessarily exist if both u_A and u_B are decreasing with respect to x_1 and increasing with respect to x_2?

c) Does an equilibrium necessarily exist if u_A is decreasing with respect to x_1 and increasing with respect to x_2, and u_B is increasing with respect to x_1 and decreasing with respect to x_2?

Answer: a) No equilibrium exists. Since both utility functions are decreasing, $\xi_A(p_1, p_2) = (0, 0) = \xi_B(p_1, p_2)$, for any price vector (p_1, p_2). Therefore both goods are in excess demand at any prices. Hence in equilibrium, both prices must be zero. Since both prices cannot be zero, by the definition of a price vector, there can be no equilibrium.

b) Yes, an equilibrium does exist. Because u_A and u_B are both decreasing with respect to x_1, neither A nor B will demand any of good 1 at any price vector, so that there will be an excess supply of that good and its price will be zero. Consumer A therefore has no income and demands nothing in equilibrium. We may take the price of the second good to be 1. Since u_B is increasing with respect to x_2, consumer B will spend all her or his income on the second good and will consume her or his endowment.

c) Yes, an equilibrium does exist. We may take the equilibrium prices of both goods to be one. The consumers will exchange endowments. Consumer A will consume $\mathbf{e}_B = (0, 1)$ and consumer B will consume $\mathbf{e}_A = (1, 0)$.

Answer to Homework Problems for Chapter 4, Problem #26

Problem: 26) a) Which of the functions, $z : \{x \in R^N \mid x > 0\} \rightarrow R^N$, listed below could be the aggregate or market excess demand function for an economy in the sense that they are homogeneous of degree 0 and satisfy Walras' Law?

i) $z(p_1, p_2) = \dfrac{(p_1, p_2)}{||p||}$.

ii) $z(p_1, p_2) = \left(\dfrac{p_2 - p_1}{p_1}, \dfrac{p_1 - p_2}{p_2}\right)$.

iii) $z(p_1, p_2) = \dfrac{(p_2, -p_1)}{p_1 + p_2}$.

iv) $z(p_1, p_2) = \dfrac{(p_2, -p_1)}{p.p}$.

b) For each of the above four functions that could be the excess demand function for an economy, find an equilibrium price vector.

Answer: a) i) $z(p_1, p_2) = \dfrac{(p_1, p_2)}{||p||}$ cannot be a market excess demand function, because it does does not satisfy Walras' law, since $(p_1, p_2).z(p_1, p_2) = p_1^2 + p_2^2 > 0$.

ii) $z(p_1, p_2) = \left(\dfrac{p_2 - p_1}{p_1}, \dfrac{p_1 - p_2}{p_2}\right)$ satisfies Walras' law and is homogeneous of degree 0 in the sense that $z(tp_1, tp_2) = z(p_1, p_2)$, for all $t > 0$. It follows that z can be a market excess demand function.

iii) $z(p_1, p_2) = \dfrac{(p_2, -p_1)}{p_1 + p_2}$ satisfies Walras' law and is homogeneous of degree 0, so that it can be a market excess demand function.

iv) $z(p_1, p_2) = \dfrac{(p_2, -p_1)}{p.p}$ is not homogeneous of degree 0 and so cannot be a market excess demand function.

Answer: b) An equilibrium price vector for case ii is $(p_1, p_2) = (1, 1)$. An equilibrium price vector for case iii is $(p_1, p_2) = (1, 0)$, since at this price vector the excess demand for good 1 is 0 and the excess demand for the second good is negative.

Answer to Homework Problems for Chapter 4, Problem #27

Problem: 27) Three next door neighbors put up flagpoles. The flagpole height chosen by each neighbor depends continuously on the heights chosen by the other two. (For instance, having too high a pole compared to the neighbors would be ostentatious, whereas having one too small would look stingy.) A town ordinance imposes an upper limit of 100 feet on flagpoles heights. The choices of flagpoles heights are in equilibrium when no one wishes to change the height of their flagpole. Prove that there exists an equilibrium.

Answer: Let h_i be the flagpole height of neighbor i, were i = 1, 2, 3. Let $H_1(h_2, h_3)$, $H_2(h_1, h_3)$, and $H_3(h_1, h_2)$ be the pole height chosen by neighbors 1, 2, and 3, respectively. The functions H_i are continuous, by assumption. Define the function

$$H: [0, 100] \times [0, 100] \times [0, 100] \rightarrow [0, 100] \times [0, 100] \times [0, 100]$$

by the equation

$$H(h_1, h_2, h_3) = (H_1(h_2, h_3), H_2(h_1, h_3), H_3(h_1, h_2)).$$

The function H is continuous and the set $[0, 100] \times [0, 100] \times [0, 100]$ is convex and compact, so that by the Brouwer fixed point theorem there exists a point $(\bar{h}_1, \bar{h}_2, \bar{h}_3)$ in the set $[0, 100] \times [0, 100] \times [0, 100]$ such that

$$H(\bar{h}_1, \bar{h}_2, \bar{h}_3) = (\bar{h}_1, \bar{h}_2, \bar{h}_3).$$

Since $\bar{h}_1 = H_1(\bar{h}_2, \bar{h}_3)$, $\bar{h}_2 = H_2(\bar{h}_1, \bar{h}_3)$, and $\bar{h}_3 = H_3(\bar{h}_1, \bar{h}_2)$, it follows that $(\bar{h}_1, \bar{h}_2, \bar{h}_3)$ is an equilibrium.

Answer to Homework Problems for Chapter 4, Problem #28

Problem: 28) Suppose a stock market analyst publishes forecasts of the prices of N stocks one month ahead. He or she knows that the price of the nth stock, p_n, is influenced by the forecast, the influence being expressed by the continuous functions $p_n = f_n(q_1, ..., q_N)$, for $n = 1, ..., N$ and where q_n is the forecast of the price of the nth stock. Assume that $f_n(q_1, ..., q_N) > 0$, for all $q_1, ..., q_N$, and that there is a $\overline{Q} > 0$ such that $f_n(q_1, ..., q_N) < \overline{Q}$, for all $q_1, ..., q_N$. Prove that the market analyst can make a correct forecast if he or she knows the functions f_n.

Answer: Let $[0, \overline{Q}]^N$ be the Cartesian product of the closed interval $[0, \overline{Q}]$ with itself N times. Define the function

$$F: [0, \overline{Q}]^N \to [0, \overline{Q}]^N$$

by the equation

$$F(q_1, ..., q_N) = (f_1(q_1, ..., q_N), f_2(q_1, ..., q_N), ..., f_N(q_1, ..., q_N)).$$

Since the functions f_n are all continuous by assumption, F is continuous. Since $[0, \overline{Q}]^N$ is convex and compact, the Brouwer fixed point theorem implies that there exists a vector $(\overline{q}_1, ..., \overline{q}_N)$ in $[0, \overline{Q}]^N$ such that $F(\overline{q}_1, ..., \overline{q}_N) = (\overline{q}_1, ..., \overline{q}_N)$. Since $f_n(\overline{q}_1, ..., \overline{q}_N) = \overline{q}_n$, for all n, $(\overline{q}_1, ..., \overline{q}_N)$ is a vector of correct forecasts.

Answer to Homework Problems for Chapter 4, Problem #29

Problem: 29) Suppose that the pure exchange economy $\mathcal{E} = ((u_i, \mathbf{e}_i)_{i=1}^{I})$ satisfies the following assumptions: i) Each utility function u_i depends directly on the price vector **p** as well as on the consumption vector $\mathbf{x}_i$, so that consumer i's utility is $u_i(\mathbf{x}_i, \mathbf{p})$. Hence $u_i: R_+^N \times (R_+^N \backslash \{0\}) \to R$. ii) For each i, u_i is continuous with respect to both **p** and $\mathbf{x}_i$ and is strictly increasing and strictly concave with respect to $\mathbf{x}_i$. iii) For each i, $\mathbf{e}_i >> 0$.

a) Prove that $\mathcal{E}$ satisfies Walras' law.

b) Prove that E has a competitive equilibrium.

c) Either prove or give a counter example to the statement that any competitive equilibrium $(\mathbf{x}, \mathbf{p})$ for $\mathcal{E}$ is Pareto optimal.

Answer: a) The proof given in the text of Walras' law (p. 98) applies without any change.

Answer: b) The proof given in section 9.8 of the existence of equilibrium applies with almost no change. In particular, the proof of the continuity of truncated demand still applies.

Answer: c) The following is one of many possible counter examples. The economy is an Edgeworth box economy with $\mathbf{e}_A = (2, 0)$, $\mathbf{e}_B = (0, 2)$, $u_A(\mathbf{x}, \mathbf{p}) = u_B(\mathbf{x}, \mathbf{p}) = x_1 x_2 + \frac{1}{||\mathbf{p}||}$. All equilibria for this economy are of the form

$$(\overline{\mathbf{x}}_A, \overline{\mathbf{x}}_B, \mathbf{p}) = ((1, 1), (1, 1), (t, t)),$$

where $t > 0$. The smaller is t, the higher is the utility of both consumers, so that no equilibrium is Pareto optimal.

Answer to Homework Problems for Chapter 5, Problem #1

Problem: 1) Consider the Edgeworth box economy with $\mathbf{e}_A = (1, 0)$, $\mathbf{e}_B = (0, 1)$, $u_A(x_1, x_2) = \min(4x_1, x_2)$, and $u_B(x_1, x_2) = x_1 + 2x_2$. Find the equilibrium with transfer payments, $(\mathbf{x}, \mathbf{p}, \tau)$, that has $u_B(x_{B1}, x_{B2}) = 1$ and $p_1 = 1$.

Answer: The relevant figure appears below. The heavy line is the set of Pareto optimal allocations. Two indifference curves for person A are shown as right angles with apexes on the heavy line. Two indifference curves for person B are shown as negatively sloped solid lines. A Pareto optimal allocation to person B is of the form $\mathbf{x}_B = (3/4 + t, 4t)$, where $0 \le t \le 1/4$.

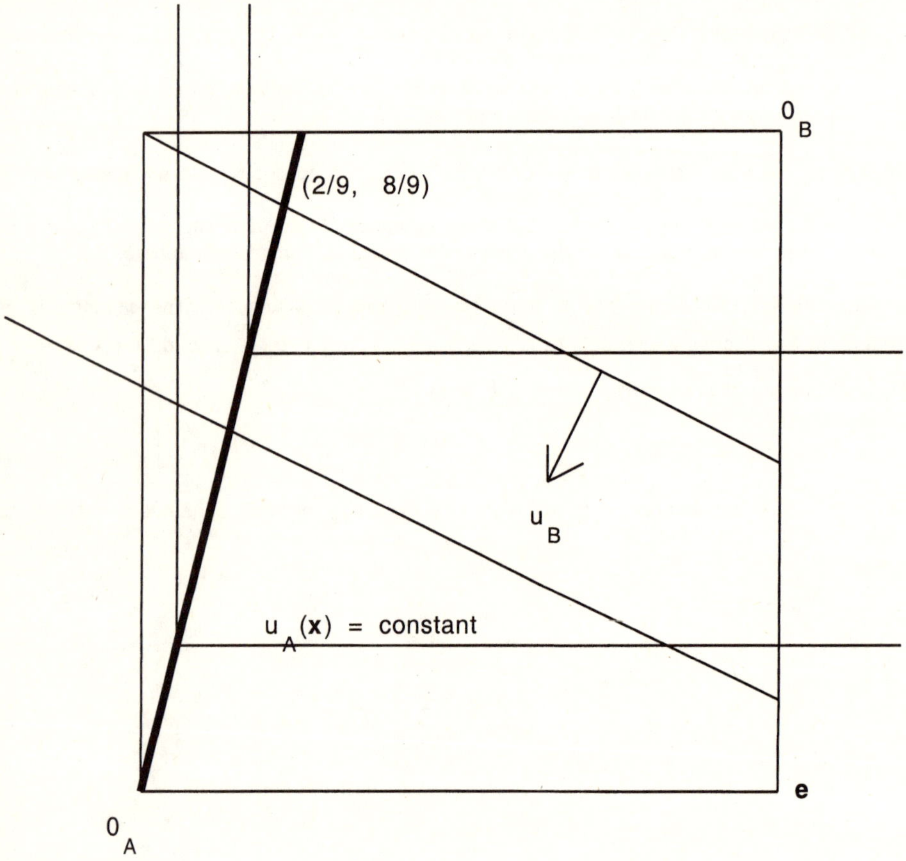

Such an allocation gives person B utility $u_B(\mathbf{x}_B) = 3/4 + 9t$. If this utility is 1, then $t = 1/36$. Therefore, the desired allocation is $(\mathbf{x}_A, \mathbf{x}_B) = ((2/9, 8/9), 7/9, 1/9))$. The budget line in the corresponding equilibrium with transfer payments must be parallel to B's indifference curve, so that the equilibrium price vector is $\mathbf{p} = (1, 2)$. The transfer payment of person A is

$$\tau_A = \mathbf{p}.(\mathbf{e}_A - \mathbf{x}_A) = (1, 2).[(1, 0) - (2/9, 8/9)] = -1.$$

It follows that $\tau_B = 1$. Hence the full equilibrium with transfer payments is

$$((\mathbf{x}_A, \mathbf{x}_B), \mathbf{p}, (\tau_A, \tau_B)) = ((2/9, 8/9), (7/9, 1/9), (1, 2), (-1, 1)).$$

Answer to Homework Problems for Chapter 5, Problem #2

Problem: 2) Consider the following economy with three commodities, 1, 2, and 3, two firms, firms 2 and 3, and two consumers, A and B.

$$u_A(x_1, x_2, x_3) = \ln(x_2) + \ln(x_3) = u_B(x_1, x_2, x_3).$$

$$\mathbf{e}_A = (2, 0, 0). \quad \mathbf{e}_B = (0, 0, 0).$$

Firm 2 produces good 2 from good 1 with the production function $y_2 = 2(-y_{21})$, where $y_{21} \le 0$ and y_{21} is firm 2's input of good 1. Firm 3 produces good 3 from good 1 with the production function $y_3 = -y_{31}$, where $y_{31} \le 0$ and y_{31} is firm 3's input of good 1. (Notice that there is constant returns to scale in production, so that there are no profits in equilibrium and hence no need to assign ownership shares to consumers.)

a) Compute an allocation that maximizes the sum of the utilities of the two consumers.

b) Find an equilibrium with transfer payments the allocation of which is the one calculated in part a. Let the price of good 1 be 1.

Answer: a) The welfare maximization problem is

$$\max_{\substack{x_{A2} \ge 0,\, x_{A3} \ge 0, \\ x_{B2} \ge 0,\, x_{B3} \ge 0, \\ y_{21} \le 0,\, y_{31} \le 0}} [\ln(x_{A2}) + \ln(x_{A3}) + \ln(x_{B2}) + \ln(x_{B3})]$$

$$\text{s.t. } x_{A2} + x_{B2} \le -y_{21}$$

$$x_{A3} + x_{B3} \le -y_{31}$$

$$-y_{21} - y_{31} \le 2.$$

The problem is symmetric with respect to the consumptions of consumers A and B, so that we may assume that $x_{A2} = x_{B2} = x_2$ and $x_{A3} = x_{B3} = x_3$. Since the utility functions are increasing, we may also assume that the constraints hold with equality. After making these assumptions and dividing the objective function by 2, the problem becomes

$$\max_{x_2 \geq 0,\, x_3 \geq 0,\, y_{21} \leq 0} [\ln(x_2) + \ln(x_3)]$$

$$\text{s.t. } x_2 = -y_{21}$$

$$x_3 = \frac{2 + y_{21}}{2}.$$

After substitution of the constraints into the objective function, the problem becomes

$$\max_{y_{21} \leq 0} [\ln(-y_{21}) + \ln\left(\frac{2 + y_{21}}{2}\right).$$

The first order conditions for this problem are

$$-\frac{1}{y_{21}} - \frac{1}{2 + y_{21}} = 0,$$

so that $y_{21} = -1$. Therefore $x_{A2} = x_{B2} = 1$, $x_{A3} = x_{B3} = 1/2$, and $y_{31} = -1$. So the full allocation is

$$((x_{A2}, x_{A3}), (x_{B2}, x_{B3}), (y_{21}, y_2), (y_{31}, y_3)) = ((1, 1/2), (1, 1/2), (-1, 2), (-1, 1)).$$

<u>Answer</u>: b) Because there is constant returns to scale in production, profits are zero in equilibrium, and therefore $p_2 = p_1/2 = 1/2$ and $p_3 = p_1 = 1$. The wealth of each consumer is 2. The transfer payments are

$$\tau_A = w_A - \mathbf{p.x}_A = 2 - (1/2, 1).(1, 1) = 2 - 1 = 1$$

$$\tau_B = -\tau_A = -1.$$

Hence the full equilibrium with transfer payments is

$$((x_{A2}, x_{A3}), (x_{B2}, x_{B3}), (y_{21}, y_2), (y_{31}, y_3), (p_1, p_2, p_3), (\tau_A, \tau_B))$$

$$= ((1,\ 1/2),\ (1,\ 1/2),\ (-1,\ 2),\ (-1,\ 1),\ (1,\ 1/2,\ 1),\ (1,\ -1)).$$

Answer to Homework Problems for Chapter 5, Problem #3

Problem:

3) Consider the Edgeworth box economy with $\mathbf{e}_A = (1, 0)$, $\mathbf{e}_B = (0, 1)$, $u_A(x_1, x_2) = x_1^{1/3}x_2^{2/3} = u_B(x_1, x_2)$. Calculate the function τ from $\Delta^1 = \{(v_A, v_B) \in R^2_+ \mid v_A + v_B = 1\}$ to $H = \{(t_1, t_2) \in R^2 \mid t_1 + t_2 = 0\}$ and defined by the equation

$$\tau(v_A, v_B) = (\tau_A, \tau_B) = (\mathbf{p}.(\mathbf{e}_A - \mathbf{x}_A), \mathbf{p}.(\mathbf{e}_B - \mathbf{x}_B)),$$

where $(\mathbf{x}_A, \mathbf{x}_B)$ is a Pareto optimal allocation such that $(u_A(\mathbf{x}_A), u_B(\mathbf{x}_B)) = \lambda(v_A, v_B)$, for some positive number λ, and $\mathbf{p}$ is a price vector such that $((\mathbf{x}_A, \mathbf{x}_B), \mathbf{p}, (\tau_A, \tau_B))$ is an equilibrium with transfer payments and $p_1 + p_2 = 1$.

Answer: Because the two consumers have the same linearly homogeneous utility function, the set of Pareto optimal allocations is the diagonal of the Edgeworth box. The Pareto optimal allocation giving consumer A utility v_A is $((x_{A1}, x_{A2}), (x_{B1}, x_{B2})) = ((v_A, v_A), (1 - v_A, 1 - v_A))$. The marginal rate of substitution of both consumers at a point (v_A, v_A) on the diagonal equals

$$\frac{\partial u_A(v_A, v_A)/\partial x_1}{\partial u_A(v_A, v_A)/\partial x_2} = \frac{\frac{1}{3}\left(\frac{v_A}{v_A}\right)^{2/3}}{\frac{2}{3}\left(\frac{v_A}{v_A}\right)^{2/3}} = \frac{1}{2},$$

so that an equilibrium price vector $\mathbf{p}$ satisfies $p_1/p_2 = 1/2$. The appropriate price vector, therefore, is $\mathbf{p} = (1/3, 2/3)$. The transfer payment of person A corresponding to the point (v_A, v_A) is

$$\tau_A = \left(\frac{1}{3}, \frac{2}{3}\right).[(1, 0) - (v_A, v_A)] = \frac{1}{3} - v_A.$$

Therefore the transfer payment of person B is $\tau_B = -\tau_A = -\frac{1}{3} + v_A$, and so

$$\tau(v_A, v_B) = \left(\frac{1}{3} - v_A, -\frac{1}{3} + v_A\right).$$

Answer to Homework Problems for Chapter 5, Problem #4

Problem: 4) Suppose that $(\overline{\mathbf{x}}, \overline{\mathbf{y}}, \overline{\mathbf{p}})$ is a competitive equilibrium for an economy $((u_i, \mathbf{e}_i)_{i=1}^{I}, (Y_j)_{j=1}^{J}, (\theta_{ij}))$ with locally non-satiated utility functions. Let Y_0 be another input-output possibility set containing 0 and satisfying

$$\max_{y \in Y_0} \overline{\mathbf{p}}.\mathbf{y} = 0$$

and let $(\mathbf{x}, \mathbf{y}, \mathbf{p})$ be an equilibrium for the economy $((u_i, \mathbf{e}_i)_{i=1}^{I}, (Y_j)_{j=0}^{J}, (\theta_{ij}))$, which is, the original economy with Y_0 adjoined. Is it possible that $(\mathbf{x}, \mathbf{y})$ Pareto dominates the allocation $(\overline{\mathbf{x}}, \overline{\mathbf{y}})$? In other words, is it possible to use a new production process earning zero profit to make everyone at least as well off and someone better off? Demonstrate your answer by means of a proof or counter example.

Answer: Since $\max_{y \in Y_0} \overline{\mathbf{p}}.\mathbf{y} = 0$, the vector $\mathbf{0}$ is profit maximizing in Y_0. Therefore an equilibrium for the economy with Y_0 adjoined is $(\mathbf{x}, \mathbf{y}, \mathbf{p})$, where $\mathbf{x}_i = \overline{\mathbf{x}}_i$, for all i, $\mathbf{y}_0 = \mathbf{0}$, $\mathbf{y}_j = \overline{\mathbf{y}}_j$, for j = 1, ... , J, and $\mathbf{p} = \overline{\mathbf{p}}$. Since the utility functions are locally non-satiated, the allocation of this equilibrium is Pareto optimal. Therefore, it cannot be Pareto dominated by any other feasible allocation. Hence the allocation $(\overline{\mathbf{x}}, \overline{\mathbf{y}})$ cannot be Pareto dominated by any other feasible allocation.

Answer to Homework Problems for Chapter 5, Problem #5

Problem: 5) Consider an economy with two consumer, two goods, and no firms. The endowment vectors of consumers A and B are $\mathbf{e}_A$ and $\mathbf{e}_B$, respectively, where $\mathbf{e}_A >> 0$ and $\mathbf{e}_B >> 0$. Assume that the utility of each consumer depends on the consumption of the other consumer as well as on his or her own consumption. That is, each consumer cares about what the other consumes, out of sympathy, envy, or because the other's consumption interferes with or helps his or her own life. For instance, each neighbor might want the other to paint his or her house, but dislike smoke from his or her barbecue. Such effects are known as consumption externalities. More formally, if $\mathbf{x}_A$ and $\mathbf{x}_B$ are the consumption bundles of consumers A and B, respectively, then their utilities are $u_A(\mathbf{x}_A, \mathbf{x}_B)$ and $u_B(\mathbf{x}_B, \mathbf{x}_A)$, respectively. Assume that u_A and u_B are continuous and that for i = A and B, u_i is strictly increasing and strictly concave with respect to $\mathbf{x}_i$. (That is, $u_A(\mathbf{x}_A, \mathbf{x}_B)$ is both strictly increasing and strictly concave with respect to $\mathbf{x}_A$, but not necessarily so with respect to $\mathbf{x}_B$, and the symmetric statement applies to u_B.) In an equilibrium, consumer A chooses $\mathbf{x}_A$ so as to solve the problem

$$\max_{\mathbf{x} \in R^2_+} u_A(\mathbf{x}, \mathbf{x}_B)$$

$$\text{s.t. } \mathbf{p}.\mathbf{x} \le \mathbf{p}.\mathbf{e}_A,$$

That is, consumer A holds $\mathbf{x}_B$ fixed when considering how to choose $\mathbf{x}_A$. Similarly, consumer B chooses $\mathbf{x}_B$ so as to solve the problem

$$\max_{\mathbf{x} \in R^2_+} u_B(\mathbf{x}_A, \mathbf{x})$$

$$\text{s.t. } \mathbf{p}.\mathbf{x} \le \mathbf{p}.\mathbf{e}_B.$$

In addition, the market excess demand for each good is non-positive and the price of any good in excess supply is zero.

a) Prove that an equilibrium exists.

b) Is an equilibrium allocation Pareto optimal? Give a proof or counter example.

Answer: The proof is similar to that of theorem 4.24, and I will not fill in the details that can be found in that proof. First of all, we must truncate the commodity space suitably. Let b be a positive number such that $e_{An} + e_{Bn} < b$, for n = 1, ... , N. Let $B = \{x \in R^N_+ \mid x_n \le b, \text{ for all } n\}$.

For each $\mathbf{x}_B \in R^N_+$ and $\mathbf{p} \in \Delta^{N-1}$, let

$\xi^T_A(\mathbf{x}_B, \mathbf{p}) = \{\mathbf{x} \in B \mid \mathbf{p}.\mathbf{x} \le \mathbf{p}.\mathbf{e}_A$ and $u_A(\mathbf{x}, \mathbf{x}_B) \ge u_A(\mathbf{z}, \mathbf{x}_B)$, for all $\mathbf{z} \in B$ such that

$\mathbf{p}.\mathbf{z} \le \mathbf{p}.\mathbf{e}_A\}$.

Symmetrically, for each $\mathbf{x}_A \in R^N_+$, let

$\xi^T_B(\mathbf{x}_A, \mathbf{p}) = \{\mathbf{x} \in B \mid \mathbf{p}.\mathbf{x} \le \mathbf{p}.\mathbf{e}_B$ and $u_B(\mathbf{x}, \mathbf{x}_A) \ge u_B(\mathbf{z}, \mathbf{x}_A)$, for all $\mathbf{z} \in B$ such that

$\mathbf{p}.\mathbf{z} \le \mathbf{p}.\mathbf{e}_B\}$.

A first task is to show that ξ^T_A and ξ^T_B are continuous functions. I give the proof for ξ^T_A. Since is convex and compact and $u(\mathbf{x}, \mathbf{x}_B)$ is continuous and strictly concave with respect to $\mathbf{x}$, it follows that $\xi^T_A(\mathbf{x}_B, \mathbf{p})$ exists and contains a single point. To show that ξ^T_A is continuous, let $(\mathbf{x}^n_B, \mathbf{p}^n)$ be a convergent sequence in $B \times \Delta^{N-1}$ converging to $(\mathbf{x}_B, \mathbf{p})$. I must show that $\lim_{n \to \infty} \xi^T_A(\mathbf{x}^n_B, \mathbf{p}^n) = \xi^T_A(\mathbf{x}_B, \mathbf{p})$. If $\xi^T_A(\mathbf{x}^n_B, \mathbf{p}^n)$ does not converge to $\xi^T_A(\mathbf{x}_B, \mathbf{p})$, then there exists a positive number ε and a subsequence $\xi^T_A(\mathbf{x}^{n_k}_B, \mathbf{p}^{n_k})$ such that $\left\|\xi^T_A(\mathbf{x}^{n_k}_B, \mathbf{p}^{n_k}) - \xi^T_A(\mathbf{x}_B, \mathbf{p})\right\| > \varepsilon$, for all k. By the Bolzano-Weierstrass theorem, we may assume that $\xi^T_A(\mathbf{x}^{n_k}_B, \mathbf{p}^{n_k})$ converges to some vector $\mathbf{x}_A$. Then $\left\|\mathbf{x}_A - \xi^T_A(\mathbf{x}_B, \mathbf{p})\right\| \ge \varepsilon$. Since $\mathbf{p}^{n_k}.\xi^T_A(\mathbf{x}^{n_k}_B, \mathbf{p}^{n_k}) \le \mathbf{p}^{n_k}.\mathbf{e}_A$, for all k, it follows that $\mathbf{p}.\mathbf{x} \le \mathbf{p}.\mathbf{e}_A$. Let $\mathbf{x} \in B$ be such that $\mathbf{p}.\mathbf{x} \le \mathbf{p}.\mathbf{e}_A$. I show that $u_A(\mathbf{x}_A, \mathbf{x}_B) \ge u_A(\mathbf{x}, \mathbf{x}_B)$. Because $\mathbf{e}_A >> 0$ and $\mathbf{p} >> 0$, it follows that $\mathbf{p}.\mathbf{e}_A > 0$. If t is such that $0 < t < 1$, then $t\mathbf{x} \in B$ and $\mathbf{p}.(t\mathbf{x}) = t\mathbf{p}.\mathbf{x} \le t\mathbf{p}.\mathbf{e}_A < \mathbf{p}.\mathbf{e}_A$. Therefore, if k is sufficiently large $\mathbf{p}^{n_k}.(t\mathbf{x}) < \mathbf{p}^{n_k}.\mathbf{e}_A$. That is, $t\mathbf{x}$ belongs to the budget set defined by $\mathbf{p}^{n_k}$ and hence $u_A(\xi^T_A(\mathbf{x}^{n_k}_B, \mathbf{p}^{n_k}), \mathbf{x}^{n_k}_B) \ge u_A(t\mathbf{x}, \mathbf{x}^{n_k}_B)$. Since u_A is continuous and $\lim_{k \to \infty} \xi^T_A(\mathbf{x}^{n_k}_B, \mathbf{p}^{n_k}) = \mathbf{x}_A$ and $\lim_{k \to \infty} \mathbf{x}^{n_k}_B = \mathbf{x}_B$, it follows that $u_A(\mathbf{x}_A, \mathbf{x}_B) \ge u_A(t\mathbf{x}, \mathbf{x}_B)$. Since t may be made arbitrarily close to 1, the continuity of u_A implies that $u_A(\mathbf{x}_A, \mathbf{x}_B) \ge u_A(\mathbf{x}, \mathbf{x}_B)$. Therefore $\mathbf{x}_A = \xi^T_A(\mathbf{x}_B, \mathbf{p})$, which contradicts the inequality $\left\|\mathbf{x}_A - \xi^T_A(\mathbf{x}_B, \mathbf{p})\right\| \ge \varepsilon > 0$. This contradiction proves that ξ^T_A is continuous.

I may now proceed with a fixed point argument. Let $\mathbf{z}\colon B \times B \times \Delta^{N-1} \to R^N$ be defined by the equation $\mathbf{z}(\mathbf{x}_A, \mathbf{x}_B, \mathbf{p}) = \xi_A(\mathbf{x}_B, \mathbf{p}) + \xi_B(\mathbf{x}_A, \mathbf{p}) - \mathbf{e}_A - \mathbf{e}_B$. Because $u_A(\mathbf{x}, \mathbf{x}_B)$ and $u_B(\mathbf{x}, \mathbf{x}_A)$ are increasing with respect to **x**, the proof of Walras' law applies. That is, $\mathbf{p}.\mathbf{z}(\mathbf{x}_A, \mathbf{x}_B, \mathbf{p}) = 0$, for all **p**. Let $g: B \times B \times \Delta^{N-1} \to R^N_+$ be defined by the equation

$$g(\mathbf{x}_A, \mathbf{x}_B, \mathbf{p}) = (\max(0, p_1 + z_1(\mathbf{x}_A, \mathbf{x}_B, \mathbf{p})), \max(0, p_2 + z_2(\mathbf{x}_A, \mathbf{x}_B, \mathbf{p}))).$$

Since $\mathbf{p}.g(\mathbf{x}_A, \mathbf{x}_B, \mathbf{p}) \geq \mathbf{p}.\mathbf{p} > 0$, it follows that $g(\mathbf{x}_A, \mathbf{x}_B, \mathbf{p}) > 0$. Let $h: B \times B \times \Delta^{N-1} \to \Delta^{N-1}$ be defined by the equation

$$h(\mathbf{x}_A, \mathbf{x}_B, \mathbf{p}) = \frac{g(\mathbf{x}_A, \mathbf{x}_B, \mathbf{p})}{g_1(\mathbf{x}_A, \mathbf{x}_B, \mathbf{p}) + g_2(\mathbf{x}_A, \mathbf{x}_B, \mathbf{p})}.$$

Let $H: B \times B \times \Delta^{N-1} \to B \times B \times \Delta^{N-1}$ be defined by the equation

$$H(\mathbf{x}_A, \mathbf{x}_B, \mathbf{p}) = (\xi^T_A(\mathbf{x}_B, \mathbf{p}), \xi^T_B(\mathbf{x}_A, \mathbf{p}), h(\mathbf{x}_A, \mathbf{x}_B, \mathbf{p})).$$

Since the function H is continuous and the set $B \times B \times \Delta^{N-1}$ is compact and convex, the Brouwer fixed point theorem implies that H has a fixed point, $(\overline{\mathbf{x}}_A, \overline{\mathbf{x}}_B, \mathbf{p})$. The argument given in the proof of theorem 4.24 implies that $\mathbf{z}(\overline{\mathbf{x}}_A, \overline{\mathbf{x}}_B, \mathbf{p}) \leq 0$. Because $\overline{\mathbf{p}}.\mathbf{z}(\overline{\mathbf{x}}_A, \overline{\mathbf{x}}_B, \mathbf{p}) = 0$, if follows that, for all n, $p_n < 0$, if $z_n(\overline{\mathbf{x}}_A, \overline{\mathbf{x}}_B, \mathbf{p}) < 0$. Because $\overline{\mathbf{x}}_A = \xi^T_A(\mathbf{x}_B, \mathbf{p})$ and $\overline{\mathbf{x}}_B = \xi^T_B(\mathbf{x}_A, \mathbf{p})$, it follows that each consumer anticipates correctly the consumption of the other. Because any feasible allocation is in the interior of B, it follows by an argument given in the proof of theorem 4.24 that

$$\overline{\mathbf{x}}_A \in \xi_A(\mathbf{x}_B, \mathbf{p}) = \{\mathbf{x} \in R^N_+ \mid \mathbf{p}.\mathbf{x} \leq \mathbf{p}.\mathbf{e}_A \text{ and } u_A(\mathbf{x}, \mathbf{x}_B) \geq u_A(\mathbf{z}, \mathbf{x}_B), \text{ for all } \mathbf{z} \in R^N_+$$
$$\text{such that } \mathbf{p}.\mathbf{z} < \mathbf{p}.\mathbf{e}_A\}.$$

That is, $\overline{\mathbf{x}}_A$ maximizes consumer A's utility in the untruncated budget set. A similar argument proves that

$$\overline{\mathbf{x}}_B \in \xi_B(\mathbf{x}_A, \mathbf{p}) = \{\mathbf{x} \in R^N_+ \mid \mathbf{p}.\mathbf{x} \leq \mathbf{p}.\mathbf{e}_B \text{ and } u_B(\mathbf{x}, \mathbf{x}_A) \geq u_B(\mathbf{z}, \mathbf{x}_A), \text{ for all } \mathbf{z} \in R^N_+$$
$$\text{such that } \mathbf{p}.\mathbf{z} \leq \mathbf{p}.\mathbf{e}_B\}.$$

Therefore $(\overline{\mathbf{x}}_A, \overline{\mathbf{x}}_B, \mathbf{p})$ is an equilibrium.

Answer to Homework Problems for Chapter 5, Problem #6

Problem: 6) Let $E = \mathcal{E} = ((u_i, \mathbf{e}_i)_{i=1}^{I})$ be a pure trade economy such that every utility function, u_i, is strictly increasing. Let $(\overline{\mathbf{x}}, \mathbf{p})$ be a competitive equilibrium for this economy. Now consider dividing the set of consumers into two disjoint groups, G_1 and G_2, where the union of G_1 and G_2 is the entire set of I consumers of $\mathcal{E}$ and each of G_1 and G_2 contains at least two people. Let $(\overline{\mathbf{x}}^1, \mathbf{p}^1)$ and $(\overline{\mathbf{x}}^2, \mathbf{p}^2)$ be competitive equilibria for the economies consisting of the people in G_1 and G_2, respectively.

a) Show that $(\overline{\mathbf{x}}^1, \overline{\mathbf{x}}^2)$ is a feasible allocation for $\mathcal{E}$.

b) Is it possible for $(\overline{\mathbf{x}}^1, \overline{\mathbf{x}}^2)$ to Pareto dominate $\overline{\mathbf{x}}$? Give an example to show that $(\overline{\mathbf{x}}^1, \overline{\mathbf{x}}^2)$ may Pareto dominate $\overline{\mathbf{x}}$ or prove that $(\overline{\mathbf{x}}^1, \overline{\mathbf{x}}^2)$ cannot Pareto dominate $\overline{\mathbf{x}}$.

Answer: a) Since $\overline{\mathbf{x}}^1$ is feasible for G_1,

$$\sum_{i \in G_1} \overline{\mathbf{x}}_i^1 \le \sum_{i \in G_1} \mathbf{e}_i.$$

Since $\overline{\mathbf{x}}^2$ is feasible for G_2,

$$\sum_{i \in G_2} \overline{\mathbf{x}}_i^2 \le \sum_{i \in G_2} \mathbf{e}_i.$$

Therefore

$$\sum_{i \in G_1} \overline{\mathbf{x}}_i^1 + \sum_{i \in G_2} \overline{\mathbf{x}}_i^2 \le \sum_{i=1}^{I} \mathbf{e}_i,$$

so that $(\overline{\mathbf{x}}^1, \overline{\mathbf{x}}^2)$ is feasible for $\mathcal{E}$.

Answer: b) Since $(\overline{\mathbf{x}}, \mathbf{p})$ is an equilibrium for $\mathcal{E}$ and the u_i are locally non-satiated, $\overline{\mathbf{x}}$ is Pareto optimal. Therefore $(\overline{\mathbf{x}}^1, \overline{\mathbf{x}}^2)$ cannot Pareto dominate $\overline{\mathbf{x}}$.

Answer to Homework Problems for Chapter 5, Problem #7

Problem: 7) Consider an economy with I consumers and N goods, where, for all i, the endowment vector of consumer i is $\mathbf{e}_i$, and the utility function of each consumer i is of the form

$$u_i(x_i, \sum_{k=1}^{I} x_k),$$

where $\mathbf{x}_i$ is the consumption vector of the ith consumer. Assume that u_i is increasing with respect to the components of $\mathbf{x}_i$.

a) Define a notion of competitive equilibrium.

b) Is an equilibrium allocation necessarily Pareto optimal? Give an argument.

Answer: a) The following is a possible definition of equilibrium.

An equilibrium consists of $(\overline{\mathbf{x}}_1, \ldots, \overline{\mathbf{x}}_I, \mathbf{p})$, where

i) $\overline{\mathbf{x}}_i \in R^N_+$, for all i, and $\sum_{i=1}^{I} \overline{\mathbf{x}}_i \leq \sum_{i=1}^{I} \mathbf{e}_i$,

ii) $\mathbf{p} \in R^N_+$ and $\mathbf{p} > 0$,

iii) for each i, $\overline{\mathbf{x}}_i$ solves the problem

$$\max_{\mathbf{x} \in R^N_+} u_i(\mathbf{x}, \sum_{k \neq i} \overline{\mathbf{x}}_k + \mathbf{x})$$

$$\text{s.t. } \mathbf{p}.\mathbf{x} \leq \mathbf{p}.\mathbf{e}_i$$

iv) for all n, $p_n = 0$, If $\sum_{i=1}^{I} \overline{x}_{in} < \sum_{i=1}^{I} e_{in}$.

Answer: No, an equilibrium allocation is not necessarily Pareto optimal. Here is a counter example.

There are two consumers, A and B, and one commodity. Each consumer is endowed with one unit of the commodity. The utility function of consumer A is

$$u_A(x_A, x_A + x_B) = x_A - \frac{2}{3}(x_A + x_B),$$

and the utility function of consumer B is

$$u_B(x_B, x_A + x_B) = x_B - \frac{2}{3}(x_A + x_B).$$

An equilibrium is $x_A = x_B = 1$, and $p = 1$. The allocation $x_A = x_B = 0$ Pareto dominates the equilibrium allocation, because the zero allocation gives each consumer a utility of zero, which exceeds the utility from the equilibrium allocation of −1/3.

Answer to Homework Problems for Chapter 5, Problem #8

Problem: 8) There are I consumers and one good, which may be used for public or private consumption. Each consumer is endowed with one unit of the good and divides this one unit between public and private consumption. That is, each consumer i, for $i = 1, \ldots, I$, chooses x_i, where $0 \leq x_i \leq 1$, and the total amount available for public consumption is $g = x_1 + x_2 + \ldots + x_I$. For all i, the utility function of consumer n is $u_i(1 - x_i, g)$, where u_i is continuous, strictly increasing, and strictly concave. In equilibrium, each consumer knows the choice of x_i for all other consumers and chooses her or his personal consumption and contribution to public consumption so as to maximize her or his own utility.

a) Describe the equilibrium formally.
b) Prove that an equilibrium exists.
c) Either prove that the equilibrium is Pareto optimal or show that it may not be by means of a counter example.

Answer: a) An equilibrium consists of $(\overline{x}_1, \ldots, \overline{x}_I)$ such that

i) $0 \leq \overline{x}_i \leq 1$, for all i, and

ii) for each i, $\overline{x}_i$ solves the problem

$$\max_{x \in [0,1]} u_i(1 - x, x + \sum_{k \neq i} \overline{x}_i).$$

Answer: b) The proof is an application of the Brouwer fixed point theorem. For each $t \in [0, I - 1]$, let $f_i(t)$ be the solution of the problem

$$\max_{x \in [0,1]} u_i(1 - x, x + t).$$

Since u_i is continuous and [0, 1] is compact, this problem has a solution. Since u_i is strictly concave, the solution is unique. Therefore f_i is a function from $[0, I - 1]$ to [0, 1]. I show that f_i is continuous. Let t_n be a sequence in [0, I – 1] that converges to t and suppose that $f_i(t_n)$ does not converge to $f_i(t)$ as n goes to infinity. Then for some positive number ε, there is a subsequence t_{n_k} such that $|f_i(t_{n_k}) - f(t)| > \varepsilon$, for all k. By the Bolzano-Weierstrass theorem, I may assume that $f_i(t_{n_k})$ converges to some y in [0, 1]. Then $|y - f_i(t)| \geq \varepsilon$. If $x \in [0, 1]$, then

$$u_i(1 - f_i(t_{n_k}), t_{n_k} + f_i(t_{n_k})) \geq u_i(1 - x, t_{n_k} + x),$$

by the definition of the function f_i. If we let k go to infinity in this inequality, we see that

$$u_i(1 - y, t + y) \geq u_i(1 - x, t + x).$$

Since x is an arbitrary point in [0, 1], it follows that y solves the problem

$$\max_{x \in [0, 1]} u_i(1 - x, t + x),$$

so that $y = f_i(t)$. This is impossible, since $|y - f_i(t)| \geq \varepsilon$. Therefore $\lim_{n \to \infty} f_i(t_n) = f_i(t)$ and so f_i is continuous.

Let $F: \times_{i=1}^{I} [0, 1] \to \times_{i=1}^{I} [0, 1]$ be the function with components

$$F_i(x_1, \ldots, x_I) = f_i(\sum_{k \neq i} x_k),$$

for i = 1, ..., I. Since the functions f_i are continuous, so is F. Since $\times_{i=1}^{I} [0, 1]$ is compact and convex, the Brouwer fixed point theorem implies that F has a fixed point, $(\bar{x}_1, \ldots, \bar{x}_I)$. The definition of F implies that $(\bar{x}_1, \ldots, \bar{x}_I)$ is an equilibrium.

Answer: c) An equilibrium may not be Pareto optimal, as the following example shows. There are two consumers, A and B. The utility function of each is of the form

$$u(1 - x, g) = 2\sqrt{1 - x} + 2g.$$

To find an equilibrium solve the problem

$$\max_{x \in [0, 1]} [2\sqrt{1 - x} + 2(\bar{x} + x)].$$

The first order condition is

$$\frac{1}{\sqrt{1 - x}} = 2,$$

so that x = 3/4. That is, the equilibrium is $\bar{x}_A = \bar{x}_B = 3/4$. The utility of each consumer in this equilibrium is $2\sqrt{1/4} + 4(3/4) = 4$. If each consumer chose $\bar{x}_A = \bar{x}_B = 15/16$, then the utility of each consumer would be $2\sqrt{1/16} + 4(15/16) = 17/4$, which exceeds 4, so that this allocation Pareto dominates the equilibrium.

Answer to Homework Problems for Chapter 6, Problem #1

Problem: 1) Compute the marginal utility of wealth, λ, for a consumer with endowment **e** = (2, 5) when prices are $(p_1, p_2) = (2, 3)$ and with the following utility functions:

a) $u(x_1, x_2) = x_1^{1/4}x_2^{1/2}$,

b) $u(x_1, x_2) = 4x_1 + x_2$,

c) $u(x_1, x_2) = 4x_1 + 6x_2$,

d) $u(x_1, x_2) = \min(3x_1, x_2)$,

e) $u(x_1, x_2) = \sqrt{\min(6x_1 + x_2, 2x_1 + 7x_2)}$.

Hint: One approach is to compute

$$V(w) = \max_{x_1 \geq 0,\, x_2 \geq 0} u(x_1, x_2)$$

$$\text{s.t. } 2x_1 + 3x_2 \leq w.$$

Then $\lambda = \dfrac{dV(19)}{dw}$.

Answer: a) The consumers wealth is w = **p**.**e** = (2, 3).(2, 5) = 19. I first compute the consumer's demands for the two goods. Because the utility function is Cobb-Douglas,

$$2x_1 = p_1x_1 = \frac{1}{3}w = \frac{19}{3},$$

so that

$$x_1 = \frac{19}{6}.$$

Similarly

$$3x_2 = \frac{2}{3}19 = \frac{38}{3},$$

so that

$$x_2 = \frac{38}{9}.$$

Therefore

$$\lambda = \frac{1}{p_1}\frac{\partial u}{\partial x_1} = \frac{1}{2}\frac{1}{4}\frac{x_2^{1/2}}{x_1^{3/4}} = \frac{1}{8}\left(\frac{38}{9}\right)^{1/2}\left(\frac{19}{6}\right)^{-3/4} = 2^{-7/4}3^{-1/4}19^{-1/4}.$$

Answer: b) The consumer will spend all her or his wealth on good 1, so that if wealth is w, consumption is

$$(x_1, x_2) = (w/p_1, 0) = (w/2, 0).$$

The consumer's utility for wealth, therefore, is $V(w) = u(w/2, 0) = 2w$. It follows that $\lambda = 2$.

Answer: c) A utility maximizing consumption in the budget set is again for the consumer to spend all of her or his wealth on good 1. It follows, as in the previous part, that $\lambda = 2$.

Answer: d) I compute the utility for wealth. At the maximum point (x_1, x_2) in the budget set, $x_2 = 3x_1$ because of the nature of the utility function. The budget equation is $2x_1 + 3x_2 = w$. Together, these equations imply that $(x_1, x_2) = (w/11, 3w/11)$. Hence the utility of wealth is $V(w) = \min(3w/11, 3w/11) = 3w/11$. Hence $\lambda = 3/11$.

Answer: e) I compute the utility for wealth. The equation $6x_1 + x_2 = 2x_1 + 7x_2$ implies that $x_2 = (2/3)x_1$. This last equation together with the budget equation $2x_1 + 3x_2 = w$ imply that $(x_1, x_2) = (w/4, w/6)$. Hence

$$V(w) = u(w/4, w/6) = \sqrt{\min((3/2)w + w/6,\ w/2 + (7/6)w)}$$

$$= \sqrt{\min((5/3)w, (5/3)w)} = \sqrt{(5/3)w}.$$

It follows that

$$\lambda = \frac{d}{dw}\sqrt{\frac{5}{3}}\sqrt{w} = \frac{1}{2}\sqrt{\frac{5}{3}}\frac{1}{\sqrt{w}} = \frac{1}{2}\sqrt{\frac{5}{3}}\frac{1}{\sqrt{19}}.$$

Answer to Homework Problems for Chapter 6, Problem #2

Problem: 2) Consider the following Edgeworth box example.

$$e_A = (2, 0),\ u_A(x_1, x_2) = 2\sqrt{x_1 x_2},$$

$$e_B = (0, 5),\ u_B(x_1, x_2) = 2\ln(x_1) + \ln(x_2).$$

a) Compute a competitive equilibrium with the price of commodity 1 equal to 1.

b) Compute the marginal utilities of unit of account for each consumer in the equilibrium.

c) Use these marginal utilities to compute weights, a_A and a_B, such that the equilibrium allocation maximizes the welfare function

$$a_A u_A(x_{A1}, x_{A2}) + a_B u_B(x_{B1}, x_{b2})$$

among all feasible allocations.

Answer: a) Because the utility functions are Cobb-Douglas and each consumer has a positive endowment of only one good, we know immediately that $x_{A1} = 1$ and $x_{B2} = 5/3$. From feasibility, it follows that $x_{B1} = 1$ and $x_{A2} = 10/3$. In order to calculate the equilibrium price for good 2, we use the budget equation for consumer A, $p_1 x_{A1} + p_2 x_{A2} = 2p_1$. Substituting the values for consumer A's consumption and 1 for p_1, we obtain $1 + (10/3)p_2 = 2$. This equation implies that $p_2 = 3/10$. Hence the equilibrium is

$$((x_{A1}, x_{A2}), (x_{B1}, x_{B2}), (p_1, p_2)) = ((1, 10/3), (1, 5/3), (1, 3/10)).$$

Answer: b)

$$\lambda_A = \frac{1}{p_1}\frac{\partial u_A(1, 10/3)}{\partial x_1} = \sqrt{\frac{10}{3}}.$$

$$\lambda_A = \frac{1}{p_1}\frac{\partial u_B(1, 5/3)}{\partial x_1} = \frac{2}{x_{B1}} = 2.$$

Answer: c)

$$a_A = \frac{1}{\lambda_A} = \sqrt{\frac{3}{10}}.\quad a_B = \frac{1}{\lambda_B} = \frac{1}{2}.$$

Answer to Homework Problems for Chapter 6, Problem #3

Problem: 3) For the economies listed below do the following:

a) compute a competitive equilibrium $(\bar{\mathbf{x}}_A, \bar{\mathbf{x}}_B, \mathbf{p})$ such that $p_1 + p_2 = 1$ and

b) find positive numbers a_A and a_B such that the equilibrium allocation $(\bar{\mathbf{x}}_A, \bar{\mathbf{x}}_B)$ solves the problem

$$\max_{(\mathbf{x}_A, \mathbf{x}_B) \geq 0} [a_A u_A(\mathbf{x}_A) + a_B u_B(\mathbf{x}_B)]$$

$$\text{s.t. } \mathbf{x}_A + \mathbf{x}_B \leq \mathbf{e}_A + \mathbf{e}_B$$

and such that, for n = 1 and 2,

$$p_n = \frac{\partial V(e_{A1} + e_{B1}, e_{A2} + e_{B2})}{\partial E_n},$$

where

$$V(E_1, E_2) = \max_{(\mathbf{x}_A, \mathbf{x}_B) \geq 0} [a_A u_A(\mathbf{x}_A) + a_B u_B(\mathbf{x}_B)]$$

$$\text{s.t. } \mathbf{x}_A + \mathbf{x}_B \leq (E_1, E_2).$$

i) $u_A(x_1, x_2) = x_1^{1/3}x_2^{2/3} = u_B(x_1, x_2)$, $\mathbf{e}_A = (12, 0)$, and $\mathbf{e}_B = (0, 12)$.

ii) $u_A(x_1, x_2) = \min(x_1, x_2) = u_B(x_1, x_2)$, $\mathbf{e}_A = (4, 1)$, and $\mathbf{e}_B = (0, 1)$.

iii) $u_A(x_1, x_2) = x_1 + 2x_2$, $u_B(x_1, x_2) = 2x_1 + x_2$, $\mathbf{e}_A = (2, 0)$, $\mathbf{e}_B = (0, 1)$.

iv) $u_A(x_1, x_2) = x_1^{6/7}x_2^{1/7}$, $\mathbf{e}_A = (7, 0)$,

$u_B(x_1, x_2) = x_1^{3/7}x_2^{4/7}$, $\mathbf{e}_B = (7, 0)$, and

$u_C(x_1, x_2) = x_1^{4/5}x_2^{1/5}$, $\mathbf{e}_C = (0, 10)$.

v) $u_A(x_1, x_2) = \frac{1}{6}\ln(x_1) + \frac{1}{3}\ln(x_2)$, $\mathbf{e}_A = (1, 2)$,

$$u_B(x_1, x_2) = \frac{1}{3}\ln(x_1) + \frac{1}{6}\ln(x_2),\ \mathbf{e}_B = (2, 1).$$

vi) $u_A(x_1, x_2) = \min(x_1 + 2x_2, 2x_1 + x_2),\ \mathbf{e}_A = (1, 1),$

$$u_B(x_1, x_2) = \sqrt{\min(x_1 + 8x_2, 2x_1 + 3x_2)},\ \mathbf{e}_B = (3, 1).$$

Answer: i) a) Because the utility functions are Cobb-Douglas and each consumer is endowed with a positive amount of only one good, we know immediately that

$$x_{A1} = \frac{1}{3}12 = 4$$

and

$$x_{B2} = \frac{2}{3}12 = 8.$$

Feasibility then implies that $x_{A2} = 8$ and $x_{A1} = 4$. To compute the prices, use the budget equation of consumer A. Since the prices sum to 1, this equation is

$$4p_1 + 4(1 - p_1) = 12p_1.$$

This equation implies that

$$p_1 = \frac{1}{3}$$

and hence

$$p_2 = \frac{2}{3}.$$

In summary, the equilibrium is

$$(\mathbf{x}_A, \mathbf{x}_B, \mathbf{p}) = ((4, 4), (8, 8), (1/3, 2/3)).$$

b) We may compute the marginal utilities of wealth of the two consumers, λ_A and λ_B, respectively, via the equations

$$\lambda_A = \frac{1}{p_1}\frac{\partial u_A(x_{A1}, x_{A2})}{\partial x_1} = \frac{1}{3p_1}\left(\frac{x_{A2}}{x_{A1}}\right)^{2/3} = 1$$

$$\lambda_B = \frac{1}{p_1}\frac{\partial u_B(x_{B1}, x_{B2})}{\partial x_1} = \frac{1}{3p_1}\left(\frac{x_{B2}}{x_{B1}}\right)^{2/3} = 1.$$

Therefore $a_A = \lambda_A^{-1} = 1 = \lambda_B^{-1} = a_B$.

Answer: ii) a) It is probably easiest to see what the equilibrium is by considering the Edgeworth box diagram below. The dashed lines are the locus of kink points in the indifference curves of consumers A and B. Sample indifference curves for the two consumers are shown as I_A and I_B. Possible equilibrium allocations are along the horizontal line through the endowment point **e**. I have picked the center point of the box, E, as an equilibrium allocation. The equilibrium price vector is **p** = (0, 1). In summary, the equilibrium is

$$(\mathbf{x}_A, \mathbf{x}_B, \mathbf{p}) = ((2, 1), (2, 1), (0, 1)).$$

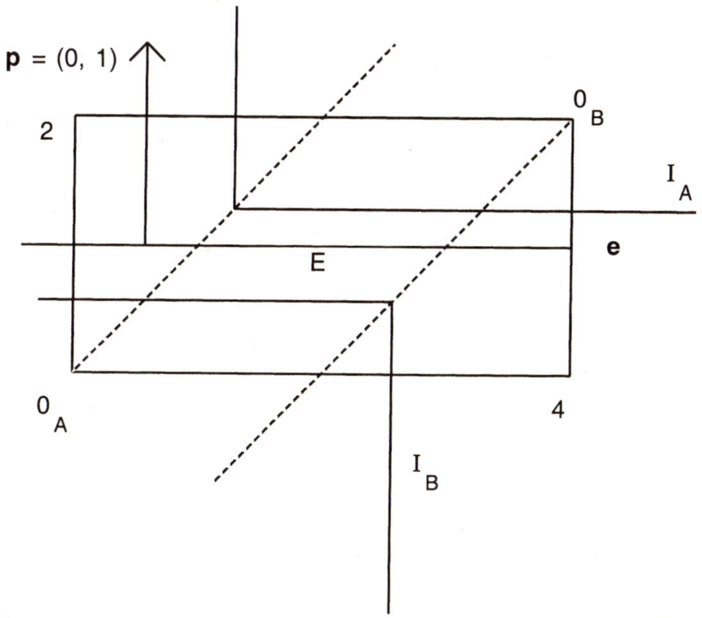

b) If the price vector is (0, 1) and either consumer has wealth w, the consumer will buy w units of good 2 and at least w units of good 1, giving a utility of w, so that the utility gained from wealth w is V(w) = w. The marginal utilities of wealth for each consumer are the derivative of this function, which is 1. Since the welfare weights are the inverses of the marginal utilities of wealth, the welfare weights are 1 as well. In summary,

$$a_A = a_B = 1.$$

Answer: iii) a) Again the equilibrium may be seen by drawing or imagining the appropriate Edgeworth box diagram, as below. It can be readily seen that the equilibrium allocation is at the point E in the diagram and that the budget line is from E to **e**. The offer curves of consumers A and B are $\mathcal{O}_A$ and $\mathcal{O}_B$, respectively, and these intersect at E. The equilibrium price vector is (1, 2), and the equilibrium is

$$(\mathbf{x}_A, \mathbf{x}_B, \mathbf{p}) = ((0, 1), (2, 0), (1, 2)).$$

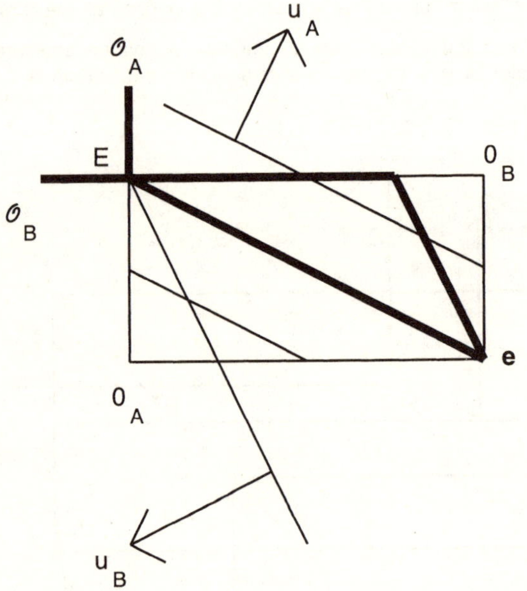

b) The maximum value of the problem

$$\max_{x_1 \geq 0,\, x_2 \geq 0} x_1 + 2x_2$$

$$\text{s.t. } x_1 + 2x_2 \leq w$$

is simply V(w) = w, so that $\lambda_A = \dfrac{dV(w)}{dw} = 1$. The solution of the problem

$$\max_{x_1 \geq 0,\, x_2 \geq 0} 2x_1 + x_2$$

$$\text{s.t. } x_1 + 2x_2 \leq w$$

is $(x_1, x_2) = (w, 0)$, so that the value of this problem is $V(w) = 2w$. It follows that $\lambda_B = 2$.

Answer: iv) a) Because the utility functions are Cobb-Douglas and each consumer has a positive endowment of only one commodity, we see immediately that

$$x_{A1} = \frac{6}{7}7 = 6$$

$$x_{B1} = \frac{3}{7}7 = 3$$

$$x_{C2} = \frac{1}{5}10 = 2.$$

From feasibility, we see that

$$x_{C1} = 14 - 6 - 3.$$

We can now use consumer C's budget equation to calculate prices. After substitution, the budget equation

$$\mathbf{p}.\mathbf{x}_C = \mathbf{p}.\mathbf{e}_C$$

becomes

$$5p_1 + 2(1 - p_1) = 10(1 - p_1).$$

This equation implies that

$$p_1 = \frac{8}{13} \text{ and } p_2 = \frac{5}{13}.$$

With knowledge of the prices and using the budget equations, we can calculate the rest of the equilibrium allocation. The budget equation for consumer A

$$\mathbf{p}.\mathbf{x}_A = \mathbf{p}.\mathbf{e}_A$$

becomes

$$6p_1 + x_{A2}(1 - p_1) = 7p_1,$$

so that

$$x_{A2} = \frac{p_1}{1 - p_1} = \frac{8/13}{5/13} = \frac{8}{5}.$$

The budget equation for consumer B

$$\mathbf{p}.\mathbf{x}_B = \mathbf{p}.\mathbf{e}_B$$

becomes

$$3p_1 + x_{B2}(1 - p_1) = 7p_1,$$

so that

$$x_{B2} = \frac{4p_1}{1 - p_1} = \frac{32/13}{5/13} = \frac{32}{5}.$$

In summary, the equilibrium is

$$(\mathbf{x}_A, \mathbf{x}_B, \mathbf{p}) = ((6, 8/5), (3, 32/5), (8/13, 5/13)).$$

b) We may compute the marginal utilities of wealth using the equations

$$\lambda_A = \frac{1}{p_1}\frac{\partial u_A(6, 8/5)}{\partial x_1} = \frac{1}{p_1}\frac{6}{7}\left(\frac{x_{A2}}{x_{A1}}\right)^{1/7} = \frac{13}{8}\frac{6}{7}\left(\frac{8/5}{6}\right)^{1/7} = \frac{39}{28}\left(\frac{4}{15}\right)^{1/7}$$

$$\lambda_B = \frac{1}{p_1}\frac{\partial u_B(3, 32/5)}{\partial x_1} = \frac{1}{p_1}\frac{3}{7}\left(\frac{x_{B2}}{x_{B1}}\right)^{4/7} = \frac{13}{8}\frac{3}{7}\left(\frac{32/5}{3}\right)^{4/7} = \frac{39}{56}\left(\frac{32}{15}\right)^{4/7}$$

$$\lambda_C = \frac{1}{p_1}\frac{\partial u_C(5, 2)}{\partial x_1} = \frac{1}{p_1}\frac{4}{5}\left(\frac{x_{C2}}{x_{C1}}\right)^{1/5} = \frac{13}{8}\frac{4}{5}\left(\frac{2}{5}\right)^{1/5} = \frac{13}{10}\left(\frac{2}{5}\right)^{1/5}.$$

Therefore

$$a_A = \frac{1}{\lambda_A} = \frac{28}{39}\left(\frac{15}{4}\right)^{1/7}$$

$$a_B = \frac{1}{\lambda_B} = \frac{56}{39}\left(\frac{15}{32}\right)^{4/7}$$

$$a_C = \frac{1}{\lambda_C} = \frac{10}{13}\left(\frac{5}{2}\right)^{1/5}.$$

Answer: v) a) Because of the Cobb Douglas nature of the utility functions,

$$p_1 x_{A1} = \frac{1}{3}(p_1, 1 - p_1).(1, 2) = \frac{1}{3}(2 - p_1) \qquad A)$$

$$p_1 x_{B1} = \frac{2}{3}(p_1, 1 - p_1).(2, 1) = \frac{2}{3}(1 + p_1). \qquad B)$$

By feasibility

$$x_{A1} + x_{B1} = 3.$$

Adding the first two equations and substituting the third, we obtain

$$3p_1 = \frac{1}{3}(2 - p_1) + \frac{2}{3}(1 + p_1).$$

This equation implies that

$$p_1 = p_2 = \frac{1}{2}.$$

We could have also determined by noticing that the prices must be equal because of the symmetry of the economy. If we substitute these prices back into equations A and B, we find that $x_{A1} = 1, x_{B1} = 2.$

The equation

$$p_2 x_{A2} = \frac{2}{3}(2 - p_1)$$

implies that

$$x_{A2} = 2$$

and hence by feasibility

$$x_{B2} = 1.$$

Hence the equilibrium is

$$(\mathbf{x}_A, \mathbf{x}_B, \mathbf{p}) = ((1, 2), (2, 1), (1/2, 1/2)).$$

b) We may compute the marginal utilities of wealth using the equations

$$\lambda_A = \frac{1}{p_1}\frac{\partial u_A(1, 2)}{\partial x_1} = \frac{1}{p_1}\frac{1}{6x_{A1}} = \frac{1}{3}$$

$$\lambda_B = \frac{1}{p_1}\frac{\partial u_B(2, 1)}{\partial x_1} = \frac{1}{p_1}\frac{1}{3x_{B1}} = \frac{1}{3}.$$

Therefore

$$a_A = \frac{1}{\lambda_A} = 3,\ a_B = \frac{1}{\lambda_B} = 3.$$

Answer: vi) a) Again it is helpful to look at an Edgeworth box diagram to see what the equilibrium is. The dashed lines are the loci of kink points in the indifference curves of the two consumers. The equilibrium point in the box, E, is at the endowment point, **e**. The diagram shows indifference curves for the two consumers through the equilibrium point. The budget line must be parallel to the facet of the indifference curve of consumer B that goes through E. The slope of this facet is –2/3. In summary, the equilibrium is

$$(\mathbf{x}_A, \mathbf{x}_B, \mathbf{p}) = ((1, 1), (3, 1), (2/5, 3/5)).$$

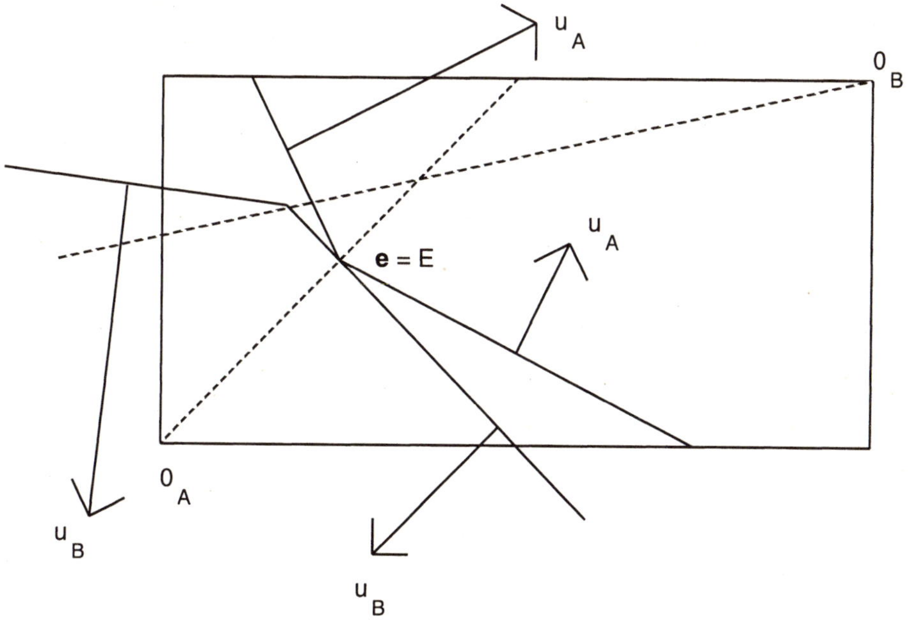

b) At the equilibrium prices, consumer A would want to buy equal amounts of each commodity. If she or he had w units of wealth, she or he would purchase w units of each commodity, and so her or his utility would be 3w. It follows that

$$\lambda_A = 3.$$

Since any budget line is parallel to one facet of consumer B's indifference curve, consumer B will purchase somewhere along that facet and the utility gained from wealth w at prices (2/5, 3/5) is $\sqrt{5w}$. Consumer B's wealth at the equilibrium allocation is 9/5. Therefore, consumer B's marginal utility of wealth in the equilibrium is

$$\lambda_B = \left.\frac{d\sqrt{5w}}{dw}\right|_{w = 9/5} = \frac{\sqrt{5}}{2\sqrt{9/5}} = \frac{5}{6}.$$

Therefore

$$a_A = \frac{1}{\lambda_A} = \frac{1}{3} \text{ and } a_B = \frac{1}{\lambda_B} = \frac{6}{5}.$$

Answer to Homework Problems for Chapter 6, Problem #4

Problem: 4) Consider a consumer who purchases two goods, goods 1 and 2. The consumer's utility function is

$$u(x_1, x_2) = \sqrt{x_1 x_2}.$$

The consumer's wealth is w, where $w > 0$. The price of each good is 1. Suppose that good 1 is rationed, so that the consumer can buy no more than r units of it, where $r \geq 0$.

a) Describe the consumer's utility maximization problem formally as a constrained maximization problem with two constraints.

b) What is the optimum quantity of each good purchased as a function of w and r?

c) Compute the consumer's maximized utility, $V(w, r)$, as a function of w and r.

d) As a function of w and r, what are the consumer's marginal utilities of wealth, λ, and of ration tickets, γ?

e) Suppose the consumer could buy on the black market more ration tickets for good 1 at a price of q per ticket. As a function of w and r, what is the minimum value of q such that the consumer would not buy any ration tickets, assuming that the ration tickets could be sold in arbitrarily small units? Hint: Think about the units in which λ, γ, and q are measured.

f) Show that if $w > 0$, then this value of q diverges to infinity as r converges to zero.

Answer: a)

$$\max_{\substack{x_1 \geq 0 \\ x_2 \geq 0}} \sqrt{x_1 x_2}$$

$$\text{s.t. } x_1 + x_2 \leq w$$

$$x_1 \leq r.$$

Answer: b) If $w/2 \leq r$, $x_1 = x_2 = w/2$, so that

$$x_1(w, r) = \begin{cases} \dfrac{w}{2}, \text{ if } \dfrac{w}{2} \leq r, \\ r, \text{ if } \dfrac{w}{2} \geq r. \end{cases}$$

$$x_2(w, r) = \begin{cases} \dfrac{w}{2}, \text{ if } \dfrac{w}{2} \le r, \\ w - r, \text{ if } \dfrac{w}{2} \ge r. \end{cases}$$

Answer: c) By substitution from part b in the utility function

$$V(w, r) = \begin{cases} \dfrac{w}{2}, \text{ if } \dfrac{w}{2} \le r, \\ \sqrt{r(w - r)}, \text{ if } \dfrac{w}{2} \ge r. \end{cases}$$

Answer: d) By differentiating V,

$$\lambda(w, r) = \frac{\partial V(w, r)}{\partial w} = \begin{cases} \dfrac{1}{2}, \text{ if } \dfrac{w}{2} \le r \\ \dfrac{1}{2}\sqrt{\dfrac{r}{w - r}}, \text{ if } \dfrac{w}{2} \ge r. \end{cases}$$

$$\gamma(w, r) = \frac{\partial V(w, r)}{\partial r} = \begin{cases} 0, \text{ if } \dfrac{w}{2} \le r \\ \dfrac{w - 2r}{2\sqrt{r(w - r)}}, \text{ if } \dfrac{w}{2} \ge r. \end{cases}$$

Answer: e) The units of q are dollars/ticket. The units of γ are utiles/ticket. The units of λ are utiles/dollar. It makes sense therefore that $q = \gamma/\lambda$. A rigorous way to see this is to notice that the marginal utility of wealth should equal the marginal utility of ration tickets divided by q, since the consumer should be indifferent between spending another cent on commodity 2 and another cent on ration tickets. Hence

$$\lambda = \frac{1}{q}\frac{\partial u(r, w - r)}{\partial r} = \frac{\gamma}{q},$$

so that

$$q(w, r) = \begin{cases} 0, \text{ if } \dfrac{w}{2} \le r \\ \dfrac{w - 2r}{r}, \text{ if } \dfrac{w}{2} \ge r. \end{cases}$$

Answer: f) If $w > 0$, then $w/2 \ge r$ if r is small enough. Therefore

$$\lim_{r \to 0} q(w, r) = \lim_{r \to 0} \frac{w - 2r}{r} = \infty.$$

Answer to Homework Problems for Chapter 6, Problem #5

Problem: 5) Let $u(x_1,x_2,x_3) = (x_1x_2x_3)^{1/3}$. Suppose that $p_1 = p_2 = p_3 = 1$ and $w = 6$ and that good 1 is rationed, so that the consumer can buy no more than one unit of it.

a) Compute the demands for goods 1, 2, and 3.

b) Suppose there is a black market for good 1. For what black market prices q would the consumer buy no more than the one unit of good 1 received at price one under rationing?

c) Suppose there was no black market. For what price p would the consumer be willing to pay for more ration tickets, assuming that the tickets could be sold in arbitrarily small units.

Answer: a) From the symmetry of the problem, we know that the consumer buys 2 units of each good, if there is no rationing, and buys 1 unit of good 1 and 5/2 units of goods 2 and 3, if she or he is rationed to buy no more than 1 unit of good 1.

Answer: b) The consumer must weigh the gain in utility from spending an additional cent on good 1 at the black market price of q versus the gain in utility from spending an additional cent on goods 2 or 3 at the market price of 1. That is, q satisfies the equation

$$\lambda = \frac{1}{q}\frac{\partial u(1, 5/2, 5/2)}{\partial x_1},$$

where λ is the consumer's marginal utility of money. This marginal utility may be calculated from the equation

$$\lambda = \frac{1}{p_2}\frac{\partial u(1, 5/2, 5/2)}{\partial x_2} = \frac{1}{3}\frac{x_3^{1/3}}{x_2^{2/3}} = \frac{1}{3}\frac{(5/2)^{1/3}}{(5/2)^{2/3}} = \frac{1}{3}\left(\frac{2}{5}\right)^{1/3}.$$

Therefore

$$q = \frac{1}{\lambda}\frac{\partial u(1, 5/2, 5/2)}{\partial x_1} = 3\left(\frac{5}{2}\right)^{1/3}\frac{1}{3}\left(\frac{5}{2}\right)^{2/3} = \frac{5}{2}.$$

Answer: c) The consumer now must weigh the gain in utility from spending an additional cent on ration tickets against the gain in utility from spending an additional cent on goods 2 or 3 at the market price of 1. In order to make this calculation, we must know the marginal utility of ration tickets. In order to calculate this marginal utility, we must solve the problem

$$\max_{r \geq 0,\, x_2 \geq 0,\, x_3 \geq 0} \quad (r x_2 x_3)^{1/3}$$

$$\text{s.t. } x_1 + x_2 + x_3 \leq 6$$

$$x_1 \leq r.$$

If $r \leq 2$, we know by symmetry that the solution to this problem is $x_1 = r$, $x_2 = x_3 = (6 - r)/2$. Therefore p satisfies the equation

$$\lambda = \frac{1}{p} \frac{\partial r^{1/3}((6 - r)/2)^{2/3}}{\partial r}\bigg|_{r=1},$$

where λ is the consumer's marginal utility of money, which we know from part b of the problem. Therefore

$$p = \frac{1}{\lambda} \frac{\partial((6 - r)/2)^{2/3} r^{1/3}}{\partial r}\bigg|_{r=1} = \frac{1}{\lambda}\left[-\frac{1}{3}\left(\frac{6 - r}{2}\right)^{-1/3} r^{1/3} + \frac{1}{3}\left(\frac{6 - r}{2r}\right)^{2/3}\right]\bigg|_{r=1}$$

$$= \frac{1}{\lambda}\left[-\frac{1}{3}\left(\frac{2}{5}\right)^{1/3} + \frac{1}{3}\left(\frac{5}{2}\right)^{2/3}\right] = 3\left(\frac{5}{2}\right)^{1/3}\left[-\frac{1}{3}\left(\frac{2}{5}\right)^{1/3} + \frac{1}{3}\left(\frac{5}{2}\right)^{2/3}\right]$$

$$= -1 + \frac{5}{2} = \frac{3}{2}.$$

This was the long way of doing the problem. A short cut is to think like a trader and notice that the black market price should be the price of the commodity plus the price of a ration ticket, so that price of the ration ticket should be 5/2 − 1 = 3/2.

Answer to Homework Problems for Chapter 6, Problem #6

Problem: 6) A firm has two processes for producing a good X. Each process uses five chemicals, A, B, C, D, and E. The first process, when operated at unit level, produces 3 tons of X and uses 5, 4, 3, 2, and 1 tons of chemicals A, B, C, D, and E, respectively. If the process is operated at level a, where a > 0, it uses 5a, 4a, 3a, 2a, and a tons of the chemicals, respectively, and produces 3a tons of X. The second process, when operated at unit level, produces 4 tons of X and uses 1, 2, 3, 4, and 5 tons, respectively, of chemicals A, B, C, D, and E. If this process is operated at level a, where a > 0, it uses a, 2a, 3a, 4a, and 5a tons, respectively, of the chemicals and produces 4a tons of X. The company has available 26 tons of each of chemicals A and E, 22 tons of each of chemicals B and D, and 21 tons of chemical C.. The price of X is $100 per ton.

a) What is the maximum amount of X the firm can produce? (Hint: The requirement that no more than a certain amount of each resource be used places linear constraints on the outputs, y_1 and y_2 produced by the two processes. Calculate and graph these constraints for each resource. The answer should then be obvious.)

b) At this optimum, how much is produced by each process?

c) What is the maximum price the firm is willing to pay for additional marginal amounts of each chemical? (Hint: Calculate the Kuhn-Tucker coefficients corresponding to each resource constraint.)

Answer: a) The problem can be described formally as

$$\max_{x_1 \geq 0,\, x_2 \geq 0} \; 3x_1 + 4x_2$$

$$\text{s.t. } 5x_1 + x_2 \leq 26$$

$$4x_1 + 2x_2 \leq 22$$

$$3x_1 + 3x_2 \leq 21$$

$$2x_1 + 4x_2 \leq 22$$

$$x_1 + 5x_2 \leq 26,$$

where x_1 and x_2 are the levels of activities 1 and 2, respectively. The diagram below describes the problem. The shaded area is the feasible set of activity level vectors **x**, that is, those that are non-negative and use no more than the available amount of each resource. The vertices or corners of the feasible set may be obtained by replacing the inequality by equality signs in neighboring pairs of inequalities in the constraints, and then solving for x_1 and x_2. The vector (3, 4) gives the amounts produced by the two activities when used at unit level. The three straight lines perpendicular to this vector are sets of activity level vectors giving a constant level of total output. It is clear from the diagram that the highest level is achieved at the vertex (3, 4) of the feasible set. That this must be the case can be seen by considering the vectors (1, 2) and (1, 1) that are perpendicular to the faces of the feasible set on either side of the vertex (3, 4). Since 3/4 is between 1/2 and 1, the vector (3, 4) points in a direction between the directions of (1, 2) and (1, 1). Therefore the maximum output must be at the vertex (3, 4). Since the activity level vector (3, 4) maximizes total output, that output is (3, 4).(3, 4) = 25.

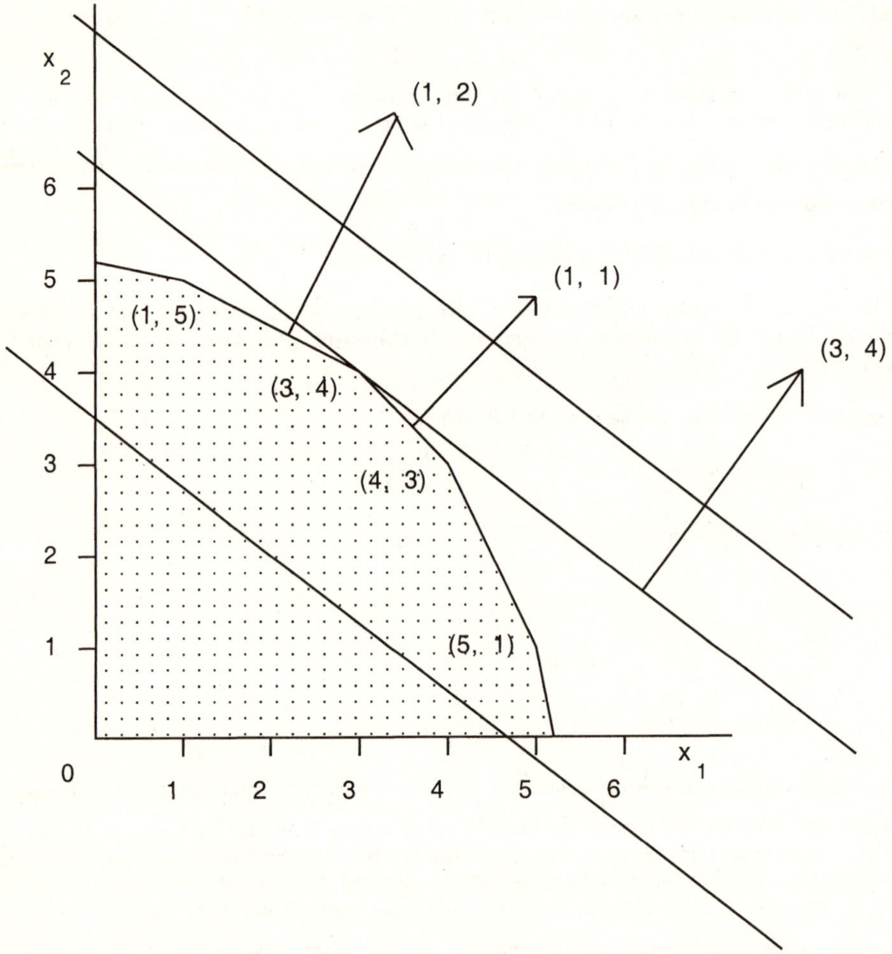

Answer: b) At the optimum, process 1 produces 3x3 = 9 and process 2 produces 4x4 = 16.

Answer: c) The prices p_n requested are the Kuhn-Tucker coefficients of the above constrained maximization problem. Since the first, second, and fifth constraints are satisfied with strict inequality, the corresponding resource prices are zero. The third and fourth constraints are satisfied with equality, since the optimum is at the vertex defined by these constraints. Hence the third and fourth prices may be non-zero. The Lagrangian therefore takes the form

$$\mathcal{L}(x_1, x_2, p_3, p_4) = 3x_1 + 4x_2 - p_3(3x_1 + 3x_2) - p_4(2x_1 + 4x_2).$$

Since the Lagrangian is maximized at positive values of x_1 and x_2, its derivative with respect to these variables is zero at the optimum. Setting these derivatives equal to zero, we obtain the equations

$$3p_3 + 2p_4 = 3$$

$$3p_3 + 4p_4 = 4.$$

The solution to these equations is $p_3 = 2/3$ and $p_4 = 1/2$. In summary, the vector of resource prices is

$$\mathbf{p} = (p_1, p_2, p_3, p_4, p_5) = (0, 0, 2/3, 1/2, 0).$$

Answer to Homework Problems for Chapter 6, Problem #7

Problem: 7) You are given the following economy with two consumers, two firms, and three commodities.

$$Y_{I} = \{(-t,\ 2t,\ t) \mid t \geq 0\}.$$

$$Y_{II} = \{(-t,\ t,\ 3t) \mid t \geq 0\}.$$

$$\mathbf{e}_A = (2, 0, 0). \qquad u_A(x_1, x_2, x_3) = \ln(x_1) + 2\ln(x_2) + 2\ln(x_3).$$

$$\mathbf{e}_B = (0, 0, 0). \qquad u_B(x_1, x_2, x_3) = 2\ln(x_1) + 2\ln(x_2) + \ln(x_3).$$

Consider the following value function of a welfare maximization problem.

$$V(e_1, e_2, e_3) = \max_{\substack{\mathbf{x}_A \in R^3_+,\, \mathbf{x}_B \in R^3_+, \\ \mathbf{y}_I \in Y_I,\, \mathbf{y}_{II} \in Y_{II}}} [u_A(\mathbf{x}_A) + u_B(\mathbf{x}_B)]$$

$$\text{s.t. } \mathbf{x}_A + \mathbf{x}_B \leq \mathbf{y}_I + \mathbf{y}_{II} + (e_1, e_2, e_3).$$

Find a subgradient for V at the point $(e_1, e_2, e_3) = \mathbf{e}_A + \mathbf{e}_B = (2, 0, 0)$. Hint: Start by computing equilibrium relative prices. There is no need to compute an equilibrium. Remember that transfer payments may be freely adjusted.

Answer: Recall that when utility functions are concave, as they are here, then the maximum of a welfare function such as $u_A(\mathbf{x}_A) + u_B(\mathbf{x}_B)$ occurs at the allocation of an equilibrium with transfer payments and, if the equilibrium prices are normalized correctly, the welfare weights are 1 divided by the consumers' marginal utilities of unit of account in the equilibrium. In this case, the price vector is a gradient of the value function V. Since the welfare weights equal 1, we want to find a price vector for an equilibrium with transfer payments such that the marginal utility of unit of account for each consumer equals 1. I use the production possibility sets to determine equilibrium relative prices and then adjust the incomes of the two consumers so that their marginal utilities of unit of account are equal at these prices. Finally I normalize the prices so that the marginal utilities of unit of account are 1.

As an initial normalization of prices, let $p_1 = 1$. Both input-output possibility sets are cones, so that profits are zero. The zero profit condition on the two input-output possibility sets yield the following two equations.

$$-p_1 + 2p_2 + p_3 = 0.$$

$$-p_1 + p_2 + 3p_3 = 0.$$

Letting $p_1 = 1$ and multiplying the second equation by 2, we obtain

$$2p_2 + p_3 = 1.$$

$$2p_2 + 6p_3 = 2.$$

Eliminating p_2 from these equations, we obtain

$$p_3 = \frac{1}{5}.$$

Substituting this value into the first equation above, we obtain

$$2p_2 + \frac{1}{5} = 1,$$

so that

$$p_2 = \frac{2}{5}.$$

Therefore a candidate equilibrium price vector is

$$\mathbf{p} = (1, \frac{2}{5}, \frac{1}{5}).$$

Using the Cobb-Douglas nature of the utility functions, we obtain

$$x_{A1} = \frac{1}{5} w_A,$$

and

$$x_{B1} = \frac{2}{5} w_B,$$

where w_A and w_B are the incomes of consumers A and B, respectively. Because $p_1 = 1$,

$$\lambda_A = p_1 \lambda_A = \frac{\partial u_A(\mathbf{x}_A)}{\partial x_1} = \frac{1}{x_{A1}} = \frac{5}{w_A},$$

and

$$\lambda_B = p_1 \lambda_B = \frac{\partial u_B(\mathbf{x}_B)}{\partial x_1} = \frac{2}{x_{B1}} = \frac{2}{\frac{2}{5} w_B} = \frac{5}{w_B},$$

where λ_A and λ_B are the marginal utilities of unit of account of consumers A and B, respectively. Therefore $\lambda_A = \lambda_B$, if and only if $w_A = w_B$. Since $w_A + w_B = p_1 e_1 = 2$, it follows that

$$w_A = w_B = 1.$$

Therefore

$$\lambda_A = \lambda_B = 5.$$

In order to obtain marginal utilities of unit of account equal to 1, we must multiply the price vector by 5, so that the final price vector is

$$5\mathbf{p} = 5(1, \frac{2}{5}, \frac{1}{5}) = (5, 2, 1).$$

This is the price vector of an equilibrium with transfer payments in which the marginal utility of account of each consumer is 1. Therefore the gradient of V at (2, 0, 0) is (5, 2, 1).

Answer to Homework Problems for Chapter 6, Problem #8

Problem: 8)[1] I introduce a government into a pure trade or exchange economy, $((u_i, \mathbf{e}_i)_{i=1}^{I})$. (An economy with no production is said to be a pure trade economy or an exchange economy.) The government chooses a consumption bundle $\mathbf{g} \in R^N_+$. An allocation consists of $(\mathbf{x}, \mathbf{g}) = (\mathbf{x}_1, \ldots, \mathbf{x}_I, \mathbf{g})$. It is feasible if $\mathbf{g} + \sum_{i=1}^{I} \mathbf{x}_i \le \sum_{i=1}^{I} \mathbf{e}_i$. For each i, u_i depends on $\mathbf{x}_i$ and $\mathbf{g}$, so that consumer I's utility is $u_i(\mathbf{x}_i, \mathbf{g})$. Assume that, for each i, u_i is differentiable, concave, and strictly increasing.

a) Define Pareto optimality of a feasible allocation.

b) Show that if $(\overline{\mathbf{x}}, \overline{\mathbf{g}})$ is a Pareto optimal allocation, then there exists an I-vector $\mathbf{a}$ such $\mathbf{a} > 0$ and $(\overline{\mathbf{x}}, \overline{\mathbf{g}})$ solves the problem

$$\max_{\substack{(\mathbf{x},\, \mathbf{g}) \text{ is a feasible} \\ \text{allocation}}} \sum_{i=1}^{I} a_i u_i(x_i, g).$$

c) Show that if $(\overline{\mathbf{x}}, \overline{\mathbf{g}})$ is a Pareto optimal allocation such that $\overline{\mathbf{x}}_i \gg 0$, for all i, and $\overline{\mathbf{g}} \gg 0$, then there exists an N-vector $\mathbf{q}$ such that $\mathbf{q} \gg 0$, $a_i \frac{\partial u_i(\overline{\mathbf{x}}_i, \overline{\mathbf{g}})}{\partial x_n} = q_n$, for all i and n, and $\sum_{i=1}^{I} a_i \frac{\partial u_i(\overline{\mathbf{x}}_i, \overline{\mathbf{g}})}{\partial g_n} = q_n$, for all n, where the a_i are as in part b.

Answer: a) The allocation $(\overline{\mathbf{x}}, \overline{\mathbf{g}})$ is Pareto optimal if it is feasible and there exists no other feasible allocation $(\mathbf{x}, \mathbf{g})$ such that $u_i(\mathbf{x}_i, \mathbf{g}) \ge u_i(\overline{\mathbf{x}}_i, \overline{\mathbf{g}})$, for all i, with $u_i(\mathbf{x}_i, \mathbf{g}) > u_i(\overline{\mathbf{x}}_i, \overline{\mathbf{g}})$, for some i.

b) Let $\mathcal{U} = \{v \in R^I \mid$ there is a feasible allocation $(\mathbf{x}, \mathbf{g})$ such that $v_i \le u_i(\mathbf{x}_i, \mathbf{g})$, for all i$\}$. I show that $\mathcal{U}$ is convex. Let $\underline{\mathbf{v}}$ and $\overline{\mathbf{v}}$ belong to $\mathcal{U}$ and let α be such that $0 < \alpha < 1$. I show that $\mathbf{v} = \alpha \underline{\mathbf{v}} + (1-\alpha)\overline{\mathbf{v}} \in \mathcal{U}$. By the definition of $\mathcal{U}$, there exist feasible allocations $(\underline{\mathbf{x}}, \underline{\mathbf{g}})$ and $(\overline{\overline{\mathbf{x}}}, \overline{\mathbf{g}})$, such that $\underline{v}_i \le u_i(\underline{\mathbf{x}}_i, \mathbf{g})$, for all i, and $\overline{v}_i \le u_i(\overline{\mathbf{x}}_i, \mathbf{g})$, for all i. Let $(\mathbf{x}, \mathbf{g}) = \alpha(\underline{\mathbf{x}}, \underline{\mathbf{g}}) + (1-\alpha)(\overline{\mathbf{x}}, \overline{\mathbf{g}})$. Then $\mathbf{x}_i = \alpha \underline{\mathbf{x}}_i + (1-\alpha)\overline{\mathbf{x}}_i \in R^N_+$, for all i since $\underline{\mathbf{x}}_i \in R^N_+$ and $\overline{\mathbf{x}}_i \in R^N_+$. Similarly $\mathbf{g} = \alpha \underline{\mathbf{g}} + (1-\alpha)\overline{\mathbf{g}} \in R^N_+$. Finally

$$\sum_{i=1}^{I} \mathbf{x}_i + \mathbf{g} = \sum_{i=1}^{I} [\alpha \underline{\mathbf{x}}_i + (1-\alpha)\overline{\mathbf{x}}_i] + \alpha \underline{\mathbf{g}} + (1-\alpha)\overline{\mathbf{g}}$$

$$= \alpha\left(\sum_{i=1}^{I} \underline{\mathbf{x}}_i + \underline{\mathbf{g}}\right) + (1-\alpha)\left(\sum_{i=1}^{I} \overline{\mathbf{x}}_i + \overline{\mathbf{g}}\right)$$

$$\leq \alpha \sum_{i=1}^{I} \mathbf{e}_i + (1-\alpha) \sum_{i=1}^{I} \mathbf{e}_i = \sum_{i=1}^{I} \mathbf{e}_i.$$

Therefore $(\mathbf{x}, \mathbf{g})$ is feasible. Next observe that because each u_i is concave,

$$u_i(\mathbf{x}_i, \mathbf{g}) = u_i(\alpha \underline{\mathbf{x}}_i + (1-\alpha)\overline{\mathbf{x}}_i, \alpha \underline{\mathbf{g}} + (1-\alpha)\overline{\mathbf{g}})$$

$$\geq \alpha u_i(\underline{\mathbf{x}}_i, \underline{\mathbf{g}}) + (1-\alpha) u_i(\overline{\mathbf{x}}_i, \overline{\mathbf{g}}) \geq \alpha \underline{v}_i + (1-\alpha)\overline{v}_i = v_i,$$

for all i. Therefore v belongs to $\mathcal{U}$.

The argument given in the proof of theorem 3.31 (section 3.5) shows that it is possible to separate the set $\mathcal{U}$ from the set $\Gamma = \{\mathbf{v} \in R^I \mid \mathbf{v} \geq \overline{\mathbf{v}}\}$, where $\overline{\mathbf{v}}$ is the vector with components $\overline{v}_i = u_i(\overline{\mathbf{x}}_i, \overline{\mathbf{g}})$ and $(\overline{\mathbf{x}}, \overline{\mathbf{g}})$ is the given Pareto optimal allocation. The argument given in the proof of theorem 3.31 also shows that the separating vector $\mathbf{a}$ is such that $\mathbf{a} > 0$ and $(\overline{\mathbf{x}}, \overline{\mathbf{g}})$ solves the problem

$$\max_{(\mathbf{x}, \mathbf{g}) \text{ is a feasible allocation}} \sum_{i=1}^{I} a_i u_i(\mathbf{x}_i, \mathbf{g}).$$

c) By part b, if $(\overline{\mathbf{x}}, \overline{\mathbf{g}})$ is a Pareto optimal allocation, it solves a problem of the form

$$\max_{\substack{\mathbf{x}_i \in R^N_+, \text{ for all i, and} \\ \mathbf{g} \in R^N_+}} \sum_{i=1}^{I} a_i u_i(\mathbf{x}_i, \mathbf{g}) \qquad \text{(A)}$$

$$\text{s.t. } \sum_{i=1}^{I} x_{in} + g_n \leq \sum_{i=1}^{I} e_{in}, \text{ for } n = 1, \ldots, N,$$

where $\mathbf{a} = (a_1, \ldots, a_I) > 0$. Since the utility functions u_i are concave, the welfare function $\sum_{i=1}^{I} a_i u_i(\mathbf{x}_i, \mathbf{g})$ is also concave and hence problem A satisfies the conditions of the Kuhn-Tucker theorem. Since $\overline{\mathbf{x}}_i >> \mathbf{0}$, for all i, and $\overline{\mathbf{g}} >> \mathbf{0}$, the allocation $\left(\frac{\overline{\mathbf{x}}}{2}, \frac{\overline{\mathbf{g}}}{2}\right)$ satisfies the strict inequalities

$$\sum_{i=1}^{I} \frac{\overline{x}_{in}}{2} + \frac{\overline{g}_n}{2} < \sum_{i=1}^{I} e_{in},$$

for all n. Therefore, problem A satisfies the constraint qualification and the necessity part of the Kuhn-Tucker theorem implies that there exist non-negative numbers $q_1, \ldots, q_N$ such that $(\overline{\mathbf{x}}, \overline{\mathbf{g}})$ solves the Lagrangian maximization problem

$$\max_{\substack{\mathbf{x}_i \in R^N_+, \text{ for all } i, \text{ and} \\ \mathbf{g} \in R^N_+}} \left[\sum_{i=1}^{I} a_i u_i(\mathbf{x}_i, \mathbf{g}) - \mathbf{q}.\left(\sum_{i=1}^{I} \mathbf{x}_i + \mathbf{g}\right)\right]. \qquad (B)$$

Since $\overline{\mathbf{x}}_i >> 0$, for all i and $\overline{\mathbf{g}} >> \mathbf{0}$ and the utility functions u_i are differentiable, all the derivatives of the above Lagrangian are zero at $(\overline{\mathbf{x}}, \overline{\mathbf{g}})$. That is,

$$a_i \frac{\partial u_i(\overline{\mathbf{x}}_i, \overline{\mathbf{g}})}{\partial x_{in}} - q_n = 0,$$

for all n, and

$$\sum_{i=1}^{I} a_i \frac{\partial u_i(\overline{\mathbf{x}}_i, \overline{\mathbf{g}})}{\partial g_n} - q_n = 0,$$

for all n, as was to be proved. Because each u_i is strictly increasing, problem B would not have a solution if some component of $\mathbf{q}$ were zero. Therefore, $\mathbf{q} >> 0$

1. This problem is based on the work of Paul Samuelson on public expenditures (1954, 1955).

Answer to Homework Problems for Chapter 7, Problem #1

Problem: 1 a) Consider an economy with two consumers, A and B, and two states, states 1 and 2. Each consumer has a von Neumann-Morgenstern utility function for lotteries of money, and for each consumer the utility of x units of money is ln(x). Consumer A believes that state 1 occurs with probability 1/4 and state 2 occurs with probability 3/4. Consumer B believes that state 1 occurs with probability 3/4 and state 2 occurs with probability 1/4. Each consumer is endowed with $1 in each state. Compute an Arrow-Debreu equilibrium.

b) In part (a), suppose that each consumer believes that each state occurs with probability 1/2, that consumer A is endowed with $2 in state 1 and $0 in state 2, and that consumer B is endowed with $0 in state 1 and $2 in state 2. Recalculate the Arrow-Debreu equilibrium.

Answer: a) The givens may be described formally as

$$u_A(x_1, x_2) = \frac{1}{4}\ln x_1 + \frac{3}{4}\ln x_2$$

$$u_B(x_1, x_2) = \frac{3}{4}\ln x_1 + \frac{1}{4}\ln x_2$$

$$\mathbf{e}_A = \mathbf{e}_B = (1, 1).$$

From the symmetry of the economy, we see immediately that the equilibrium prices for a dollar in the two states must be the same and that consumer A's purchase in state 1 will be the same as that of consumer B in state 2 and vice versa. Let the price of a unit of money in each state be 1, so that the wealth of each consumer is 2. That is, $w_A = w_B = 2$. Because the utility functions are Cobb-Douglas, we have that

$$x_{A1} = \frac{1}{4}w_A = \frac{1}{2}.$$

It follows from feasibility that

$$x_{B1} = \frac{3}{2}.$$

By symmetry, $x_{A2} = 3/2$, and $x_{B1} = 1/2$. In summary, the equilibrium is

$$(\mathbf{x}_A, \mathbf{x}_B, \mathbf{p}) = ((1/2, 3/2), (3/2, 1/2), (1, 1)).$$

Answer: b) Now the givens may be described formally as

$$u_A(x_1, x_2) = \frac{1}{2}\ln x_1 + \frac{1}{2}\ln x_2$$

$$u_B(x_1, x_2) = \frac{1}{2}\ln x_1 + \frac{1}{2}\ln x_2$$

$$\mathbf{e}_A = (2, 0), \mathbf{e}_B = (0, 2).$$

Because of the utility functions are Cobb-Douglas and each consumer has positive endowment in only one state, we know immediately that $x_{A1} = 1$ and hence the feasibility, $x_{B1} = 1$. Since the economy is symmetric with respect to the states, we know that $x_{A2} = x_{B2} = 1$. If we let the price of a unit of money in each state be 1, we obtain the equilibrium

$$(\mathbf{x}_A, \mathbf{x}_B, \mathbf{p}) = ((1, 1), (1, 1), (1, 1)).$$

Answer to Homework Problems for Chapter 7, Problem #2

Problem: 2) Consider an economy with two consumers, A and B, and two states, states 1 and 2. Each consumer has a von Neumann-Morgenstern utility function for lotteries of money. For each consumer, the utility of x units of money is $\sqrt{x}$ and each consumers believes that each state occurs with probability 1/2. Consumer A is endowed with \$2 in state 1 and \$4 in state 2. Consumer B is endowed with \$1 in state 1 and \$10 in state 2. Compute an Arrow-Debreu equilibrium for this example.

Answer: The givens may be described formally as

$$u_A(x_1, x_2) = u_B(x_1, x_2) = \frac{1}{2}\sqrt{x_1} + \frac{1}{2}\sqrt{x_2}$$

$$\mathbf{e}_A = (2, 4), \mathbf{e}_B = (1, 10).$$

Let the price of money in state 1 be 1 and that of money in state 2 be p. We do not change the consumers' demands if we multiply their objective functions by 4. Having done this, the maximization problem of consumer A becomes

$$\max_{x_1 \geq 0, x_2 \geq 0} 2\sqrt{x_1} + 2\sqrt{x_2}$$

$$\text{s.t. } x_1 + px_2 = 2 + 4p.$$

The first order conditions for this problem are

$$\frac{1}{\sqrt{x_1}} = \lambda \text{ and } \frac{1}{\sqrt{x_2}} = \lambda p.$$

Division of one of these equations by the other yields that

$$x_1 = p^2 x_2.$$

Upon substituting this equation into the budget equation, we find that

$$x_{A1} = \frac{p(2 + 4p)}{1 + p} \text{ and } x_{A2} = \frac{2 + 4p}{p(1 + p)}.$$

The utility maximization problem for consumer B is

$$\max_{x_1 \geq 0,\, x_2 \geq 0} \quad 2\sqrt{x_1} + 2\sqrt{x_2}$$

$$\text{s.t. } x_1 + px_2 = 1 + 10p.$$

We may obtain the solution for consumer B by substituting the expression 1 + 10p for 2 + 4p in the demands of consumer A, so that

$$x_{A1} = \frac{p(1 + 10p)}{1 + p} \text{ and } x_{A2} = \frac{1 + 10p}{p(1 + p)}.$$

We may obtain the price p by using the feasibility equation for money in the first state,

$$x_{A1} + x_{B1} = e_{A1} + e_{B1}.$$

Upon substitution, this equation becomes

$$\frac{p(2 + 4p)}{1 + p} + \frac{p(1 + 10p)}{1 + p} = 3,$$

which implies that

$$p(3 + 14p) = 3 + 3p$$

and so

$$14p^2 = 3$$

and hence

$$p = \sqrt{\frac{3}{14}}.$$

Thus the equilibrium is

$$(\mathbf{x}_A, \mathbf{x}_B, \mathbf{p}) = \left(\left(\frac{p(2 + 4p)}{1 + p}, \frac{2 + 4p}{p(1 + p)}\right), \left(\frac{p(1 + 10p)}{1 + p}, \frac{1 + 10p}{p(1 + p)}\right), (1, p)\right),$$

where $p = \sqrt{3/14}$.

Answer to Homework Problems for Chapter 7, Problem #3

Problem: 3) Consider the following insurance problem. There are two consumers, A and B, two events, a and b, and one period. The endowment of consumer A is

$$\mathbf{e}_A = (e_{Aa}, e_{Ab}) = (1, 0).$$

The endowment of consumer B is

$$\mathbf{e}_B = (e_{Ba}, e_{Bb}) = (0, 1).$$

The utility function of consumer A is

$$u_A(x_a, x_b) = -\frac{1}{3}e^{-x_a} - \frac{2}{3}e^{-x_b}.$$

The utility function of consumer B is

$$u_B(x_a, x_b) = \frac{1}{3}x_a + \frac{2}{3}x_b.$$

Compute an Arrow-Debreu equilibrium in which the sum of the prices is one.

Answer: Since u_B is linear, we may guess that $p_a = 1/3$ and $p_b = 2/3$. This guess will be valid if consumer B buys a positive amount of contingent claim for each of the states a and b. We may conclude that $x_{Aa} = x_{Ab}$, because u_A is a von Neumann-Morgenstern and concave utility function with probabilities equal to the prices. Since consumer A's budget equation is

$$\frac{1}{3}x_{Aa} + \frac{2}{3}x_{Ab} = \frac{1}{3},$$

we may conclude that

$$x_{Aa} = x_{Ab} = \frac{1}{3}.$$

By feasibility, it follows that

$$x_{Ba} = \frac{2}{3} \text{ and } x_{Bb} = \frac{5}{3}.$$

Since $x_B >> 0$, we were correct in assuming that the prices could be $p_a = 1/3$ and $p_b = 2/3$. In summary, the equilibrium is

$$(\mathbf{x}_A, \mathbf{x}_B, \mathbf{p}) = ((1/3, 1/3), (2/3, 5/3), (1/3, 2/3)).$$

<u>Answer to Homework Problems for Chapter 7, Problem #4</u>

<u>Problem</u>: 4) Consider the following insurance model with two states, a and b, and three consumers, A, B, and C.

$$u_A(x_a, x_b) = u_B(x_a, x_b) = u_C(x_a, x_b) = \frac{1}{3}\ln(x_a) + \frac{2}{3}\ln(x_b).$$

$$\mathbf{e}_A = (1, 4), \mathbf{e}_B = (2, 1), \mathbf{e}_C = (1, 3).$$

Compute an Arrow-Debreu equilibrium such that the sum of the prices is one. Hint: The problem can be solved quickly by noticing that the total endowment is twice as big in state b as in state a and using the fact that the utility functions are logarithmic.

<u>Answer</u>: Let the equilibrium price vector be (p_a, p_b). Because the common utility function is Cobb-Douglas, we know that consumer i's purchase of contingent claims for states a and b are

$$x_{ia} = \frac{w_i}{3p_a} \text{ and } x_{ib} = \frac{2w_i}{3p_b}, \qquad (A)$$

for i = A, B, or C, where w_i is consumer i's wealth. Therefore

$$\frac{x_{ia}}{x_{ib}} = \frac{1}{2}\frac{p_b}{p_a},$$

for all i. Since the consumer's purchases for states a and b add up to the total endowments in these states, we know

$$\frac{1}{2}\frac{p_b}{p_a} = \frac{e_{Aa} + e_{Ba} + e_{Ca}}{e_{Ab} + e_{Bb} + e_{Cb}} = \frac{1}{2}.$$

It follows that

$$p_a = p_b = \frac{1}{2}.$$

We can now calculate the wealths of the consumers to be

$$w_A = \frac{1}{2}1 + \frac{1}{2}4 = \frac{5}{2}, \ w_B = \frac{3}{2}, \ w_C = 2.$$

If we now substitute into equation A, we find the equilibrium allocation, so that the full equilibrium is $(\mathbf{x}_A, \mathbf{x}_B, \mathbf{x}_C, \mathbf{p}) = ((5/12, 5/6), (1/4, 1/2), (1/3, 2/3), (1/2, 1/2))$.

Answer to Homework Problems for Chapter 7, Problem #5

Problem: 5) Consider the following Arrow-Debreu model with production. There are two periods, periods 0 and 1. In period 1, there are two states, states a and b, each occurring with probability 1/2. There is one commodity in period 0, which is labor-leisure time. There is one commodity in period 2, which is food. With obvious notation, the utility functions are

$$u_A(\ell_0, x_{1a}, x_{1b}) = \ln(\ell_0) + \frac{1}{2}\ln(x_{1a}) + \frac{1}{2}\ln(x_{1b}) = u_B(\ell_0, x_{1a}, x_{1b}).$$

Each consumer is endowed with 15 units of labor-leisure time in period 0 and with nothing else. There is one firm. Its input-output possibility set, again using obvious notation, is

$$Y = \left\{(-L_0, y_{1a}, y_{1b}) \mid L_0 \geq 0,\ y_{1a} \leq 2\sqrt{L_0},\ y_{1b} \leq 20\sqrt{L_0}\right\},$$

where L_0 is labor input in period 0. Each consumer has a share of 1/2 in the profits of the firm. Find an Arrow-Debreu equilibrium where the price of labor-leisure time is 1.

Answer: The wealth of each consumer is $w = 15 + \pi/2$, where π is the maximum profits of the firm. The maximum profits equal

$$\pi = \max_{L_0 \geq 0} \left(2p_{1a}\sqrt{L_0} + 20p_{1b}\sqrt{L_0} - L_0\right),$$

where p_{1a} and p_{1b} are the prices of food in period 1 in states a and b, respectively. The price of labor-leisure time is 1 by assumption. The first order condition for the above profit maximization problem is

$$\frac{p_{1a}}{\sqrt{L_0}} + \frac{10p_{1b}}{\sqrt{L_0}} - 1 = 0.$$

This equation implies that

$$p_{1a} + 10p_{1b} = \sqrt{L_0},$$

so that

$$L_0 = (p_{1a} + 10p_{1b})^2.$$

Hence

$$y_{1a} = 2\sqrt{L_0} = 2p_{1a} + 20p_{1b},$$

$$y_{1b} = 20\sqrt{L_0} = 20p_{1a} + 200p_{1b},$$

and

$$\pi = p_{1a}y_{1a} + p_{1b}y_{1b} - L_0$$

$$= 2p_{1a}^2 + 20p_{1a}p_{1b} + 20p_{1a}p_{1b} + 200p_{1b}^2 - (p_{1a} + 10p_{1b})^2$$

$$= 2(p_{1a}^2 + 20p_{1a}p_{1b} + 100p_{1b}^2) - (p_{1a} + 10p_{1b})^2$$

$$= 2(p_{1a} + 10p_{1b})^2 - (p_{1a} + 10p_{1b})^2$$

$$= (p_{1a} + 10p_{1b})^2.$$

Therefore each consumer's wealth is

$$w = 15 + \frac{\pi}{2} = 15 + \frac{(p_{1a} + 10p_{1b})^2}{2}.$$

Because the utility functions are Cobb-Douglas,

$$x_{A1a} = x_{B1a} = \frac{w}{4p_{1a}} = w = \frac{15}{4p_{1a}} + \frac{(p_{1a} + 10p_{1b})^2}{8p_{1a}}.$$

Similarly

$$x_{A1b} = x_{B1b} = \frac{w}{4p_{1b}} = w = \frac{15}{4p_{1b}} + \frac{(p_{1a} + 10p_{1b})^2}{8p_{1b}}.$$

By feasibility,

$$x_{A1a} + x_{B1a} = y_{1a},$$

which after substitution becomes

$$\frac{15}{2p_{1a}} + \frac{(p_{1a} + 10p_{1b})^2}{4p_{1a}} = 2p_{1a} + 20p_{1b}.$$

On clearing the denominators in this equation, we find that

$$30 + \left(p_{1a} + 10p_{1b}\right)^2 = 8p_{1a}^2 + 80p_{1a}p_{1b}. \qquad (A)$$

Similarly the feasibility equation

$$x_{A1b} + x_{B1b} = y_{1b}$$

implies that

$$\frac{15}{2p_{1b}} + \frac{\left(p_{1a} + 10p_{1b}\right)^2}{4p_{1b}} = 20p_{1a} + 200p_{1b}.$$

After clearing denominators, we obtain the equation

$$30 + \left(p_{1a} + 10p_{1b}\right)^2 = 80p_{1a}p_{1b} + 800p_{1b}^2. \qquad (B)$$

On subtracting equation A from equation B, we obtain

$$0 = -8p_{1a}^2 + 800p_{1b}^2,$$

so that

$$p_{1a}^2 = 100p_{1b}^2$$

and so

$$p_{1a} = 10p_{1b}.$$

When we substitute this equation into equation A, we see that

$$30 + \left(20p_{1b}\right)^2 = 800p_{1b}^2 + 800p_{1b}^2,$$

so that

$$30 + 400p_{1b}^2 = 1600p_{1b}^2$$

and hence

$$p_{1b}^2 = \frac{1}{40}$$

and

$$p_{1b} = \sqrt{\frac{1}{40}} = \frac{\sqrt{10}}{20}.$$

Therefore

$$p_{1a} = \frac{\sqrt{10}}{2}.$$

By substitution, we find that

$$y_{1a} = 2p_{1a} + 20p_{1b} = 40p_{1b} = 2\sqrt{10},$$

$$y_{1b} = 10y_{1a} = 20\sqrt{10},$$

$$x_{A1a} = x_{B1a} = \frac{y_{1a}}{2} = \sqrt{10},$$

$$x_{A1b} = x_{B1b} = \frac{y_{1b}}{2} = 10\sqrt{10},$$

$$L_0 = \left(p_{1a} + 10p_{1b}\right)^2 = \left(20p_{1b}\right)^2 = 400p_{1b}^2 = 10,$$

$$\ell_{A0} = \ell_{B0} = \frac{30 - L_0}{2} = 10.$$

As a check, we can calculate that $w = 20$ and so $\ell_{A0} = \ell_{B0} = w/2 = 10$.

In summary, the equilibrium is

$$((\ell_{A0}, x_{A1a}, x_{A1b}), (\ell_{B0}, x_{B1a}, x_{B1b}), (-L_0, y_{1a}, y_{1b}), (p_0, p_{1a}, p_{1b}))$$

$$= ((10, \sqrt{10}, 10\sqrt{10}), (10, \sqrt{10}, 10\sqrt{10}), (-10, 2\sqrt{10}, 20\sqrt{10}),$$

$$(1, \sqrt{10}/2, \sqrt{10}/20)).$$

Answer to Homework Problems for Chapter 7, Problem #6

Problem: 6) Compute an Arrow-Debreu equilibrium for the following example. There are two periods, 0 and 1. There are two states, a and b, in the second period, and one commodity in each period. There are two consumers, A and B, and two firms, A and B. The input-output possibility set of firm A, using obvious notation, is

$$Y_A = \{(y_0, y_{1a}, y_{1b}) = (y_0, -y_0, 0) \mid y_0 \le 0\}.$$

The input possibility set of firm B is

$$Y_B = \{(y_0, y_{1a}, y_{1b}) = (y_0, 0, -2y_0) \mid y_0 \le 0\}.$$

Because these sets are cones, the firms earn zero profits in equilibrium, and hence there is no need to assign ownership shares in the firms to the consumers.

a) If the Arrow-Debreu price of the commodity in period 0 is 1, what are the Arrow-Debreu prices, p_{1a} and p_{1b}, respectively, of the commodity in dated events (1, a) and (1, b), if both firms produce positive amounts?

The utility function of consumer A is

$$u_A(x_0, x_{1a}, x_{1b}) = \ln(x_0) + \ln(x_{1a}) + 2\ln(x_{1b}).$$

The utility function of consumer B is

$$u_B(x_0, x_{1a}, x_{1b}) = \ln(x_0) + 2\ln(x_{1a}) + \ln(x_{1b}).$$

The endowment of each consumer is

$$(e_0, e_{1a}, e_{1b}) = (1, 0, 0).$$

b) Compute an Arrow-Debreu equilibrium,

$$((x_{A0}, x_{A1a}, x_{A1b}), (x_{B0}, x_{B1a}, x_{B1b}),$$

$$(y_{A0}, y_{A1a}, y_{A1b}), (y_{B0}, y_{B1a}, y_{B1b}), (p_0, p_{1a}, p_{1b})),$$

in which the price of the commodity in period 0 is 1.

Answer: a) Because profits are zero, if firm A produces a positive amount, then we know that $(1, p_{1a}, p_{1b}).(y_0, -y_0, 0) = 0$, for some $y_0 < 0$. It follows that $p_{1a} = 1$. A similar reasoning applied to firm B shows that $p_{1b} = 1/2$.

Answer: b) We know that the wealth of each consumer is

$$w = (1, p_{1a}, p_{1b}) \cdot \mathbf{e} = (1, p_{1a}, p_{1b}) \cdot (1, 0, 0) = 1.$$

Because the utility function is Cobb-Douglas, we can calculate the consumer demands as follows.

$$x_{A0} = \frac{1}{4} = x_{B0}.$$

$$p_{1a}x_{A1a} = \frac{1}{4}w,$$

so that

$$x_{A1a} = \frac{1}{4}.$$

$$p_{1b}x_{B1b} = \frac{1}{2}w,$$

so that

$$\frac{1}{2}x_{A1b} = \frac{1}{2},$$

and so

$$x_{A1b} = 1.$$

A similar reasoning shows that

$$x_{B1a} = \frac{1}{2} \text{ and } x_{B1b} = \frac{1}{2}.$$

By feasibility,

$$y_{A1a} = x_{A1a} + x_{B1a} = \frac{1}{4} + \frac{1}{2} = \frac{3}{4}$$

$$y_{B1b} = x_{A1b} + x_{B1b} = 1 + \frac{1}{2} = \frac{3}{2}.$$

In order to produce this output, we must have

$$y_{A0} = -\frac{3}{4} = y_{B0}.$$

As a check, we verify that the market for the commodity in period 0 clears.

$$x_{A0} + x_{B0} = \frac{1}{4} + \frac{1}{4} = \frac{1}{2} = 1 + 1 - \frac{3}{4} - \frac{3}{4} = e_{A0} + e_{B0} + y_{A0} + y_{B0}.$$

3

Answer to Homework Problems for Chapter 7, Problem #7

Problem: 7) There are two states, 1 and 2, two consumers, A and B, and one good in each state. The two states occur with equal probability. The endowment of consumer A is two in state 1 and zero in state 2. The endowment of consumer B is zero in state 1 and one in state 2. Both consumers have von Neumann - Morgenstern utility functions. Let u_A and u_B be the utility functions of consumers A and B, respectively, for the one good in either state. Suppose that $u_A(x) = \ln(x)$.

a) Compute an Arrow-Debreu equilibrium if $u_B(x) = \ln(x)$.

b) Compute an Arrow-Debreu equilibrium if $u_B(x) = x$.

c) Is there an equilibrium if $u_B(x) = e^x$? If so calculate it. If not, show why there is no equilibrium. A good drawing would suffice in this case.

Answer: a) The utility functions are Cobb-Douglas and each consumer has a positive endowment of only one of the two commodities. We know, therefore, that

$$x_{A1} = e_{A1}/2 = 1$$

and

$$x_{B2} = e_{B2}/2 = 1/2.$$

It follows from feasibility that

$$x_{B1} = 1$$

and

$$x_{A2} = \frac{1}{2}.$$

Normalize the prices so that they sum to 1. We can calculate the price p_1 of the commodity in state 1 from the budget set of person A.

$$p_1 x_{A1} + (1 - p_1) x_{A2} = p_1 e_{A1} + (1 - p_1) e_{A2}.$$

On substitution, this equation becomes

$$p_1 + \frac{1 - p_1}{2} = 2p_1.$$

This equation implies that

$$p_1 = \frac{1}{3}.$$

Hence the full equilibrium is

$$(\mathbf{x}_A, \mathbf{x}_B, \mathbf{p}) = ((1, 1/2), (1, 1/2), (1/3, 2/3)).$$

The risk in the aggregate endowment is shared equally between consumers A and B.

Answer: b) Since consumer B is risk neutral, we can guess that consumer B will bear all the risk and that the Arrow-Debreu prices will be proportional to the probabilities. So let

$$p_1 = p_2 = \frac{1}{2}.$$

Since consumer A has a strictly concave von Neumann-Morgenstern utility function and the prices are proportional (indeed equal to) the probabilities of the two states, we know that consumer A's consumption will be the same for both states. Since her or his wealth is 1 at the given prices,

$$x_{A1} = x_{A2} = 1$$

at these prices. Since consumer B is risk neutral and the prices are proportional to the probabilities, she or he is indifferent to all points on the budget line, that is, to all points satisfying the budget equation

$$\frac{1}{2}x_{B1} + \frac{1}{2}x_{B2} = \frac{1}{2}e_{B1} + \frac{1}{2}e_{B2} = \frac{1}{2}.$$

One such point is $(x_{B1}, x_{B2}) = (1, 0)$. Since this demand point plus $(x_{A1}, x_{A2}) = (1, 1)$ equals the total endowment $(e_{A1}, e_{A2}) + (e_{B1}, e_{B2}) = (2, 1)$, B's demand $(x_{B1}, x_{B2}) = (1, 0)$ is an equilibrium demand. Therefore the full equilibrium is

$$(\mathbf{x}_A, \mathbf{x}_B, \mathbf{p}) = ((1, 1), (1, 0), (1/2, 1/2)).$$

The risk neutral consumer, consumer B, bears all the risk.

Answer: c)

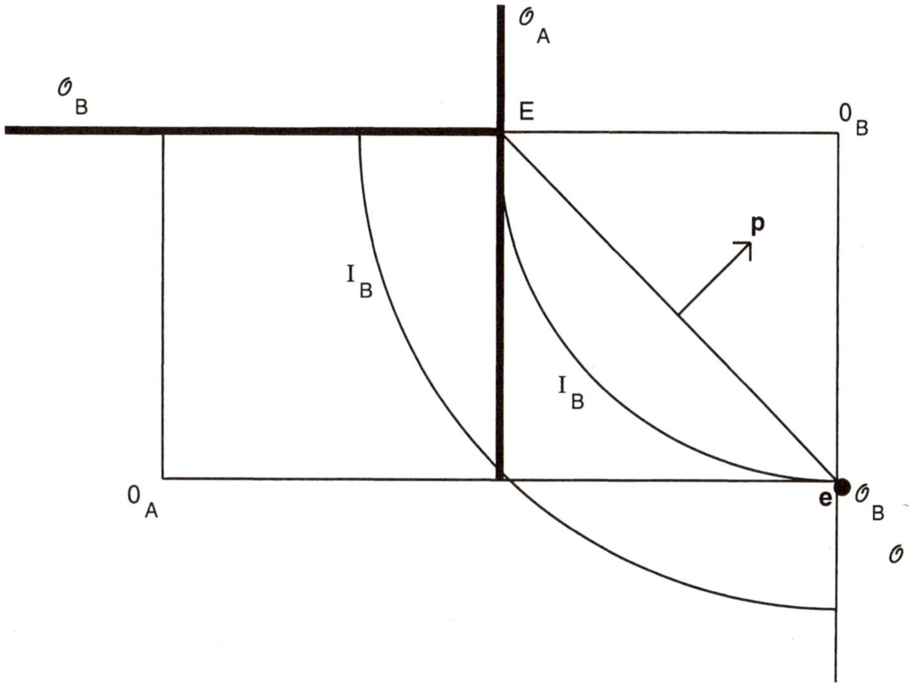

Suppose that the prices sum to 1. At any price p_1 such that $0 < p_1 < 1$, consumer A's demand is

$$\xi_A(p_1, 1 - p_1) = \left(1, \frac{p_1}{1 - p_1}\right).$$

If $p_1 < 1/2$, then

$$\xi_B(p_1, 1 - p_1) = \left(\frac{1 - p_1}{p_1}, 0\right).$$

Clearly this demand plus the demand of person A does not add up to the total endowment of $(2, 1)$. If $p_1 > 1/2$, then

$$\xi_B(p_1, 1 - p_1) = (0, 1),$$

and this demand plus that of consumer A does not add up to (2, 1) either. If $p_1 = 1/2$, then

$$\xi_B(1/2, 1/2) = \{(1, 0), (0, 1)\},$$

and

$$\xi_A(1/2, 1/2) = (1, 1),$$

and demands $x_A = (1, 1)$ and $x_B = (1, 0)$ do add up to the total endowment of (2, 1). Therefore, the full equilibrium is

$$(\mathbf{x}_A, \mathbf{x}_B, \mathbf{p}) = ((1, 1), (1, 0), (1/2, 1/2)).$$

So there exists an equilibrium and it is an equilibrium in which consumer B bears all the risk, which makes sense since B is risk loving. The above diagram illustrates the equilibrium. The offer curve of consumer A is $\mathcal{O}_A$ and that of consumer B is $\mathcal{O}_B$. Notice that the offer curve of B jumps from the point E to the endowment point **e**. The offer curves intersect at the equilibrium allocation E. The budget line for consumer B connects points E and **e**. Two indifference curves for consumer B are indicated as I_B.

Answer to Homework Problems for Chapter 7, Problem #8

Problem: 8) Compute an Arrow-Debreu equilibrium for the following economy. There are three consumers, A, B, and C, and one good, money. The endowment of each consumer is 1 with probability 1/2 and 0 with probability 1/2. The endowments of the three consumers are independently distributed. Each consumer has a von Neumann-Morgenstern utility function, where the utility of an amount of money, x, in any one state is ln(x + 1).

Answer: Describe a state as $s = (s_A, s_B, s_C)$, where s_A, s_B, and s_C are the endowments of consumers A, B, and C, respectively. The state space is

$$S = \{(s_A, s_B, s_C) \mid s_i = 0 \text{ or } 1, \text{ for } i = A, B, \text{ or } C\}.$$

There are 8 members of this state space and each has probability 1/8. Since the consumers all have the same risk averse utility function and their endowments are symmetric, we can guess that they will all consume the same amount in each state. Therefore the equilibrium allocation **x** is such that

$$x_{As} = x_{Bs} = x_{Cs} = \frac{s_A + s_B + s_C}{3}, \qquad \text{(A)}$$

for all $s \in S$. By the first order conditions for utility maximization over a budget set, we have the equations

$$\lambda_i p_s = \frac{1}{8}\left(\frac{1}{1 + x_{is}}\right) = \frac{1}{8}\left(\frac{3}{3 + s_A + s_B + s_C}\right),$$

for all s, where λ_i is a positive number, p_s is the price of a contingent claim on state s, and i = A, B, or C. Normalize prices so that

$$p_{(0,0,0)} = 1,$$

and hence $\lambda_i = 1/8$, for all i, and

$$p_s = \frac{3}{3 + s_A + s_B + s_C}. \qquad \text{(B)}$$

Equations A and B describe the equilibrium. For instance, if the state is s = (0, 1, 0), every consumer's consumption is 1/3 and the price for a contingent claim on the state is 3/4.

Answer to Homework Problems for Chapter 7, Problem #9

Problem: 9) a) Consider the following economy. There is no production. There are two consumers, A and B, two states, 1 and 2, one time period, and one consumption good in each state. Each consumer has a von Neumann-Morgenstern utility function. The probability of each state is one half. Each consumer's utility of consuming x units of the good in one state is $u(x) = \ln(x)$. The endowment of consumer A is $e_A = (e_{A1}, e_{A2}) = (24, 0)$. The endowment of consumer B is $e_B = (e_{B1}, e_{B2}) = (8, 8)$.

Compute an Arrow-Debreu equilibrium for this economy. Who bears the risk in the equilibrium?

b) In the economy of part (a), change the utility function of consumer B for consumption of the good to be $u(x) = x$. Leave the utility function of consumer A as it is in part (a). Compute an Arrow-Debreu equilibrium for the new economy. Who bears the risk in the equilibrium? Why?

c) Imagine that person A is the victim of a flood in the bad state, state 2, and that the flood may be prevented by constructing a dam. You might believe that there would be no point in building the dam if the consumers were insured against flood damage, as they are in the equilibrium of parts (a) and (b). This problem is meant to contradict this wrong idea. Suppose that if a dam is built, the endowment of consumer A is $e_A = (e_{A1}, e_{A2}) = (20, 20)$, and the endowment of consumer B is $e_B = (e_{B1}, e_{B2}) = (4, 4)$. That is, the dam costs each consumer 4 units of consumption in each state, but prevents the loss of 24 units to consumer A in state 2. Suppose that the utility functions are as in part (a). Suppose also that consumer A gives c units of the good to consumer B in each state to compensate consumer B for the cost of dam construction. Assume that $0 \le c \le 20$.

> i) Compute the equilibrium if the dam is built and consumer A pays c units of the good to consumer B in each state.
>
> ii) For what values of c, if any, does the equilibrium of part (i) Pareto dominate the equilibrium of part (a)?

Answer: a) Because consumer A's utility function is Cobb-Douglas and she or he has a positive endowment only of the good in state 1, we know that $x_{A1} = 12$. Because the total endowment in state 1 is 32, we know by feasibility that $x_{B1} = 20$. Let us normalize prices so that they sum to 1. Then consumer B's wealth is $8p_1 + 8p_2 = 8p_1 + 8(1 - p_1) = 8$. Because consumer B's utility function is Cobb-Douglas, we know that

$$p_1 x_{B1} = \frac{1}{2} 8 = 4,$$

so that

$$p_1 = \frac{4}{x_{B1}} = \frac{4}{20} = \frac{1}{5}.$$

Therefore

$$p_2 = 1 - p_1 = \frac{4}{5}.$$

Consumer A's wealth is $24p_1$. Since consumer A's utility function is Cobb-Douglas, we know that

$$\frac{4}{5}x_{A2} = \frac{1}{2}24p_1 = \frac{12}{5}.$$

Therefore

$$x_{A2} = 3,$$

and hence by feasibility

$$x_{B2} = 5.$$

The full equilibrium is therefore

$$(\mathbf{x}_A, \mathbf{x}_B, \mathbf{x}_C, \mathbf{p}) = ((12, 3), (20, 5), (1/5, 4/5)).$$

The two consumers share the risk. Notice that the ratio of their consumptions in the two states is the same.

Answer: b) Perhaps the quickest way to solve this problem is to draw an Edgeworth box diagram like that below. The offer curves of consumers A and B are shown as $\mathcal{O}_A$ and $\mathcal{O}_B$, respectively. These intersect at the equilibrium allocation E. If we normalize the prices of contingent claims so that they sum to 1, then the price of the claim on state 1, p_1, can be calculated from the budget equation for consumer A

$$12p_1 + 8(1 - p_1) = 24p_1.$$

This equation implies that

$$p_1 = \frac{2}{5},$$

and hence

$$p_2 = \frac{3}{5}.$$

The full equilibrium is

$$(\mathbf{x}_A, \mathbf{x}_B, \mathbf{x}_C, \mathbf{p}) = ((12,\ 8), (20,\ 0), (2/5,\ 3/5)).$$

Both consumers share the risk. Consumer B is not wealthy enough to bear all the risk, despite being risk neutral.

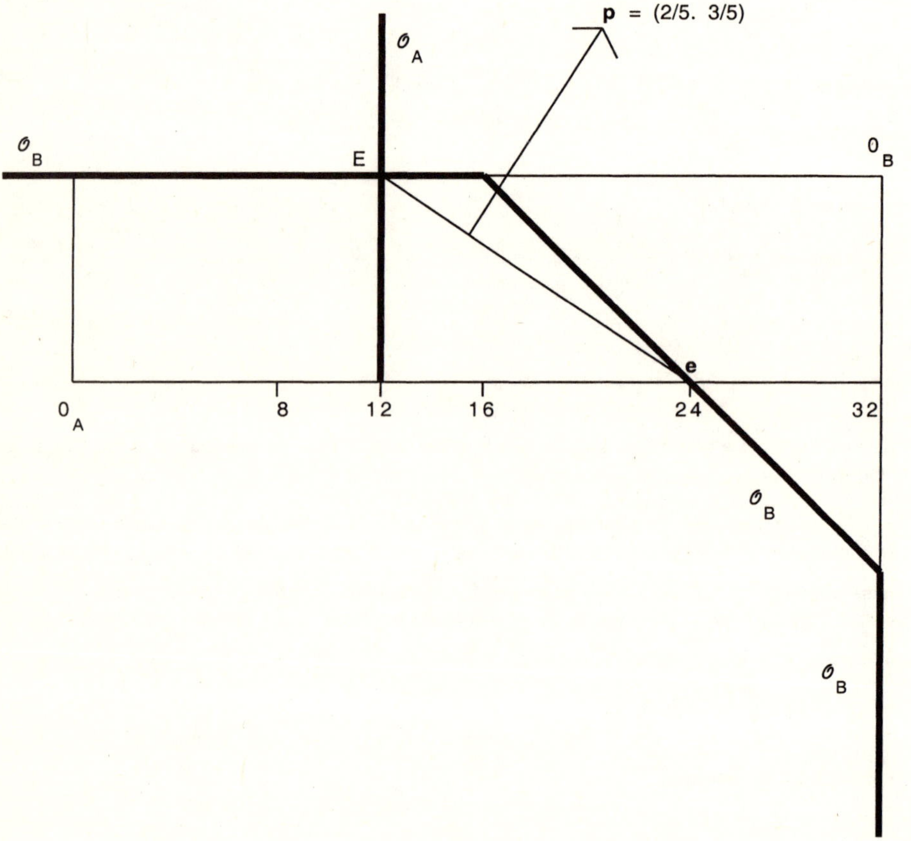

Answer: c) i) It is immediate that if we normalize prices to add to 1, then the equilibrium is

$$(\mathbf{x}_A, \mathbf{x}_B, \mathbf{x}_C, \mathbf{p}) = ((20 - c, 20 - c), (4 + c, 4 + c), (1/2, 1/2)).$$

Answer: c) ii) In the equilibrium of part a, the utilities of consumers A and B are, respectively,

$$\underline{v}_A = \frac{1}{2}\ln(12) + \frac{1}{2}\ln(3) = \frac{1}{2}\ln(36) = \ln(6)$$

and

$$\underline{v}_B = \frac{1}{2}\ln(20) + \frac{1}{2}\ln(5) = \ln(10).$$

In the equilibrium of part c, the utilities of consumers A and B are, respectively,

$$v_A = \ln(20 - c)$$

and

$$v_B = \ln(4 + c).$$

It follows that the equilibrium of part c Pareto dominates that of part a if $20 - c \geq 6$ and $4 + c \geq 10$, with strict inequality in at least one of the inequalities. That is, the equilibrium of part c Pareto dominates that of part a if $6 \leq c \leq 14$.

Answer to Homework Problems for Chapter 7, Problem #10

Problem: 10) There are two farmers, A and B, in a valley. There are two states, flood and no flood, and each occurs with probability 1/2. Each farmer has a von Neumann-Morgenstern utility function with the utility of an amount, x, of the crop in any one state being ln(x). The harvest of farmer A equals 10 if there is no flood and equals 5 if there is a flood. The harvest of farmer B equals 10 whether there is a flood or not.

> a) Compute an Arrow-Debreu equilibrium with the price of the crop being 1 if there is no flood.

Now suppose that a dam can be built that would prevent the flood. That is, if the dam were built, the crop of each farmer would be 10 in both states. The dam would cost a certain amount, say t, of crop payable after the dam was built and after the harvest and in either state.

> b) Suppose there is no insurance and, hence, no Arrow-Debreu markets, so that each farmer's consumption equals his or her crop in either state. How much would each farmer be willing to pay for the dam, assuming that he pays for it alone?
>
> c) Suppose there is insurance, so that the farmers would consume their allocation under the Arrow-Debreu equilibrium. How much would each farmer be willing to pay for the dam, assuming that he pays for it alone? For each farmer, does insurance increase or decrease his willingness to pay for the dam?

Answer: a) We have that

$$u_A(x) = u_B(x) = \frac{1}{2}\ln(x_{NF}) + \frac{1}{2}\ln(x_F)$$

and

$$\mathbf{e}_A = (10,\ 5) \text{ and } \mathbf{e}_B = (10,\ 10)\ ,$$

where the notation should be obvious. We assume that $p_{NF} = 1$. The wealth of consumer A is $10 + 5p_{NF}$ and the wealth of consumer B is $10 + 10p_{NF}$. Because the utility function is Cobb-Douglas, we know that

$$x_{A,NF} = \frac{1}{2}(10 + 5p_{NF})$$

and

$$x_{B,NF} = \frac{1}{2}(10 + 10p_{NF}).$$

By feasibility,

$$x_{A,\,NF} + x_{B,\,NF} = 20.$$

These three equations together imply that

$$p_{NF} = \frac{4}{3}.$$

It now follows that

$$x_{A,\,NF} = \frac{1}{2}\left(10 + 5\frac{4}{3}\right) = \frac{25}{3}$$

$$x_{AF} = \frac{3}{4}\left(\frac{1}{2}\right)\left(10 + 5\frac{4}{3}\right) = \frac{25}{4}$$

$$x_{B,\,NF} = \frac{1}{2}\left(10 + 10\frac{4}{3}\right) = \frac{35}{3}$$

$$x_{AF} = \frac{3}{4}\left(\frac{1}{2}\right)\left(10 + 10\frac{4}{3}\right) = \frac{35}{4}.$$

The full equilibrium is

$$(\mathbf{x}_A, \mathbf{x}_B, \mathbf{p}) = ((25/3,\ 25/4),\ (35/3,\ 35/4),\ (1,\ 4/3)).$$

<u>Answer</u>: b) If consumer A has neither insurance nor dam, her or his utility is

$$\frac{1}{2}\ln(10) + \frac{1}{2}\ln(5) = \ln(\sqrt{50}).$$

If there is a dam and consumer A pays t_A for it, her or his utility is

$$\frac{1}{2}\ln(10 - t_A) + \frac{1}{2}\ln(10 - t_A) = \ln(10 - t_A).$$

Setting the two right-hand sides equal, we see that

$$\sqrt{50} = 10 - t_A,$$

so that

$$t_A = 10 - \sqrt{50} \cong 2.929.$$

If consumer B has neither insurance nor dam, her or his utility is ln(10). If there is a dam and consumer B pays t_B for it, her or his utility is $\ln(10 - t_B)$. Setting these two quantities equal, we see that $t_B = 0$.

<u>Answer</u>: c) If there is no dam, but there is insurance, then consumer A's utility is

$$\frac{1}{2}\ln\left(\frac{25}{3}\right) + \frac{1}{2}\ln\left(\frac{25}{4}\right) = \frac{1}{2}\ln\left(\frac{625}{12}\right) = \ln\left(\frac{25}{2\sqrt{3}}\right).$$

If there is a dam and consumer A pays t_A for it, her or his utility is $\ln(10 - t_A)$. Setting these two quantities equal, we see that

$$t_A = 10 - \frac{25}{2\sqrt{3}} \cong 2.783 .$$

If there is no dam, but there is insurance, then consumer B's utility is

$$\frac{1}{2}\ln\left(\frac{35}{3}\right) + \frac{1}{2}\ln\left(\frac{35}{4}\right) = \frac{1}{2}\ln\left(\frac{1225}{12}\right) = \ln\left(\frac{35}{2\sqrt{3}}\right).$$

If there is a dam and consumer B pays t_B for it, her or his utility is $\ln(10 - t_B)$. Setting the two quantities equal, we see that

$$t_B = 10 - \frac{35}{2\sqrt{3}} \cong -0.104.$$

Consumer B would want to be compensated for the construction of the dam, because she or he gains from selling insurance to consumer A when there is no dam.

Answer to Homework Problems for Chapter 7, Problem #11

Problem: 11) Texas cotton farmers suffer from hail storms. The federal government provides hail insurance. An entrepreneur has discovered a way to seed thunderclouds so as to prevent them from producing hail. The entrepreneur wishes to sell its invention to the government or to a cotton farmers organization. Both argue that because farmers can buy insurance against hail damage, there is no need to spend money to prevent hail storms. Is this argument correct? Make a case for your answer.

Answer: The argument is false. Crop insurance redistributes the loss from hail storms among farmers, but does not eliminate the loss from the point of the whole economy.

Answer to Homework Problems for Chapter 7, Problem #12

Problem: 12) Two men agree to insure each other against heart attack, which would incapacitate but not kill them. For simplicity, treat this as a one period problem. The probability that the first man will have a heart attack is 1/10, as is the probability that the second will have one. For simplicity again, assume that it is impossible for them to have a heart attack simultaneously. Only one or neither will have one. Each man earns 100 if healthy and nothing after a heart attack. Each has a von Neumann - Morgenstern utility function, with the utility for money or income, x, being ln(x).

a) Compute the Arrow-Debreu equilibrium and the expected utility of the men after trading in insurance, but before the state is revealed, i.e., before it is known whether either has a heart attack and if so who does. What is the expected utility of each man in this equilibrium?

b) Suppose that a new medical technology makes it possible to know in advance who will and who will not have a heart attack. This knowledge is available at the time trading in contingent claims occurs. Describe the outcome of Arrow-Debreu trading in the new situation. What are the expected utilities of the two men in this situation, where the expectation is calculated from the point of view of a moment just before the new technology provides the information about who is going to have a heart attack? Does the new medical technology increase their expected utility? Give an intuitive explanation of why or why not.

Answer: a) Let the state in which consumer A has a heart attack be s_A, let the state in which consumer B has a heart attack be s_B, and let the state in which neither has a heart attack be s_N. Then Prob(s_A) = Prob(s_B) = 1/10, and Prob(s_N) = 8/10. Write a consumption bundle as $\mathbf{x} = (x_{s_A}, x_{s_N}, x_{s_B})$, where the notation should be obvious. Then the endowment of consumer A is $\mathbf{e}_A = (0, 100, 100)$, and the endowment of consumer B is $\mathbf{e}_B = (100, 100, 0)$. Since the consumers have the same risk averse von Neumann-Morgenstern utility function, they are going to fully insure each other, so that the equilibrium consumption bundle of each will be $\mathbf{x} = (50, 100, 50)$. Normalize the prices so that $p_{s_A} = 1$. By symmetry, $p_{s_B} = 1$. To compute p_{s_N}, notice that by the first order conditions for utility maximization over a budget set

$$\frac{1}{10x_{A,s_A}} = \frac{1}{10}\frac{du_A(x_{A,s_A})}{dx} = \lambda_A p_{s_A} = \lambda_A,$$

so that

$$\lambda_A = \frac{1}{10x_{A,s_A}} = \frac{1}{500}.$$

Similarly

$$\frac{8}{10x_{A,s_N}} = \frac{8}{10}\frac{du_A(x_{A,s_N})}{dx} = \lambda_A p_{s_N},$$

so that

$$p_{s_N} = 500\left(\frac{8}{10}\right)\left(\frac{1}{100}\right) = 4.$$

Therefore the full equilibrium is

$$(\mathbf{x}_A, \mathbf{x}_B, \mathbf{x}_N) = ((50,\ 100,\ 50),\ (50,\ 100,\ 50),\ (1,\ 4,\ 1)).$$

The expected utility of either consumer is

$$\frac{1}{10}\ln(50) + \frac{8}{10}\ln(100) + \frac{1}{10}\ln(50) = \frac{1}{5}\ln(50) + \frac{8}{10}\ln(100).$$

Answer: b) No insurance is possible, because the outcome is known. There are three Arrow-Debreu equilibria, depending on the state. For instance, if the state is s_A, then $x_A = 0$, $x_B = 100$, and $p = 1$. Similarly if the state is s_B, then $x_A = 100$, $x_B = 0$, and $p = 1$, and if the if the state is s_N, then $x_A = 100 = x_B$, and $p = 1$. The expected utility of both consumers is

$$\frac{1}{10}\ln(0) + \frac{9}{10}\ln(100) = -\infty,$$

which is infinitely smaller than the expected utility with insurance, $(1/5)\ln(50) + (8/10)\ln(100)$.

Answer to Homework Problems for Chapter 7, Problem #13

Problem: 13) Consider a world with N consumers, with N equally probable states, where $N \geq 2$, and with one good, money. The consumers all have identical von Neumann-Morgenstern utility functions, with the utility for \$x being $2\sqrt{x}$. In state n, for n = 1, ... , N, the endowment of consumer n is \$0, whereas the endowment of every other consumer is \$1.

a) Compute the Arrow-Debreu equilibrium with prices that sum to 1.
b) In the equilibrium, what insurance premium do consumers pay when they have an endowment of \$1? What insurance benefit do they receive when their endowment is \$0?

Suppose that in this world, a public agency can transfer wealth from those with money to the person without any. There is leakage, however, in that if \$x is taken from a wealthy consumer, only \$x/2 is given to the needy one. Suppose that the social objective is to maximize the expected utility of a typical consumer.

c) If there are complete Arrow-Debreu insurance markets, what is the socially optimal transfer by the public agency?

d) If there is no insurance, what is the socially optimal transfer by the public agency?

Suppose now that it is possible for the government agency to determine and to announce, before the trade in insurance contracts occurs, who is going to have an endowment of \$0.

e) What would be the outcome of Arrow-Debreu trading if the announcement were made?

f) Would the expected utility of consumers be improved by the announcement, where the expectation is calculated from the point of view of a moment before the announcement was made?

Answer: a) Because the utility function is strictly concave and the problem is symmetric with respect to the states and consumers, we know that the Arrow-Debreu equilibrium is such that

$$x_{in} = \frac{N-1}{N},$$

for i = 1, ... , N and n = 1, ... , N, and

$$p_n = \frac{1}{N},$$

for n = 1, ... , N.

Answer: b) The premium is \$1/N. The benefit is \$(N – 1)/N.

Answer: c) There are no transfers in this case, since the allocation of the Arrow-Debreu equilibrium maximizes the social objective.

Answer: d) The socially optimal transfer is the value of t that solves the problem

$$\max_{t \geq 0} \left[\frac{2}{N} \sqrt{\frac{(N-1)t}{2}} + \frac{(N-1)2}{N} \sqrt{1-t} \right].$$

If we multiply the objective function by $\frac{N}{\sqrt{N-1}}$, the problem becomes

$$\max_{t \geq 0} \left[\frac{2}{\sqrt{2}} \sqrt{t} + 2\sqrt{N-1}\sqrt{1-t} \right].$$

The first order condition for the optimum is

$$\frac{1}{\sqrt{2t}} = \frac{\sqrt{N-1}}{\sqrt{1-t}}.$$

After cross multiplication, this equation becomes

$$\sqrt{1-t} = \sqrt{N-1}\sqrt{2t}.$$

On squaring both sides of this equation, we obtain

$$1 - t = (N - 1)2t = (2N - 2)t,$$

so that

$$1 = (2N - 1)t$$

and hence

$$t = \frac{1}{2N-1}.$$

This is the socially optimal transfer.

Answer: e) There would be no Arrow-Debreu trading and hence no insurance.

Answer: f) Without the announcement and with insurance, a consumer's expected utility is

$$2\sqrt{\frac{N-1}{N}}.$$

If the announcement is made and kills insurance, a consumer's expected utility is

$$\left(\frac{N-1}{N}\right)2\sqrt{1} + \frac{1}{n}0 = 2\left(\frac{N-1}{N}\right).$$

Since

$$\sqrt{\frac{N-1}{N}} > \frac{N-1}{N},$$

the announcement decreases expected utility.

Answer to Homework Problems for Chapter 7, Problem #14

Problem: 14) Three workers reach a mutual insurance agreement for one period. They know that exactly one of them will be unemployed in that period and each is equally likely to be the one that is unemployed. Each worker earns 10 when employed and nothing when unemployed. Each worker consumes exactly what they earn in the period plus benefits from or minus payments for the insurance. There are two commodities, leisure and consumption. Each worker has three units of leisure if unemployed and one unit of leisure if employed. The workers set up Arrow-Debreu markets to insure each other against unemployment. The utility function of each worker has the form

$$Eu(\ell(s),\ x(s)),$$

where $\ell(s)$ is the consumption of leisure, $x(s)$ is the consumption of income, s is the state of the world, and E is the expected value.

For each of the following functions, u, find an Arrow-Debreu equilibrium and point out whether workers consume more when unemployed or unemployed or the same in both cases.

a) $u(\ell, x) = \ell^{1/3}x^{2/3}$.

b) $u(\ell, x) = \frac{1}{3}\ln(\ell) + \frac{2}{3}\ln(x)$.

Hint: Make use of symmetry. If you set the problem up with variables for each worker and each state and a price for each state, you will have 12 equations for 12 variables and waste time. By using symmetry, you can reduce the problem to one involving only two variables, the consumption, x_u, of an unemployed worker and the consumption, x_e, of an employed worker.

Answer: Because of the symmetry of the problem, all consumers have the same marginal utility of consumption in an Arrow-Debreu equilibrium and so the equilibrium allocation maximizes the sum of their expected utilities among all feasible allocations. Because the allocation in one state does not affect the allocation or its utility in any other state, an allocation that maximizes the total expected utility, maximizes the total utility in each state, given the feasibility constraint. Therefore the Arrow-Debreu equilibrium allocation may be found by solving the problem

$$\max_{x_u \geq 0,\, x_e \geq 0} \left[u(3, x_u) + 2u(1, x_e)\right] \qquad \text{(A)}$$
$$\text{s.t. } x_u + 2x_e = 20.$$

Answer: a) Problem A is now

$$\max_{x_u \geq 0,\, x_e \geq 0} \left[3^{1/3}x_u^{2/3} + 2x_e^{2/3}\right]$$

$$\text{s.t. } x_u + 2x_e = 20.$$

Its Lagrangian is

$$\mathcal{L} = 3^{1/3}x_u^{2/3} + 2x_e^{2/3} - \lambda(x_u + 2x_e).$$

The first order conditions for optimality are

$$\frac{2}{3}3^{1/3}x_u^{-1/3} = \lambda$$

$$\frac{4}{3}x_e^{-1/3} = 2\lambda.$$

These two equations imply that

$$\frac{4}{3}3^{1/3}x_u^{-1/3} = \frac{4}{3}x_e^{-1/3},$$

so that

$$x_u^{1/3} = 3^{1/3}x_e^{1/3},$$

and hence

$$x_u = 3x_e.$$

Since

$$x_u + 2x_e = 20,$$

we have that

$$x_e = 4 \text{ and } x_u = 12.$$

Let the consumers be A, B, and C and let p_A, p_B, or p_C be the Arrow-Debreu price for consumption in the state in which consumer A, B, or C, respectively, is unemployed. By the symmetry of the problem, all these prices are equal and we may let them be 1. Therefore in the Arrow-Debreu equilibrium, the price of a contingent claim for consumption in each of the three states equals 1, and each of the three consumers consumes 4 when employed and 12 when unemployed. Consumers consume more when unemployed than when employed, because leisure and consumption are complementary commodities.

Answer: b) Problem A is now

$$\max_{x_u \geq 0,\, x_e \geq 0} \left[\ln(x_u) + 2\ln(x_e)\right]$$

$$\text{s.t. } x_u + 2x_e = 20.$$

Its Lagrangian is

$$\mathcal{L} = \ln(x_u) + 2\ln(x_e) - \lambda(x_u + 2x_e).$$

The first order conditions for optimality are

$$\frac{1}{x_u} = \lambda$$

$$\frac{2}{x_e} = 2\lambda,$$

so that

$$x_u = x_e.$$

Substituting this equation into the constraint, we see that

$$x_u = x_e = \frac{20}{3}.$$

The consumers consume the same whether employed or unemployed. As in part a, we may let the price be 1 for a contingent claim on consumption in each of the three states. These consumptions and prices define the Arrow-Debreu equilibrium.

Answer to Homework Problems for Chapter 7, Problem #15

Problem: 15) One hundred workers in the shipping department of a large factory randomly select one of their member to be their representative to management during the year. Each worker is equally likely to be selected. The job of representative is miserable, as it entails abuse from both management and fellow employees. In order to induce workers to accept the job, the company pays the representative an income of 10 during the year, whereas every other worker is paid only 1. In order to further compensate the representative for his suffering, the workers consider setting up an Arrow-Debreu insurance market to protect the worker who is chosen. The utility function of a worker for the year has the form

$$Eu(x(s), \ s),$$

where x(s) is income, s is the state of the world, and E is expected value. Suppose that

$$u(x(s), s) = 2\sqrt{x(s)} - 100,$$

if the worker is selected as representative in state s, and

$$u(x(s), s) = 2\sqrt{x(s)},$$

if the worker is not selected in state s.

Compute an Arrow-Debreu equilibrium. Would the representative be better off with the insurance arrangement or without it or would it make not affect his welfare? Would insurance increase, reduce, or leave unchanged a worker's expected utility for the year, calculated before the selection of a representative?

Hint: Make use of symmetry to reduce the problem to one involving only two variables, the consumption, x_r, of a worker randomly selected to be a representative and the consumption, x_o, of a worker not selected.

Answer: Let the set of states be S = {1, 2, ..., 100}, where each worker n, for n = 1, 2, ... , 100, is the representative when the state is s, if and only if s = n. The endowment of the nth worker is the function $e_n: S \to R$, where $e_n(s) = 1$, if $s \neq n$ and $e_n(n) = 10$. From the symmetry of the model, we know that each worker will have the same marginal utility of unit of account in an Arrow-Debreu equilibrium, so that the equilibrium allocation will maximize the total utility of all the workers among feasible allocations. Because the allocation in one state does not affect the allocation or its utility in any other state, an allocation that maximizes the total expected utility, maximizes the total utility in each state, given the feasibility constraint. By the symmetry of the problem, this maximization problem is the same for each state, up to a permutation of the names of the workers. Therefore the maximization problem is

$$\max_{x_r \geq 0,\, x_w \geq 0} \left[(2\sqrt{x_r} - 100) + (99)\, 2\sqrt{x_w}\right]$$

$$\text{s.t. } x_r + 99x_w = 109,$$

where x_r is the consumption of the worker who is the representative and x_w is the consumption of any other worker. Because the square root function is strictly concave, it should be obvious that the unique solution of this problem is to give every worker the same consumption, so that

$$x_r = x_w = \frac{109}{100}.$$

By the symmetry of the problem, we know that the price of a contingent claim on consumption in any state is the same, so that we may let all of these Arrow-Debreu prices be 1.

The worker who is a representative receives an income of 10 if there is no insurance and the smaller income of 109/100 if there is insurance. In both cases, the representative suffers the loss of utility of 100 from acting as representative. Therefore the representative is worse off with insurance than without.

Because the square root function is strictly concave, we know that the expected utility of a worker before the selection of a representative is higher with insurance than without. We can also calculate directly that this is so. If there is no insurance, a worker's expected utility is

$$\frac{99}{100} 2\sqrt{1} + \frac{1}{100}(2\sqrt{10} - 100) = 2\left(\frac{99}{100} + \frac{\sqrt{10}}{100}\right) - 1 \cong 1.043.$$

If there is insurance, a worker's expected utility is

$$2\sqrt{\frac{109}{100}} - \frac{100}{100} = 1.088.$$

Therefore a worker's expected utility is greater with insurance.

The point of the problem is that the loss of utility from the psychological burden of being a representative is not insurable. Only fluctuations in wealth are insurable. Since the representative is richer than the other workers, she or he is actually hurt by insurance. Insurance increases only the expected utility calculated before the representative is chosen.

Answer to Homework Problems for Chapter 7, Problem #16

16) This problem has to do with the time consistency of consumer choice in the context of the Arrow model. In the Arrow model, consumers have the opportunity at each dated event to change their consumption plans. The question is whether they would want to do so. If their preferences are determined by a single preference ordering or utility function of lifetime consumption plans, they would not ever change plans. The proof of this fact in a full model with uncertainty involves lots of notation, but the essential insight required may be grasped by making a proof for the following simple example. Suppose that there are T time periods, there are N commodities in each period, and that there is no uncertainty and consider the utility maximization problem of a single consumer in an Arrow equilibrium. Assume the price of an Arrow security is 1 in every period. That is, the cost of an Arrow security in the succeeding period is always 1, so that buying and selling Arrow securities is the same as saving money that earns no interest. A consumer's problem is

$$\max_{\substack{\mathbf{x}_t \in R^N_+ \text{ and } M_t \in R, \\ \text{for } t = 1, \ldots, T.}} u(\mathbf{x}_1, \ldots, \mathbf{x}_T)$$

$$\begin{aligned} \text{s.t. } & P_1 . \mathbf{x}_1 + M_1 \le w_1, \\ & P_2 . \mathbf{x}_2 + M_2 \le w_2 + M_1, \\ & \quad \cdot \\ & \quad \cdot \\ & P_{T-1} . \mathbf{x}_{T-1} + M_{T-1} \le w_{T-1} + M_{T-2} \\ & P_T . \mathbf{x}_T \le w_T + M_{T-1}, \end{aligned} \tag{7.34}$$

where u is the utility function of the consumer, $\mathbf{x}_t$ is the consumption vector of period t, $\mathbf{P}_t$ is the N-vector of spot prices for commodities in period t, M_t is the amount of money saved (or loaned if $M_t < 0$) in period t, and w_t is the consumer's income in period t. By adding the T budget conditions, we see that the above problem yields the same optimal consumptions as the Arrow-Debreu consumption choice problem

$$\max_{\mathbf{x}_t \in R^N_+, \text{for } t = 1, \ldots, T.} u(\mathbf{x}_1, \ldots, \mathbf{x}_T)$$

$$\begin{aligned} \text{s.t. } & P_1 . \mathbf{x}_1 + P_2 . \mathbf{x}_2 + \ldots + P_T . \mathbf{x}_T \\ & \le w_1 + w_2 + \ldots + w_T. \end{aligned}$$

Allowing for T budget constraints, as in problem (7.34) makes us aware that choice might not be intertemporally consistent. Let $(\bar{\mathbf{x}}_1, \bar{\mathbf{x}}_2, \ldots, \bar{\mathbf{x}}_T)$ be the optimal path of consumption chosen in either problem. Assume that the utility function u is locally non-satiated. Then if the path $(\bar{\mathbf{x}}_1, \bar{\mathbf{x}}_2, \ldots, \bar{\mathbf{x}}_T)$ is followed, the amount of money saved in period t is

$\overline{M}_t = w_1 + ... + w_t - P_1.\overline{x}_1 - .... - P_t.\overline{x}_t$. Prove that for each t = 1, 2, ..., T, the vector $(\overline{x}_t, \overline{x}_{t+1}, ... , \overline{x}_T)$ and the money holdings $(\overline{M}_t, ... , \overline{M}_T)$ solve the problem

$$\max_{\substack{x_s \in R^N_+ \text{ and } M_s \in R, \\ \text{for } s = t, ... , T.}} u(\overline{x}_1, ... , \overline{x}_{t-1}, x_t, ... , x_T)$$

$$\text{s.t. } P_t.x_t + M_t \le w_t + \overline{M}_{t-1},$$

$$P_{t+1}.x_{t+1} + M_{t+1} \le w_{t+1} + M_t,$$

.

.

$$P_{T-1}.x_{T-1} + M_{T-1} \le w_{T-1} + M_{T-2}$$

$$P_T.x_T \le w_T + M_{T-1}.$$

That is, the consumer desires in each period to stick to her or his original consumption plan.

<u>Answer</u>: Suppose that $(x_t, x_{t+1}, ... , x_T)$ and $(M_t, M_{t+1}, ... , M_{T-1})$ satisfy the constraints

$$P_t.x_t + M_t \le w_t + \overline{M}_{t-1},$$

$$P_{t+1}.x_{t+1} + M_{t+1} \le w_{t+1} + M_t,$$

. .

. .

. .

. .

$$P_{T-1}.x_{T-1} + M_{T-1} \le w_{T-1} + M_{T-2}$$

$$P_T.x_T \le w_T + M_{T-1}$$

and that

$$u(\overline{x}_1, \overline{x}_2, ... , \overline{x}_{t-1}, x_t, ... , x_T) > u(\overline{x}_1, \overline{x}_2, ... , \overline{x}_T).$$

Then $(\overline{x}_1, ..., \overline{x}_{t-1}, x_t, ... , x_T)$ and $(\overline{M}_1, ... , \overline{M}_{t-1}, M_t, ... , M_{T-1})$ satisfy all the constraints of problem 7.34) and yet $(\overline{x}_1, ..., \overline{x}_{t-1}, x_t, ... , x_T)$ is preferred to $(\overline{x}_1, ... , \overline{x}_T)$. This implication contradicts the assumption that $(\overline{x}_1, ... , \overline{x}_T)$ and $(M_1, ... , M_{T-1})$ solve problem 7.34. This completes the proof.

Answer to Homework Problems for Chapter 8, Problem #1

Problem: 1) For each of the utility functions listed below, compute the short-run demand function, ξ^s as a function of the price vector. That is, compute the functions $x_1 = \xi_1^s(P_1, P_2)$ and $x_2 = \xi_2^s(P_1, P_2)$ that satisfy the equations

$$\frac{\partial u(x_1, x_2)}{\partial x_1} = \lambda P_1 \text{ and } \frac{\partial u(x_1, x_2)}{\partial x_2} = \lambda P_2,$$

where λ is a positive constant.

a) $u(x_1, x_2) = a \ln(x_1) + b \ln(x_2)$, where $a > 0$ and $b > 0$.

b) $u(x_1, x_2) = Ax_1^a x_2^b$, where $A > 0$, $a > 0$, $b > 0$, and $a + b < 1$.

c) $u(x_1, x_2) = a\sqrt{x_1} + b\sqrt{x_2}$, where $a > 0$, $b > 0$.

d) $u(x_1, x_2) = ax_1 - bx_1^2 + cx_2 - dx_2^2 + ex_1x_2$, where $a > 0$, $b > 0$, $c > 0$, $d > 0$, and $4bd - e^2 > 0$.

Answer: a) The equation

$$\frac{\partial u(x_1, x_2)}{\partial x_1} = \lambda P_1$$

becomes

$$\frac{a}{x_1} = \lambda P_1,$$

so that

$$\xi_1^s(P_1, P_2) = x_1 = \frac{a}{\lambda P_1}.$$

Similarly

$$\xi_2^s(P_1, P_2) = x_2 = \frac{b}{\lambda P_2}.$$

Answer: b) The equations

$$\frac{\partial u(x_1, x_2)}{\partial x_1} = \lambda P_1 \text{ and } \frac{\partial u(x_1, x_2)}{\partial x_2} = \lambda P_2,$$

become

$$aAx_1^{a-1}x_2^b = \lambda P_1 \text{ and } bAx_1^a x_2^{b-1} = \lambda P_2.$$

Dividing the second equation by the first, we obtain

$$\frac{bx_1}{ax_2} = \frac{P_2}{P_1},$$

so that

$$x_2 = \frac{bP_1}{aP_2}x_1.$$

Substituting this equation into the equation $aAx_1^{a-1}x_2^b = \lambda P_1$, we obtain

$$aAx_1^{a-1}\left(\frac{bP_1}{aP_2}\right)^b x_1^b = \lambda P_1,$$

so that

$$\xi_1^s(P_1, P_2) = x_1 = \left(\frac{A}{\lambda}\right)^{\frac{1}{1-a-b}}\left(\frac{a}{P_1}\right)^{\frac{1-b}{1-a-b}}\left(\frac{b}{P_2}\right)^{\frac{b}{1-a-b}}.$$

If we substitute this equation into the equation $x_2 = bP_1x_1/aP_2$, we obtain

$$\xi_2^s(P_1, P_2) = x_2 = \left(\frac{A}{\lambda}\right)^{\frac{1}{1-a-b}}\left(\frac{a}{P_1}\right)^{\frac{a}{1-a-b}}\left(\frac{b}{P_2}\right)^{\frac{1-a}{1-a-b}}.$$

Answer: c) The equation

$$\frac{\partial u(x_1, x_2)}{\partial x_1} = \lambda P_1$$

becomes

$$\frac{a}{2\sqrt{x_1}} = \lambda P_1,$$

and hence

$$\xi_1^s(P_1, P_2) = x_1 = \left(\frac{a}{2\lambda P_1}\right)^2.$$

Similarly

$$\xi_2^s(P_1, P_2) = x_2 = \left(\frac{b}{2\lambda P_2}\right)^2.$$

Answer: d) The equations

$$\frac{\partial u(x_1, x_2)}{\partial x_1} = \lambda P_1 \text{ and } \frac{\partial u(x_1, x_2)}{\partial x_2} = \lambda P_2,$$

become

$$a - 2bx_1 + ex_2 = \lambda P_1$$

$$c - 2dx_2 + ex_1 = \lambda P_2.$$

On solving these two simultaneous linear equations for x_1 and x_2, we find that

$$\xi_1^s(P_1, P_2) = x_1 = \frac{ce + 2ad - 2d\lambda P_1 - e\lambda P_2}{4bd - e^2}$$

and

$$\xi_2^s(P_1, P_2) = x_2 = \frac{ae + 2bc - e\lambda P_1 - 2b\lambda P_2}{4bd - e^2}.$$

Answer to Homework Problems for Chapter 8, Problem #2

Problem: 2) For each of the utility functions in problem 1, compute the short run demand curve for good 1 when $\lambda = P_2 = 1$. That is, calculate the function $\xi_1^s(P_1, 1)$.

Answer: a) $\xi_1^s(P_1, 1) = \dfrac{1}{P_1}$.

Answer: b) $\xi_1^s(P_1, 1) = A^{1/(1-a-b)} a^{(1-b)/(1-a-b)} b^{b/(1-a-b)} \dfrac{1}{P_1^{(1-b)/(1-a-b)}}$.

Answer: c) $\xi_1^s(P_1, 1) = \left(\dfrac{a}{2P_1}\right)^2$.

Answer: d) $\xi_1^s(P_1, 1) = \dfrac{(c-1)e + 2ad - 2dP_1}{4bd - e^2}$.

Answer to Homework Problems for Chapter 8, Problem #3

Problem: 3) For each of the utility functions in problem 1, compute the surplus function

$$h(P_1, P_2) = \lambda^{-1} u_i(\xi^s(P_1, P_2)) - P_1[\xi_1^s(P_1, P_2) - e_1] - P_2[\xi_2^s(P_1, P_2) - e_2],$$

where $\mathbf{e} = (e_1, e_2)$ is a positive endowment vector.

Answer: a) $h(P_1, P_2) = \lambda^{-1}\left[a \ln\left(\frac{a}{\lambda P_1}\right) + b \ln\left(\frac{b}{\lambda P_2}\right)\right] - P_1\left(\frac{a}{\lambda P_1} - e_1\right) - P_2\left(\frac{b}{\lambda P_2} - e_2\right)$

$$= \lambda^{-1}[a \ln(a) + b \ln(b) - (a+b)\ln(\lambda) - a \ln(P_1) - b \ln(P_2)] - \lambda^{-1}(a+b) + \mathbf{P}.\mathbf{e}$$

$$= \lambda^{-1}[a(\ln(a) - 1) + b(\ln(b) - 1) - (a+b)\ln(\lambda)] - a \ln(P_1) - b \ln(P_2) + \mathbf{P}.\mathbf{e}.$$

Answer: b) $h(P_1, P_2) = \left(\frac{A}{\lambda}\right)\left(\frac{A}{\lambda}\right)^{\frac{a}{1-a-b}}\left(\frac{a}{P_1}\right)^{\frac{a-ab}{1-a-b}}\left(\frac{b}{P_2}\right)^{\frac{ab}{1-a-b}}\left(\frac{A}{\lambda}\right)^{\frac{b}{1-a-b}}\left(\frac{a}{P_1}\right)^{\frac{ab}{1-a-b}}\left(\frac{b}{P_2}\right)^{\frac{b-ab}{1-a-b}}$

$$- P_1\left(\frac{A}{\lambda}\right)^{\frac{1}{1-a-b}}\left(\frac{a}{P_1}\right)^{\frac{1-b}{1-a-b}}\left(\frac{b}{P_2}\right)^{\frac{b}{1-a-b}} - P_2\left(\frac{A}{\lambda}\right)^{\frac{1}{1-a-b}}\left(\frac{a}{P_1}\right)^{\frac{a}{1-a-b}}\left(\frac{b}{P_2}\right)^{\frac{1-a}{1-a-b}} + \mathbf{P}.\mathbf{e}$$

$$= \left(\frac{A}{\lambda}\right)^{\frac{1}{1-a-b}}\left(\frac{a}{P_1}\right)^{\frac{a}{1-a-b}}\left(\frac{b}{P_2}\right)^{\frac{b}{1-a-b}} - a\left(\frac{A}{\lambda}\right)^{\frac{1}{1-a-b}}\left(\frac{a}{P_1}\right)^{\frac{a}{1-a-b}}\left(\frac{b}{P_2}\right)^{\frac{b}{1-a-b}}$$

$$- b\left(\frac{a}{P_1}\right)^{\frac{a}{1-a-b}}\left(\frac{b}{P_2}\right)^{\frac{b}{1-a-b}} + \mathbf{P}.\mathbf{e}$$

$$= (1 - a - b)\left(\frac{A}{\lambda}\right)^{\frac{1}{1-a-b}}\left(\frac{a}{P_1}\right)^{\frac{a}{1-a-b}}\left(\frac{b}{P_2}\right)^{\frac{b}{1-a-b}} + \mathbf{P}.\mathbf{e}.$$

Answer: c) $h(P_1, P_2) = \lambda^{-1}\left[a\left(\frac{a}{2\lambda P_1}\right) + b\left(\frac{b}{2\lambda P_2}\right)\right] - P_1\left(\frac{a}{2\lambda P_1}\right)^2 - P_2\left(\frac{b}{2\lambda P_2}\right)^2 + \mathbf{P}.\mathbf{e}$

$$= \frac{a^2}{2\lambda^2 P_1} + \frac{b^2}{2\lambda^2 P_2} - \frac{a^2}{4\lambda^2 P_1} - \frac{b^2}{4\lambda^2 P_2} = \frac{a^2}{4\lambda^2 P_1} + \frac{b^2}{4\lambda^2 P_2} + \mathbf{P}.\mathbf{e}.$$

Answer: d) $$h(P_1, P_2) = \lambda^{-1}\left[a\left(\frac{ce + 2ad - 2d\lambda P_1 - e\lambda P_2}{4bd - e^2}\right) - b\left(\frac{ce + 2ad - 2d\lambda P_1 - e\lambda P_2}{4bd - e^2}\right)^2 \right.$$

$$+ c\left(\frac{ae + 2bc - e\lambda P_1 - 2b\lambda P_2}{4bd - e^2}\right) - d\left(\frac{ae + 2bc - e\lambda P_1 - 2b\lambda P_2}{4bd - e^2}\right)^2$$

$$\left. + e\left(\frac{ce + 2ad - 2d\lambda P_1 - e\lambda P_2}{4bd - e^2}\right)\left(\frac{ae + 2bc - e\lambda P_1 - 2b\lambda P_2}{4bd - e^2}\right)\right]$$

$$- P_1\left(\frac{ce + 2ad - 2d\lambda P_1 - e\lambda P_2}{4bd - e^2}\right) - P_2\left(\frac{ae + 2bc - e\lambda P_1 - 2b\lambda P_2}{4bd - e^2}\right) + \mathbf{P.e.}$$

Answer to Homework Problems for Chapter 8, Problem #4

Problem: 4) Verify that in each of the utility functions of problem 1,

$$\frac{\partial h(P_1, P_2)}{\partial P_k} = e_k - \xi_k^S(P_1, P_2),$$

for k = 1 and 2.

Answer: a) $\dfrac{\partial h(P_1, P_2)}{\partial P_1}$

$$= \frac{\partial}{\partial P_1}\lambda^{-1}\Big\{[a(\ln(a) - 1) + b(\ln(b) - 1) - (a + b)\ln(\lambda)])$$

$$- a\ln(P_1) - b\ln(P_2) + \mathbf{P}.\mathbf{e}\Big\}$$

$$= -\frac{a}{\lambda P_1} + e_1 = e_1 - \xi_1^S(P_1, P_2).$$

$$\frac{\partial h(P_1, P_2)}{\partial P_2} = \frac{\partial}{\partial P_2}\lambda^{-1}\Big\{[a(\ln(a) - 1) + b(\ln(b) - 1) - (a + b)\ln(\lambda)]$$

$$- a\ln(P_1) - b\ln(P_2) + \mathbf{P}.\mathbf{e}\Big\}$$

$$= -\frac{b}{\lambda P_2} + e_2 = e_2 - \xi_2^S(P_1, P_2).$$

Answer: b) $\dfrac{\partial h(P_1, P_2)}{\partial P_1}$

$$= \frac{\partial}{\partial P_1}\left[(1 - a - b)\left(\frac{A}{\lambda}\right)^{\frac{1}{1-a-b}} a^{\frac{a}{1-a-b}} b^{\frac{b}{1-a-b}} P_1^{\frac{a}{a+b-1}} P_2^{\frac{b}{a+b-1}} + \mathbf{P}.\mathbf{e}\right]$$

$$= (1 - a - b)\left(\frac{A}{\lambda}\right)^{\frac{1}{1-a-b}} a^{\frac{a}{1-a-b}} b^{\frac{b}{1-a-b}}\left(\frac{a}{a + b - 1}\right) P_1^{\frac{a}{a+b-1} - 1} P_2^{\frac{b}{a+b-1}} + e_1$$

$$= -\left(\frac{A}{\lambda}\right)^{\frac{1}{1-a-b}} a^{1 + \frac{a}{1-a-b}} b^{\frac{b}{1-a-b}} P_1^{\frac{a}{a+b-1} - 1} P_2^{\frac{b}{a+b-1}} + e_1$$

$$= -\left(\frac{A}{\lambda}\right)^{\frac{1}{1-a-b}} a^{\frac{1-b}{1-a-b}} b^{\frac{b}{1-a-b}} P_1^{\frac{1-b}{a+b-1}} P_2^{\frac{b}{a+b-1}} + e_1$$

$$= -\left(\frac{A}{\lambda}\right)^{\frac{1}{1-a-b}} \left(\frac{a}{P_1}\right)^{\frac{1-b}{1-a-b}} \left(\frac{b}{P_2}\right)^{\frac{b}{1-a-b}} + e_1$$

$$= e_1 - \xi_1^s(P_1, P_2).$$

$$\frac{\partial h(P_1, P_2)}{\partial P_2} = \frac{\partial}{\partial P_2}\left[(1-a-b)\left(\frac{A}{\lambda}\right)^{\frac{1}{1-a-b}} a^{\frac{a}{1-a-b}} b^{\frac{b}{1-a-b}} P_1^{\frac{a}{a+b-1}} P_2^{\frac{b}{a+b-1}} + \mathbf{P}.\mathbf{e}\right]$$

$$= (1-a-b)\left(\frac{A}{\lambda}\right)^{\frac{1}{1-a-b}} a^{\frac{a}{1-a-b}} b^{\frac{b}{1-a-b}} P_1^{\frac{a}{a+b-1}} \left(\frac{b}{a+b-1}\right) P_2^{\frac{b}{a+b-1}-1} + e_2$$

$$= -\left(\frac{A}{\lambda}\right)^{\frac{1}{1-a-b}} a^{\frac{a}{1-a-b}} b^{1+\frac{b}{1-a-b}} P_1^{\frac{a}{a+b-1}} P_2^{\frac{b}{a+b-1}-1} + e_2$$

$$= -\left(\frac{A}{\lambda}\right)^{\frac{1}{1-a-b}} a^{\frac{a}{1-a-b}} b^{\frac{1-a}{1-a-b}} P_1^{\frac{a}{a+b-1}} P_2^{\frac{1-a}{a+b-1}} + e_2$$

$$= -\left(\frac{A}{\lambda}\right)^{\frac{1}{1-a-b}} \left(\frac{a}{P_1}\right)^{\frac{a}{1-a-b}} \left(\frac{b}{P_2}\right)^{\frac{1-a}{1-a-b}} + e_2$$

$$= e_2 - \xi_2^s(P_1, P_2).$$

<u>Answer</u>: c) $\dfrac{\partial h(P_1, P_2)}{\partial P_1} = \dfrac{\partial}{\partial P_1}\left(\dfrac{a^2}{4\lambda^2 P_1} + \dfrac{b^2}{4\lambda^2 P_2} + \mathbf{P}.\mathbf{e}\right) = -\dfrac{a^2}{4\lambda^2 P_1^2} + e_1$

$$= -\left(\frac{a}{2\lambda P_1}\right)^2 + e_1 = e_1 - \xi_1^s(P_1, P_2).$$

$$\frac{\partial h(P_1, P_2)}{\partial P_2} = \frac{\partial}{\partial P_2}\left(\frac{a^2}{4\lambda^2 P_1} + \frac{b^2}{4\lambda^2 P_2} + \mathbf{P}.\mathbf{e}\right) = -\frac{b^2}{4\lambda^2 P_2^2} + e_2$$

$$= -\left(\frac{a}{2\lambda P_2}\right)^2 + e_2 = e_2 - \xi_1^s(P_1, P_2).$$

Answer: d) $\dfrac{\partial h(P_1, P_2)}{\partial P_1}$

$$= \frac{\partial}{\partial P_1}\left\{\lambda^{-1}\left[a\left(\frac{ce + 2ad - 2d\lambda P_1 - e\lambda P_2}{4bd - e^2}\right) - b\left(\frac{ce + 2ad - 2d\lambda P_1 - e\lambda P_2}{4bd - e^2}\right)^2\right.\right.$$

$$+ c\left(\frac{ae + 2bc - e\lambda P_1 - 2b\lambda P_2}{4bd - e^2}\right) - d\left(\frac{ae + 2bc - e\lambda P_1 - 2b\lambda P_2}{4bd - e^2}\right)^2$$

$$\left. + e\left(\frac{ce + 2ad - 2d\lambda P_1 - e\lambda P_2}{4bd - e^2}\right)\left(\frac{ae + 2bc - e\lambda P_1 - 2b\lambda P_2}{4bd - e^2}\right)\right]$$

$$\left. - P_1\left(\frac{ce + 2ad - 2d\lambda P_1 - e\lambda P_2}{4bd - e^2}\right) - P_2\left(\frac{ae + 2bc - e\lambda P_1 - 2b\lambda P_2}{4bd - e^2}\right) + \mathbf{P}.\mathbf{e}\right\}$$

$$= -\frac{2ad}{4bd - e^2} - \frac{2b\lambda^{-1}}{(4bd - e^2)^2}(-2d\lambda)(ce + 2ad - 2d\lambda P_1 - e\lambda P_2)$$

$$-\frac{ce}{4bd - e^2} - \frac{2d\lambda^{-1}}{(4bd - e^2)^2}(-e\lambda)(ae + 2bc - e\lambda P_1 - 2b\lambda P_2)$$

$$+ \frac{e\lambda^{-1}}{(4bd - e^2)^2}(-e\lambda)(ce + 2ad - 2d\lambda P_1 - e\lambda P_2)$$

$$+ \frac{e\lambda^{-1}}{(4bd - e^2)^2}(-2d\lambda)(ae + 2bc - e\lambda P_1 - 2b\lambda P_2)$$

$$- \frac{ce + 2ad - 2d\lambda P_1 - e\lambda P_2}{4bd - e^2} + \frac{2d\lambda P_1}{4bd - e^2} + \frac{e\lambda P_2}{4bd - e^2} + e_1$$

$$= (4bd - e^2)^{-1}(-2ad - ce - ce - 2ad + 2d\lambda P_1 + 2e\lambda P_2 + 2d\lambda P_1)$$

$$+ (4bd - e^2)^{-2}(4bcde + 8abd^2 - 8bd^2\lambda P_1 - 4bde\lambda P_2 + 2ade^2 + 4bcde - 2de^2\lambda P_1$$

$$- 4bde\lambda P_2 - ce^3 - 2ade^2 + 2de^2\lambda P_1 + e^3\lambda P_2$$

$$- 2ade^2 - 4bcde + 2de^2\lambda P_1 + 4bde\lambda P_2) + e_1$$

$$= (4bd - e^2)^{-1}(-4ad - 2ce + 4d\lambda P_1 + 2e\lambda P_2)$$

$$+ (4bd - e^2)^{-2}[8abd^2 - ce^3 - 2ade^2 + 4bcde$$

$$- (8bd^2 - 2de^2)\lambda P_1 - (4bde - e^3)\lambda P_2] + e_1$$

$$= (4bd - e^2)^{-1}(-4ad - 2ce + 4d\lambda P_1 + 2e\lambda P_2)$$

$$+ (4bd - e^2)^{-2}[(4bd - e^2)(2ad + ce) - (4bd - e^2)2d\lambda P_1 - (4bd - e^2)e\lambda P_2] + e_1$$

$$= (4bd - e^2)^{-1}(-4ad - 2ce + 4d\lambda P_1 + 2e\lambda P_2 + 2ad + ce - 2d\lambda P_1 - e\lambda P_2) + e_1$$

$$= (4bd - e^2)^{-1}(-2ad - ce + 2d\lambda P_1 + e\lambda P_2) + e_1$$

$$= e_1 - \xi_1^s(P_1, P_2).$$

$$\frac{\partial h(P_1, P_2)}{\partial P_2}$$

$$= \frac{\partial}{\partial P_2}\left\{\lambda^{-1}\left[a\left(\frac{ce + 2ad - 2d\lambda P_1 - e\lambda P_2}{4bd - e^2}\right) - b\left(\frac{ce + 2ad - 2d\lambda P_1 - e\lambda P_2}{4bd - e^2}\right)^2\right.\right.$$

$$+ c\left(\frac{ae + 2bc - e\lambda P_1 - 2b\lambda P_2}{4bd - e^2}\right) - d\left(\frac{ae + 2bc - e\lambda P_1 - 2b\lambda P_2}{4bd - e^2}\right)^2$$

$$\left. + e\left(\frac{ce + 2ad - 2d\lambda P_1 - e\lambda P_2}{4bd - e^2}\right)\left(\frac{ae + 2bc - e\lambda P_1 - 2b\lambda P_2}{4bd - e^2}\right)\right]$$

$$\left. - P_1\left(\frac{ce + 2ad - 2d\lambda P_1 - e\lambda P_2}{4bd - e^2}\right) - P_2\left(\frac{ae + 2bc - e\lambda P_1 - 2b\lambda P_2}{4bd - e^2}\right) + \mathbf{P}.\mathbf{e}\right\}$$

$$= -\frac{ae}{4bd - e^2} - \frac{2b\lambda^{-1}}{(4bd - e^2)^2}(-e\lambda)(ce + 2ad - 2d\lambda P_1 - e\lambda P_2)$$

$$-\frac{2bc}{4bd - e^2} - \frac{2d\lambda^{-1}}{(4bd - e^2)^2}(-2b\lambda)(ae + 2bc - e\lambda P_1 - 2b\lambda P_2)$$

$$+ \frac{e\lambda^{-1}}{(4bd - e^2)^2}(-e\lambda)(ae + 2bc - e\lambda P_1 - 2bc\lambda P_2)$$

$$+ \frac{e\lambda^{-1}}{(4bd - e^2)^2}(-2b\lambda)(ce + 2ad - 2d\lambda P_1 - e\lambda P_2)$$

$$- \frac{ae + 2bc - e\lambda P_1 - 2b\lambda P_2}{4bd - e^2} + \frac{e\lambda P_1}{4bd - e^2} + \frac{2b\lambda P_2}{4bd - e^2} + e_2$$

$$= (4bd - e^2)^{-1}(-2ae - 4bc + 2e\lambda P_1 + 4b\lambda P_2)$$

$$+ (4bd - e^2)^{-2}(2bce^2 + 4abde - 4bde\lambda P_1 - 2be^2\lambda P_2 + 4abde + 8b^2cd - 4bde\lambda P_1$$

$$- 8b^2d\lambda P_2 - ae^3 - 2bce^2 + e^3\lambda P_1 + 2be^2\lambda P_2$$

$$- 2bce^2 - 4abde + 4bde\lambda P_1 + 2be^2\lambda P_2) + e_2$$

$$= (4bd - e^2)^{-1}(-2ae - 4bc + 2e\lambda P_1 + 4b\lambda P_2)$$

$$+ (4bd - e^2)^{-2}(4abde + 8b^2cd - ae^3 - 2bce^2 - 4bde\lambda P_1 + e^3\lambda P_1$$

$$- 8b^2d\lambda P_2 + 2be^2\lambda P_2) + e_2$$

$$= (4bd - e^2)^{-1}(-2ae - 4bc + 2e\lambda P_1 + 4b\lambda P_2)$$

$$+ (4bd - e^2)^{-2}[(4bd - e^2)(ae + 2bc) - (4bd - e^2)e\lambda P_1 - (4bd - e^2)2b\lambda P_2] + e_2$$

$$= (4bd - e^2)^{-1}(-2ae - 4bc + 2e\lambda P_1 + 4b\lambda P_2 + ae + 2bc - e\lambda P_1 - 2b\lambda P_2) + e_2$$

$$= (4bd - e^2)^{-1}(-ae - 2bc + e\lambda P_1 + 2b\lambda P_2) + e_2$$

$$= e_2 - \xi_2^s(P_1, P_2).$$

Answer to Homework Problems for Chapter 8, Problem #5

Problem: 5) Consider a consumer with utility function

$$u(x_1, x_2) = x_1 - \frac{x_1^2}{2} + 5x_2 - \frac{x_2^2}{2}$$

and with endowment **e** = (0, 1). Let the price of good 1 be p and the price of good 2 be 1.

a) Calculate the consumer's Walrasian demand, $x_1(p)$, for good 1 as a function of p.

b) Calculate the price, $\bar{p}$, such that $x_1(\bar{p}) = \frac{1}{2}$.

c) Calculate the consumer's surplus when the price is $\bar{p}$, where the surplus is defined using the demand function $x_1(p)$.

d) Calculate the consumer's marginal utility of money, $\bar{\lambda}$, when $p = \bar{p}$.

e) Calculate the consumer's short-run demand function, $x_1^s(p)$, when his or her marginal utility of money is $\bar{\lambda}$.

f) Calculate the consumer's surplus when $p = \bar{p}$, where the surplus is defined using the demand function $x_1^s(p)$.

Answer: a) The problem to be solved is

$$\max_{x_1 \geq 0,\ x_2 \geq 0} \left(x_1 - \frac{x_1^2}{2} + 5x_2 - \frac{x_2^2}{2} \right)$$

$$\text{s.t. } px_1 + x_2 \leq 1.$$

The first order conditions are

$$1 - x_1 = \lambda p$$

$$5 - x_2 = \lambda,$$

so that

$$x_1 = 1 - \lambda p$$

$$x_2 = 5 - \lambda.$$

If we substitute these equations into the budget equation, we obtain

$$p(1 - \lambda p) + 5 - \lambda = 1,$$

so that

$$\lambda = \frac{p + 4}{p^2 + 1}.$$

Therefore

$$x_1 = 1 - \frac{p^2 + 4p}{p^2 + 1} = \frac{p^2 + 1 - p^2 - 4p}{p^2 + 1} = \frac{1 - 4p}{p^2 + 1},$$

if $0 \le p \le 1/4$. In summary,

$$x_1 = \begin{cases} \dfrac{1 - 4p}{1 + p^2}, \text{ if } 0 \le p \le \dfrac{1}{4} \\ 0, \text{ if } p \ge \dfrac{1}{4}. \end{cases}$$

<u>Answer</u>: b) The equation to be solved is

$$\frac{1 - 4p}{1 + p^2} = \frac{1}{2}.$$

After cross multiplication, this equation becomes

$$p^2 + 8p - 1 = 0,$$

so that

$$\bar{p} = \frac{-8 + \sqrt{64 + 4}}{2} = 0.1231056256.$$

<u>Answer</u>: c) The surplus is

$$\int_0^{\bar{p}} \frac{1 - 4p}{1 + p^2} dp - \frac{\bar{p}(1 - 4\bar{p})}{1 + \bar{p}^2} = \tan^{-1}(\bar{p}) - 2\log(\bar{p}^2 + 1) - \frac{\bar{p}(1 - 4\bar{p})}{1 + \bar{p}^2}$$

$= 0.0740012305.$

Answer: d) The calculation is

$$\bar{\lambda} = \frac{4 + \bar{p}}{1 + \bar{p}^2} = 4.061552813.$$

Answer: e) Since

$$1 - x_1^s = \bar{\lambda}\, p,$$

it follows that

$$x_1^s = 1 - \bar{\lambda}\, p = 1 - 4.061552813p\ .$$

Answer: f) The calculation is

$$\int_0^{\bar{p}} (1 - \bar{\lambda}\, p)\, dp - \frac{\bar{p}(1 - 4\bar{p})}{1 + \bar{p}^2} = \bar{p}^2 - \bar{\lambda}\frac{\bar{p}^2}{2} - \frac{\bar{p}(1 - 4\bar{p})}{1 + \bar{p}^2}$$

$$= 0.307764064.$$

Answer to Homework Problems for Chapter 8, Problem #6

Problem: 6) Let $u(x) = ax - \frac{b}{2}x^2$, be the utility of a single consumer for a single commodity, where $a > 0$ and $b > 0$. Let $\lambda = 1$ be the consumer's marginal utility of unit of account.

a) Compute the consumer's short-run demand function, $\xi^s(P)$, where P is a positive number.

b) Let e be the consumer's endowment of the single commodity. Compute the equilibrium price, $\overline{P}$, at which $\xi^s(\overline{P}) = e$.

c) Compute the solution of the differential equation $\frac{dP(t)}{dt} = \xi^s(P(t)) - e$ for an arbitrary initial condition and show that it converges to $\overline{P}$.

Answer: a) The equation to be solved is

$$a - bx = P,$$

so that

$$\xi^s(P) = x = ab^{-1} - Pb^{-1}.$$

Answer: b) The equation to be solved is

$$\xi^s(P) = ab^{-1} - Pb^{-1} = e,$$

so that

$$P = a - be.$$

Answer: c) The differential equation to be solved is

$$\frac{dP(t)}{dt} = b^{-1}a - b^{-1}P(t) - e = -b^{-1}P(t) + b^{-1}(a - be).$$

The solution to this differential equation is

$$P(t) = Ae^{-\frac{t}{b}} + (a - be),$$

where $A = P(0) - a + be$. It is clear that

$$\lim_{t \to \infty} P(t) = a - be.$$

Answer to Homework Problems for Chapter 8, Problem #7

Problem: 7) Let there be two commodities, let the utility function of a consumer be

$$u(x_1, x_2) = x_1 - x_1^2 + x_2 - x_2^2 + x_1 x_2,$$

let the endowment of the consumer be

$$\mathbf{e} = \left(\frac{1}{2}, \frac{1}{2}\right),$$

and let the consumer's marginal utility of unit of account be $\lambda = 1$.

a) Compute the consumer's short-run demand function for both commodities,

$$(\xi_1^s(P_1, P_2), \xi_2^s(P_1, P_2)).$$

b) Compute the equilibrium price vector $(\overline{P}_1, \overline{P}_2)$ that satisfies the equation

$$(\xi_1^s(\overline{P}_1, \overline{P}_2), \xi_2^s(\overline{P}_1, \overline{P}_2)) = \left(\frac{1}{2}, \frac{1}{2}\right).$$

c) Compute the solution to the equations

$$\frac{dP_1(t)}{dt} = \xi_1^s(P_1(t), P_2(t)) - \frac{1}{2}$$

and

$$\frac{dP_2(t)}{dt} = \xi_2^s(P_1(t), P_2(t)) - \frac{1}{2}$$

with arbitrary initial conditions and show that it converges to $(\overline{P}_1, \overline{P}_2)$.

Answer: a) The equations to be solved are

$$\frac{\partial u(x_1, x_2)}{\partial x_1} = P_1$$

$$\frac{\partial u(x_1, x_2)}{\partial x_2} = P_2,$$

which after substitution become

$$1 - 2x_1 + x_2 = P_1$$

$$1 - 2x_2 + x_1 = P_2.$$

The solution of these equations is

$$\xi_1^s(P_1, P_2) = x_1 = 1 - \frac{2}{3}P_1 - \frac{1}{3}P_2$$

$$\xi_2^s(P_1, P_2) = x_2 = 1 - \frac{1}{3}P_1 - \frac{2}{3}P_2.$$

Answer: b) The equations to be solved are

$$1 - \frac{2}{3}P_1 - \frac{1}{3}P_2 = \frac{1}{2}$$

$$1 - \frac{1}{3}P_1 - \frac{2}{3}P_2 = \frac{1}{2}.$$

The solution of these equations is

$$P_1 = P_2 = \frac{1}{2}.$$

Answer: c) The differential equations to be solved are

$$\frac{dP_1(t)}{dt} = \frac{1}{2} - \frac{2}{3}P_1(t) - \frac{1}{3}P_2(t)$$

$$\frac{dP_2(t)}{dt} = \frac{1}{2} - \frac{1}{3}P_1(t) - \frac{2}{3}P_2(t).$$

These may be written as the vector differential equation

$$\frac{d\mathbf{P}(t)}{dt} = -A\mathbf{P}(t) + \mathbf{b},$$

where $\mathbf{P}(t)$ is the vector $\begin{pmatrix} P_1(t) \\ P_2(t) \end{pmatrix}$, $\mathbf{b}$ is the vector $\begin{pmatrix} 1/2 \\ 1/2 \end{pmatrix}$, and A is the matrix $\begin{pmatrix} 2/3 & 1/3 \\ 1/3 & 2/3 \end{pmatrix}$. The solution to this differential equation is

$$\mathbf{P}(t) = e^{-At}\mathbf{c} + A^{-1}\mathbf{b},$$

where $A^{-1} = \begin{pmatrix} 2 & -1 \\ -1 & 2 \end{pmatrix}$ is the inverse of A and $\mathbf{c}$ is the vector $\mathbf{P}(0) - A^{-1}\mathbf{b}$. From the theory of linear differential equations, we know that $\lim_{t \to \infty} e^{-At} = 0$, if the real parts of the eigenvalues of characteristic values of the matrix $-A$ are negative. The eigenvalues are the roots of the polynomial in y

$$\det\begin{pmatrix} (-\frac{2}{3} - y) & -\frac{1}{3} \\ -\frac{1}{3} & (-\frac{2}{3} - y) \end{pmatrix} = \frac{1}{3} + \frac{4}{3}y + y^2$$

and they are $-1/3$ and -1. Therefore $\lim_{t \to \infty} e^{-At} = 0$, and we can conclude that $\lim_{t \to \infty} \mathbf{P}(t) = A^{-1}\mathbf{b}$. Since $A^{-1}\mathbf{b} = \mathbf{b} = \begin{pmatrix} 1/2 \\ 1/2 \end{pmatrix} = \begin{pmatrix} \overline{P}_1 \\ \overline{P}_2 \end{pmatrix}$, we have shown that $\lim_{t \to \infty} \mathbf{P}(t) = (\overline{P}_1, \overline{P}_2)$.

The rows of the matrix e^{-At} solve the differential equation

$$\frac{d\mathbf{x}(t)}{dt} = A\mathbf{x}(t),$$

where $\mathbf{x}(t)$ is a 2-vector. Any solutions of this equation are linear combinations of the functions $e^{-\frac{1}{3}t}$ and e^{-t}, since $-1/3$ and -1 are the eigenvalues of A. The initial condition of the first row is $\mathbf{x}(0) = (1, 0)$, and the initial condition of the second row is $\mathbf{x}(0) = (0, 1)$. Using this information, it is not hard to calculate that

$$e^{-At} = \begin{pmatrix} \frac{1}{2}e^{-\frac{1}{3}t} + \frac{1}{2}e^{-t} & -\frac{1}{2}e^{-\frac{1}{3}t} + \frac{1}{2}e^{-t} \\ -\frac{1}{2}e^{-\frac{1}{3}t} + \frac{1}{2}e^{-t} & \frac{1}{2}e^{-\frac{1}{3}t} + \frac{1}{2}e^{-t} \end{pmatrix}.$$

This matrix clearly converges to zero as t goes to infinity.

Answer to Homework Problems for Chapter 9, Problem #1

Problem: 1) Consider a Samuelson model in which consumers are endowed with one unit of good in youth and none in old age and where their utility functions are

$$u(x_0, x_1) = \ln(x_0) + (0.5)\ln(x_1).$$

a) Compute formulas for a stationary spot price equilibrium, $(\overline{x}_0, \overline{x}_1, P, r, G, T)$, with non-negative interest rate r and with P = 1.

b) Show on a diagram all feasible stationary allocations and those allocations that are Pareto optimal. Show in similar diagrams the allocations and budget sets for the equilibria with interest rates r = 0 and r = 1. Indicate the tax payments on the diagrams for each of these equilibria.

Answer: a) To find the stationary equilibrium allocation, we must solve the equations

$$(1 + r)\frac{\partial u(x_0, x_1)}{\partial x_1} = \frac{\partial u(x_0, x_1)}{\partial x_0}$$

$$x_0 + x_1 = e_0 + e_1.$$

The first equation is the first order condition for utility maximization over the budget set. The second equation is the feasibility condition. On substituting for the utility function u and the endowment **e**, these equations become

$$\frac{1 + r}{2}\frac{1}{x_1} = \frac{1}{x_0}$$

$$x_0 + x_1 = 1.$$

The solution of these equations is

$$x_0 = \frac{2}{3 + r} \text{ and } x_1 = \frac{1 + r}{3 + r}.$$

Letting the price be P = 1, the tax T satisfies the budget equation

$$x_0 + \frac{x_1}{1 + r} = 1 - T.$$

Therefore

$$T = 1 - \left(x_0 + \frac{x_1}{1 + r}\right) = 1 - \frac{2}{3 + r} - \frac{1}{3 + r} = \frac{r}{3 + r}.$$

It follows that the government debt is

$$G = \frac{T}{r} = \frac{1}{3 + r}.$$

In summary, the equilibrium is

$$((\bar{x}_0, \bar{x}_1), P, r, G, T) = \left(\left(\frac{2}{3 + r}, \frac{1 + r}{3 + r}\right), 1, r, \frac{1}{3 + r}, \frac{r}{3 + r}\right).$$

Answer: b) The feasible stationary allocations are the points on the line segment connecting the points at distance 1 from the origin on the coordinate axes. The set of Pareto optimal allocations are the heavy part of this line.

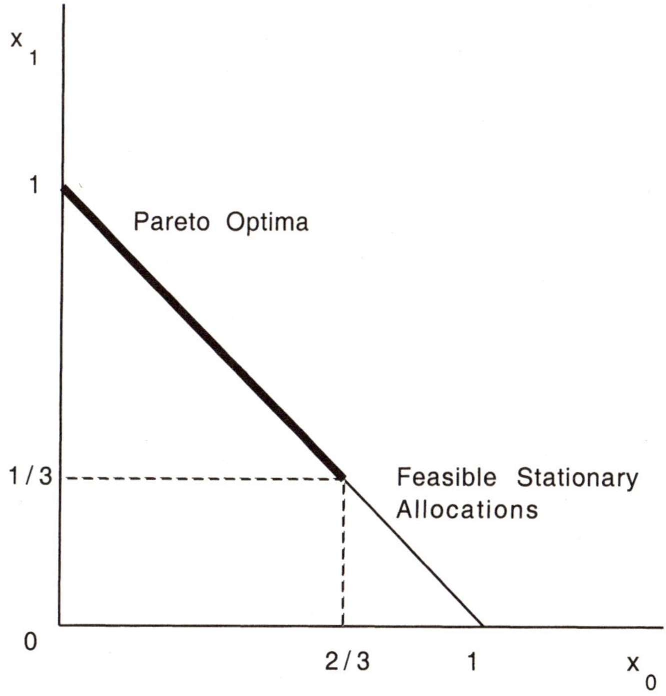

The next diagram portrays the stationary equilibrium with interest rate zero. The budget set is shaded and the equilibrium allocation is **x** = (2/3, 1/3). There is no tax.

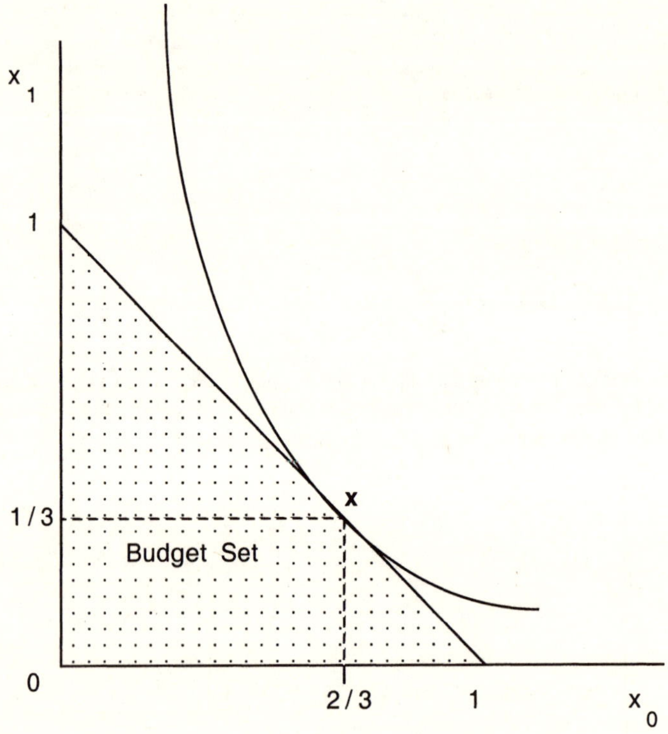

The next diagram portrays the stationary equilibrium with interest rate 1. The budget set is shaded and the equilibrium allocation is **x** = (1/2, 1/2). The tax is 1/4 and can be thought of as the distance from 3/4 to 1 on the horizontal axis.

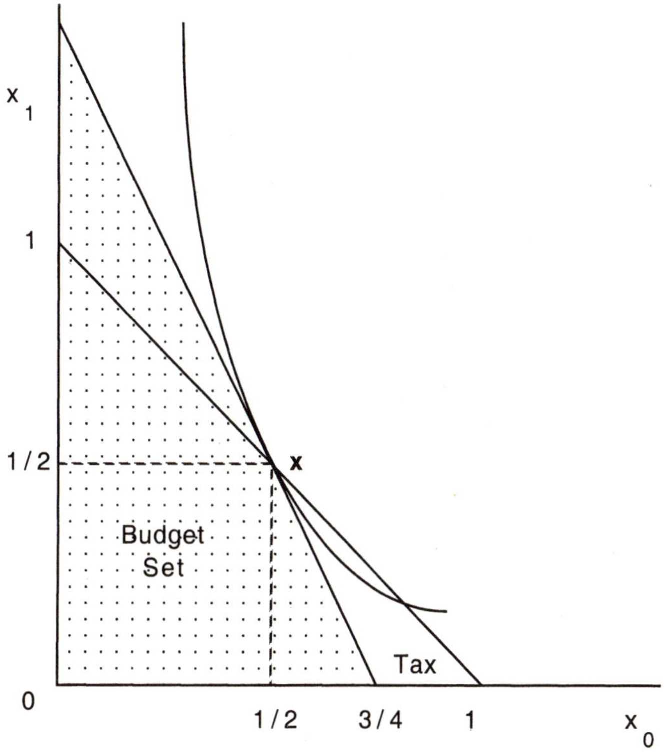

Answer to Homework Problems for Chapter 9, Problem #2

Problem: 2) Consider a Samuelson model with one commodity in each period and where the endowment of every consumer is e = (1, 0). Let the utility function of every consumer be

$$u(x_0, x_1) = x_0 + 2x_1.$$

a) Draw a diagram that shows the set of feasible stationary allocations, the endowment, and sample indifference curves.

b) Indicate on a second copy of the diagram which of the feasible stationary allocations are Pareto optimal.

c) Compute a stationary spot price equilibrium, $(\overline{x}_0, \overline{x}_1, P, r, G, T)$, for this economy with positive interest rate r and with P = 1.

d) State a social welfare maximization problem that is solved by the allocation of the stationary spot price equilibrium that you just found.

Answer: a)

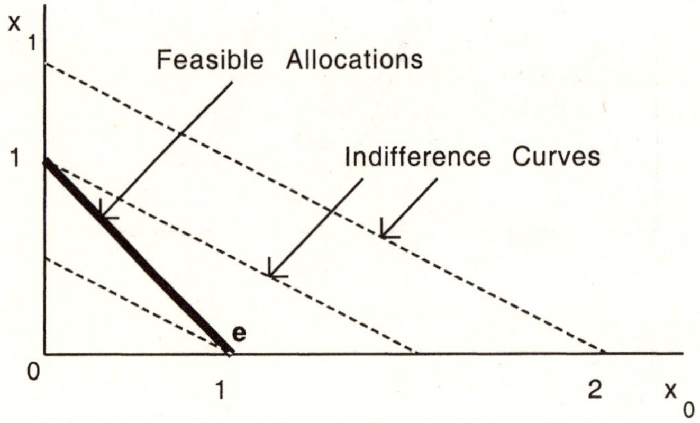

Answer: b)

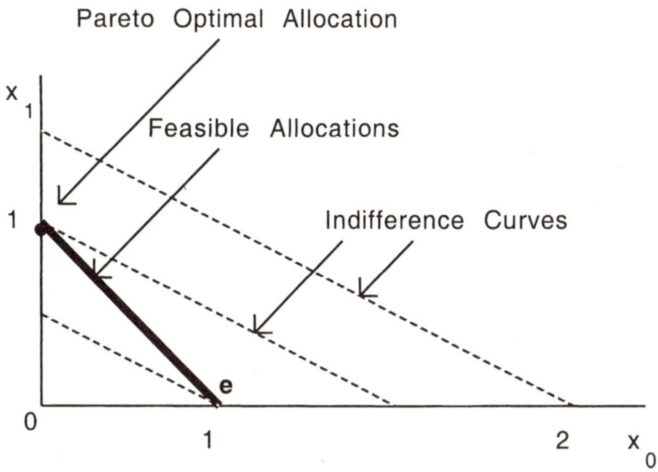

Answer: c) The allocation is the only Pareto optimal allocation, namely, $(\bar{x}_0, \bar{x}_1) = (0, 1)$. The government debt, G, satisfies the equation

$$(1 + r)G = Px_1.$$

Since $P = 1$ and $x_1 = 1$,

$$G = \frac{1}{1 + r}.$$

The tax is

$$T = rG = \frac{r}{1 + r}.$$

In summary, the equilibrium is

$$((\bar{x}_0, \bar{x}_1), P, r, G, T) = ((0, 1), 1, r, 1/(1 + r), r/(1 + r))$$

Answer: d) $(1 + r)2x_{-1,1} + \sum_{t=0}^{\infty} (1 + r)^{-t}[x_{t0} + 2x_{t1}]$.

Answer to Homework Problems for Chapter 9, Problem #3

Problem: 3) Consider a Samuelson model with one commodity in each period and where each consumer is endowed with one unit of the commodity in youth and none in old age. The utility function of each consumer is

$$u(x_0, x_1) = 2\sqrt{x_0} + 2\sqrt{x_1}.$$

a) Compute a stationary spot price equilibrium, $(\overline{x}_0, \overline{x}_1, P, r, G, T)$, with $r = P = 1$.

b) Compute a stationary spot price equilibrium, $(\overline{x}_0, \overline{x}_1, P, r, G, T)$, with $P = 1$ and $r = 0$.

c) Show that the allocation of the equilibrium of part (a) is Pareto optimal.

d) Compute the utility of a typical consumer in each of the equilibria of parts (a) and (b).

e) Why is the allocation of the equilibrium of part (a) not Pareto dominated by that of part (b)?

f) Show the equilibrium allocations of parts (a) and (b) in a two-dimensional diagram.

Answer: I first compute a stationary spot price equilibrium with interest rate r and with $P = 1$. The equilibrium allocation satisfies the equations

$$(1 + r)\frac{\partial u(x_0, x_1)}{\partial x_1} = \frac{\partial u(x_0, x_1)}{\partial x_0}$$

$$x_0 + x_1 = 1.$$

On substituting the actual utility function, the first of these equations becomes

$$\frac{1 + r}{\sqrt{x_1}} = \frac{1}{\sqrt{x_0}},$$

which implies that

$$(1 + r)\sqrt{x_0} = \sqrt{x_1}$$

and hence

$$x_1 = (1 + r)^2 x_0.$$

Substituting this equation into the feasibility equation, we obtain

$$x_0 + (1 + r)^2 x_0 = 1,$$

so that

$$x_0 = \frac{1}{2 + 2r + r^2} \text{ and } x_1 = \frac{(1 + r)^2}{2 + 2r + r^2}.$$

Government debt, G, satisfies the equation

$$G = \frac{Px_1}{1 + r} = \frac{x_1}{1 + r} = \frac{1 + r}{2 + 2r + r^2}.$$

The tax is then

$$T = rG = \frac{r(1 + r)}{2 + 2r + r^2}.$$

In summary, the equilibrium is

$$((\overline{x}_0, \overline{x}_1), r, P, G, T)$$

$$= \left(\left(\frac{1}{2 + 2r + r^2}, \frac{(1 + r)^2}{2 + 2r + r^2}\right), r, 1, \frac{1 + r}{2 + 2r + r^2}, \frac{r(1 + r)}{2 + 2r + r^2}\right)$$

Answer: a) On substituting r = 1 into the above formula, we obtain

$$((\overline{x}_0, \overline{x}_1), P, r, G, T) = ((1/5, 4/5), 1, 1, 2/5, 2/5).$$

Answer: b) On substituting r = 0 into the above formula, we obtain

$$((\overline{x}_0, \overline{x}_1), P, r, G, T) = ((1/2, 1/2), 1, 0, 1/2, 0).$$

Answer: c) The allocation of the equilibrium of part a is Pareto optimal, because it maximizes over the set of feasible allocations a social welfare function that gives positive weight to every consumer. This social welfare function is

$$4\sqrt{x_{-1,1}} + \sum_{t=0}^{\infty} 2^{-t}(2\sqrt{x_{t0}} + 2\sqrt{x_{t1}}).$$

Answer: d) If $r = 1$, the utility level of a consumer is

$$2\sqrt{\frac{1}{5}} + 2\sqrt{\frac{4}{5}} = 6\frac{\sqrt{5}}{5}.$$

If $r = 0$, the utility level of a consumer is

$$2\sqrt{\frac{1}{2}} + 2\sqrt{\frac{1}{2}} = 2\sqrt{2}.$$

Notice that

$$2\sqrt{2} > \frac{6}{5}\sqrt{5},$$

since

$$10\sqrt{2} > 6\sqrt{5},$$

because if we square both sides of this inequality, we find that

$$200 > 36(5) = 180.$$

Answer: e) In order to switch from the stationary allocation $(x_0, x_1) = (1/5, 4/5)$ to the stationary allocation $(x_0, x_1) = (1/2, 1/2)$, the old person at the time of the switch must give up $4/5 - 1/2 = 3/10$ units of consumption.

Answer: f) In the figure that follows, the feasibility line is heavy and the budget line for the equilibrium with r = 1 is the steeper line of normal thickness. The vector (1, 1/2) is perpendicular to the budget line.

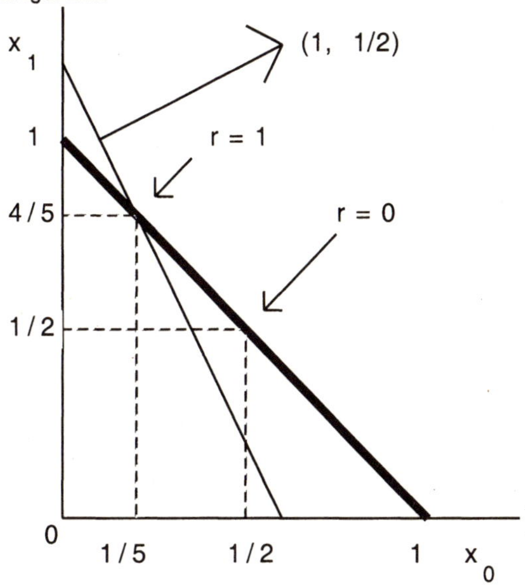

Answer to Homework Problems for Chapter 9, Problem #4

Problem: 4) Consider a Samuelson model with one commodity in each period and where each consumer has utility function

$$u(x_0, x_1) = 2\sqrt{x_0 x_1}.$$

and endowment

$$e = (10, 0).$$

a) Show the set of feasible stationary allocations in a diagram.

b) Indicate which of these are Pareto optimal.

c) Find a stationary spot price equilibrium, $(\bar{x}_0, \bar{x}_1, P, r, G, T)$, the allocation of which maximizes the social welfare function

$$(1.1)\,u(x_{-1,0}, x_{-1,1}) + \sum_{t=0}^{\infty} (1.1)^{-t} u(x_{t0}, x_{t1})$$

among feasible allocations and with $x_{-1,0}$ given. Notice that you have to choose $x_{-1,0}$, so that the equilibrium is stationary.

d) Is the allocation of this equilibrium Pareto optimal? Why or why not?

Answer: a)

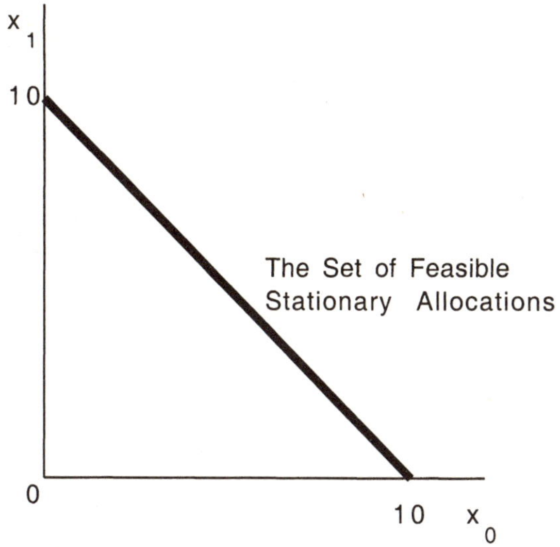

Answer: b)

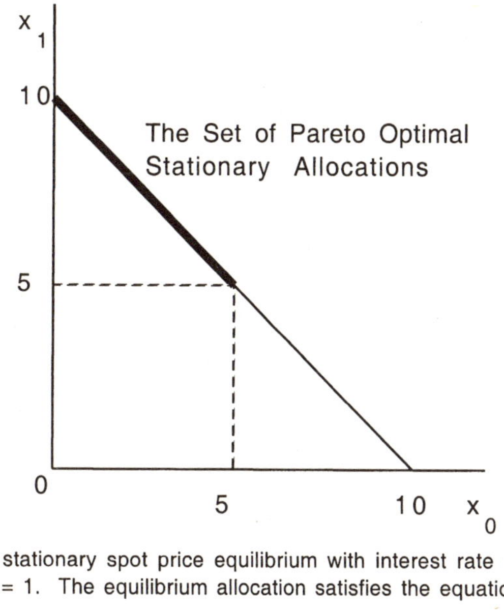

Answer: c) I find a stationary spot price equilibrium with interest rate r and then substitute in 0.1 for r and with P = 1. The equilibrium allocation satisfies the equations

$$(1+r)\frac{\partial u(x_0, x_1)}{\partial x_1} = \frac{\partial u(x_0, x_1)}{\partial x_0}$$

$$x_0 + x_1 = 10.$$

On substituting the actual utility function, the first of these equations becomes

$$(1+r)\sqrt{\frac{x_0}{x_1}} = \sqrt{\frac{x_1}{x_0}},$$

so that

$$x_1 = (1+r)x_0.$$

If we substitute this equation into the feasibility equation, we obtain

$$x_0 + (1+r)x_0 = 10,$$

so that

$$x_0 = \frac{10}{2+r} \text{ and } x_1 = \frac{10(1+r)}{2+r}.$$

The government debt is

$$G = \frac{x_1}{1+r} = \frac{10}{2+r}.$$

Hence the tax is

$$T = rG = \frac{10r}{2+r}.$$

In summary, the equilibrium is

$$((\overline{x}_0, \overline{x}_1), P, r, G, T) = \left(\left(\frac{10}{2+r}, \frac{10(1+r)}{2+r}\right), 1, r, \frac{10}{2+r}, \frac{10r}{2+r}\right).$$

If I substitute $r = 0.1$, I obtain

$$((\overline{x}_0, \overline{x}_1), P, r, G, T) = \left(\left(\frac{10}{2.1}, \frac{11}{2.1}\right), 1, 0.1, \frac{10}{2.1}, \frac{1}{2.1}\right).$$

Answer: d) This equilibrium allocation is Pareto optimal, because it maximizes over all feasible allocations a welfare function that gives positive weight to every consumer.

Answer to Homework Problems for Chapter 9, Problem #5

Problem: 5) Consider the Samuelson overlapping generations model with one commodity and with

$$u(x_0, x_1) = 4x_0^{1/3} + x_1^{1/3} \text{ and } (e_0, e_1) = (1, 8).$$

a) Draw a diagram showing the set of feasible stationary allocations and indicate on the diagram which of these are Pareto optimal. In addition, give a precise formula for the set of Pareto optimal stationary allocations.

b) Define a stationary spot price equilibrium, $(\bar{x}_0, \bar{x}_1, P, r, G, T)$, such that $P = 1$ and the endowment allocation, $(x_0, x_1) = (e_0, e_1) = (1, 8)$ is the equilibrium allocation. Be sure to state the equilibrium interest rate.

Answer: a) In order to determine which of the stationary allocations are Pareto optimal, we must find the stationary allocation that maximizes the utility of a consumer. That is, we must solve the problem

$$\max_{x_0 \geq 0,\, x_1 \geq 0} [4x_0^{1/3} + x_1^{1/3}]$$

$$\text{s.t. } x_0 + x_1 \leq 9.$$

The Lagrangian for this problem is

$$\mathcal{L} = 4x_0^{1/3} + x_1^{1/3} - \lambda(x_0 + x_1).$$

Therefore the first order conditions for optimality are

$$\frac{4}{3}x_0^{-2/3} = \lambda$$

$$\frac{1}{3}x_1^{-2/3} = \lambda.$$

It follows that

$$\frac{4x_0^{-2/3}}{x_1^{-2/3}} = 1.$$

Hence

$$4x_1^{2/3} = x_0^{2/3}$$

and so

$$4^{3/2}x_1 = x_0$$

and

$$x_0 = 8x_1.$$

Since

$$x_0 + x_1 = 9,$$

it follows that

$$x_1 = 1 \text{ and } x_0 = 8.$$

The set of Pareto optimal allocations is $\{(x_0, x_1) \in R_+^2 \mid x_0 + x_1 = 9 \text{ and } 0 \leq x_0 \leq 8\}$. It is portrayed in the figure below.

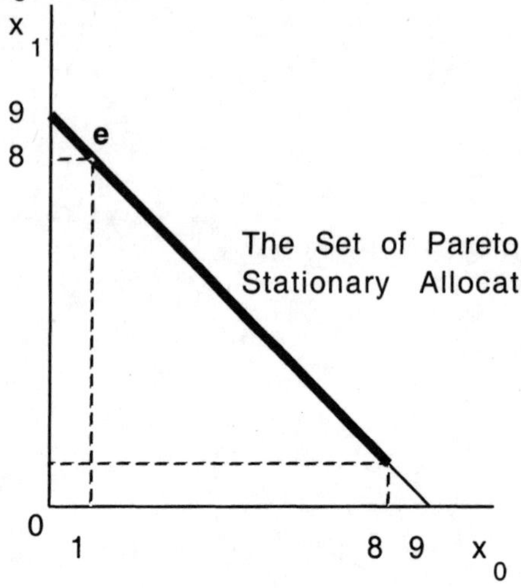

Answer: b) The key difficulty here is to find the appropriate interest rate, r. That interest rate satisfies the equation

$$1 + r = \frac{\frac{\partial u(1, 8)}{\partial x_0}}{\frac{\partial u(1, 8)}{\partial x_1}} = \frac{\frac{4}{3} 1^{-2/3}}{\frac{1}{3} 8^{-2/3}} = 4(8^{2/3}) = 16,$$

so that $r = 15$. Since the allocation is equal to the endowment, the tax and government debt are zero. Therefore the equilibrium is

$$((\bar{x}_0, \bar{x}_1), P, r, G, T) = ((1, 8), 1, 15, 0, 0).$$

Answer to Homework Problems for Chapter 9, Problem #6

Problem: 6) Consider the following one commodity Samuelson model.

$\mathbf{e} = (1, 1)$, $u(x_0, x_1) = \min(3x_0 + x_1, 2x_0 + 5x_1)$.

a) Show the set of feasible stationary allocations in a diagram. Show indifference curves in the diagram.

b) Show in a separate copy of the same diagram which of the feasible stationary allocations is Pareto optimal.

c) Find a stationary spot price equilibrium, $(\overline{x}_0, \overline{x}_1, P, r, G, T)$, in which $P = 1$, where the endowment is the equilibrium allocation.

d) Find a stationary spot price equilibrium, $(\overline{x}_0, \overline{x}_1, P, r, G, T)$, such that $P = 1$ and the stationary allocation $(\overline{x}_0, \overline{x}_1) = (0, 2)$ is the equilibrium allocation.

e) What social welfare function is maximized by the endowment allocation?

Answer: a)

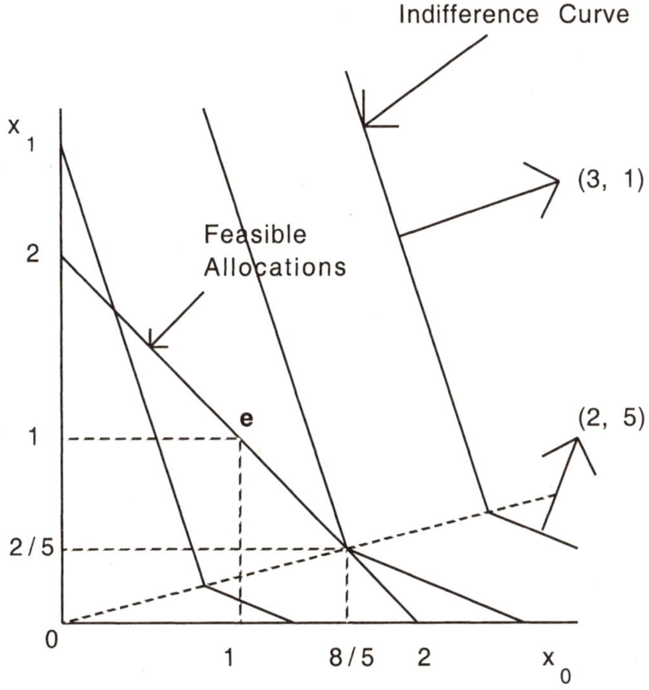

The dotted positively sloped line is the guideline for the indifference curves, where the functions $3x_0 + x_1$ and $2x_0 + 5x_1$ are equal. Setting these two functions equal yields the equation $x_1 = x_0/4$.

Answer: b) The Pareto optimal allocations are shown as a heavy line in the next diagram.

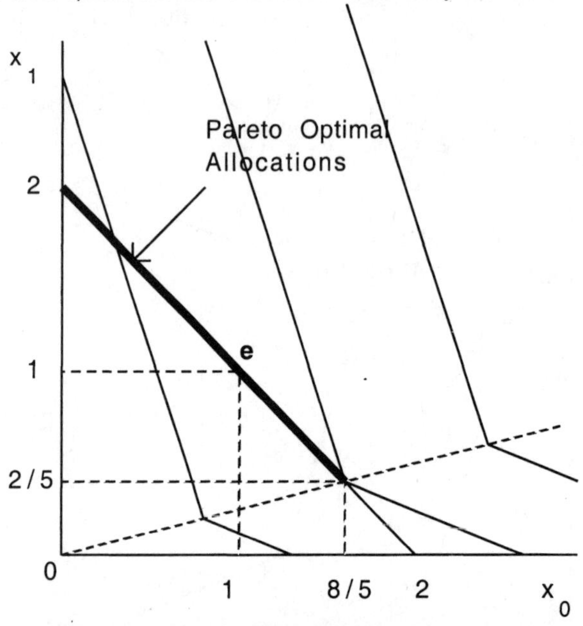

Answer: c) We can see from the above diagram that the endowment lies in the region where the indifference curves are steepest. These steep segments satisfy the equation

$$x_0 + \frac{x_1}{3} = \text{constant.}$$

The equation for a budget line is

$$x_0 + \frac{x_1}{1 + r} = \text{constant.}$$

Since the indifference curves are straight in the region around **e**, this point can be a maximum point in a budget set only if the budget line and indifference curve are parallel there. That is, $1 + r = 3$ or $r = 2$. Once we know r, we know everything. In summary, the equilibrium is

$$((\bar{x}_0, \bar{x}_1), P, r, G, T) = ((1, 1), 1, 2, 0, 0).$$

Answer: d) The interest rate is 2 for the same reason that it was in part c. The government debt is

$$G = \frac{x_1 - e_1}{1 + r} = \frac{2 - 1}{3} = \frac{1}{3},$$

and the tax is

$$T = rG = \frac{2}{3}.$$

In summary, the equilibrium is

$$((\bar{x}_0, \bar{x}_1), P, r, G, T) = ((0, 2), 1, 2, 1/3, 2/3).$$

Answer: e)

$$\min(3 + x_{-1,1}, 2 + 5x_{-1,1}) + \sum_{t=0}^{\infty} 3^{-t}\min(3x_{t0} + x_{t1}, 2x_{t0} + 5x_{t1}).$$

Answer to Homework Problems for Chapter 9, Problem #7

Problem: 7) Consider a Samuelson model with one commodity in each period, where each consumer is endowed with one unit of the commodity in youth and none in old age and has utility function

$$u(x_0, x_1) = \min(2x_0 + x_1, x_0 + 2x_1).$$

Compute all the stationary spot price equilibria, $(\overline{x}_0, \overline{x}_1, P, r, G, T)$, in which $P = r = 1$.

Answer: If we set $2x_0 + x_1$ equal to $x_0 + 2x_1$, we obtain the equation $x_1 = x_0$. It follows that the diagram for this example is as below. The allocations of stationary spot price equilibria with interest rate 1 are shown as a heavy line. If $(x_0, x_1) = (x_0, 1 - x_0)$ is such an allocation, then the corresponding government debt is $G(x_0) = x_1/(1 + r) = (1 - x_0)/2$. Since the interest rate

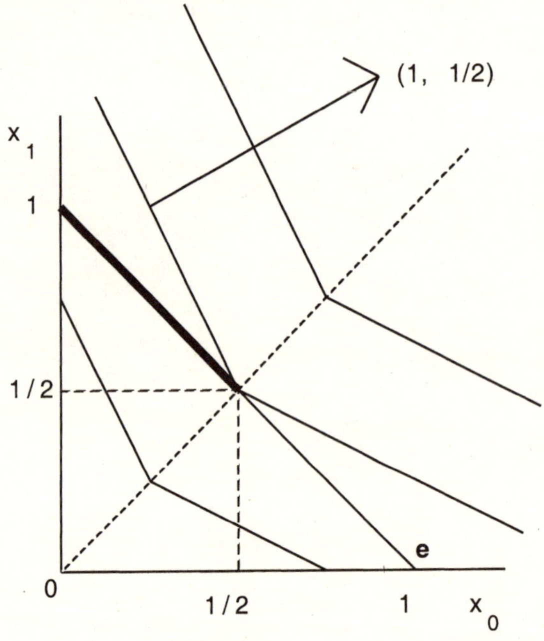

is 1, the tax is the same as the government debt. In summary, the set of stationary spot price equilibria is

$$\{((\overline{x}_0, \overline{x}_1), P, r, G, T) = ((\overline{x}_0, 1 - \overline{x}_0), 1, 1, (1 - \overline{x}_0)/2, (1 - \overline{x}_0)/2) \mid 0 \le \overline{x}_0 \le 1/2\}.$$

Answer to Homework Problems for Chapter 9, Problem #8

Problem: 8) Consider a Samuelson model with two commodities, commodities 1 and 2, respectively, in each period. Each consumer is endowed with one unit of each commodity in youth and none in old age. The utility function of each consumer is

$$u(x_{01}, x_{02}, x_{11}, x_{12}) = 2\ln(x_{01}) + \ln(x_{02}) + \ln(x_{11}) + 2\ln(x_{12}).$$

a) Compute a stationary spot price equilibrium, $(\overline{\mathbf{x}}_0, \overline{\mathbf{x}}_1, \mathbf{P}(r), r, G, T)$, with non-negative interest rate r and with $P_1(r) + P_2(r) = 1$.

b) Does the ratio $P_1(r)/P_2(r)$ increase, decrease, or remain constant as r increases? Give an intuitive explanation for what occurs.

Answer: a) The allocation of a stationary spot price equilibrium satisfies the equations

$$x_{01} + x_{11} = 1$$

$$(1 + r)\frac{\partial u(x_{01}, x_{02}, x_{11}, x_{12})}{\partial x_{11}} = \frac{\partial u(x_{01}, x_{02}, x_{11}, x_{12})}{\partial x_{01}}$$

$$x_{02} + x_{12} = 1$$

$$(1 + r)\frac{\partial u(x_{01}, x_{02}, x_{11}, x_{12})}{\partial x_{12}} = \frac{\partial u(x_{01}, x_{02}, x_{11}, x_{12})}{\partial x_{02}}.$$

The second equation becomes

$$\frac{1 + r}{x_{11}} = \frac{2}{x_{01}},$$

so that

$$x_{11} = \frac{1 + r}{2}x_{01}.$$

On substituting this equation into the first, we obtain

$$x_{01} = \frac{2}{3 + r},$$

so that

$$x_{11} = 1 - x_{01} = \frac{1 + r}{3 + r}.$$

Proceeding in the same way with the allocation for the second commodity, we find that

$$x_{02} = \frac{1}{3 + 2r}, \; x_{12} = \frac{2(1 + r)}{3 + 2r}.$$

The ratio of the two prices is

$$\frac{P_1}{P_2} = \frac{\dfrac{\partial u(x_{01}, x_{02}, x_{11}, x_{12})}{\partial x_{01}}}{\dfrac{\partial u(x_{01}, x_{02}, x_{11}, x_{12})}{\partial x_{02}}} = \frac{\dfrac{2}{x_{01}}}{\dfrac{1}{x_{02}}} = \frac{2x_{02}}{x_{01}}.$$

Therefore

$$\frac{P_1}{P_2} = \frac{\dfrac{2}{3 + 2r}}{\dfrac{2}{3 + r}} = \frac{3 + r}{3 + 2r},$$

and hence

$$P_1 = \frac{3 + r}{3 + 2r} P_2 = \frac{3 + r}{3 + 2r}(1 - P_1).$$

Solving this equation, we find that

$$P_1 = \frac{3 + r}{3(2 + r)}, \; P_2 = \frac{3 + 2r}{3(2 + r)}.$$

Government debt satisfies the equation

$$(1 + r)G = P_1 x_{11} + P_2 x_{12} = \left(\frac{3 + r}{3(2 + r)}\right)\left(\frac{1 + r}{3 + r}\right) + \left(\frac{3 + 2r}{3(2 + r)}\right)\left(\frac{2(1 + r)}{3 + r}\right) = \frac{1 + r}{2 + r}.$$

Hence

$$G = \frac{1}{2 + r}.$$

The tax is then

$$T = rG = \frac{r}{1 + r}.$$

In summary, the equilibrium is

$$((\bar{x}_0, \bar{x}_1), (P_1(r), P_2(r)), r, G, T) = \left(\left(\left(\frac{2}{3 + r}, \frac{1}{3 + r}\right), \left(\frac{1 + r}{3 + r}, \frac{2(1 + r)}{3 + 2r}\right)\right),\right.$$

$$\left.\left(\frac{3 + r}{3(2 + r)}, \frac{3 + 2r}{3(2 + r)}\right), r, \frac{1}{2 + r}, \frac{r}{2 + r}\right).$$

Answer: b)

$$\frac{P_1(r)}{P_2(r)} = \frac{\dfrac{3 + r}{3(2 + r)}}{\dfrac{3 + 2r}{3(2 + r)}} = \frac{3 + r}{3 + 2r}.$$

$$\frac{d}{dr}\left(\frac{P_1(r)}{P_2(r)}\right) = \frac{d}{dr}\left(\frac{3 + r}{3 + 2r}\right) = -\frac{3}{(3 + 2r)^2} < 0.$$

The ratio decrease. As r increases, the old become relatively wealthier compared to the young. Since the old value commodity 2 relative to commodity 1 more highly than do the young, the price of commodity 2 rises relative to that of commodity 1 as the old become relatively wealthier with the increase in r.

Answer to Homework Problems for Chapter 9, Problem #9

Problem: 9) We know that the allocation of a stationary spot price equilibrium in the Samuelson model is Pareto optimal if its sequence of equilibrium prices is summable when discounted to period 0 at market interest rates. This fact might lead you to suspect that stationary equilibrium allocations would be Pareto optimal if some asset were present that yielded a fixed positive return indefinitely, for then the price of the asset would be finite and equal to the discounted present value of its future returns. The following problem tests this idea.

Consider a Samuelson model with one commodity in every period and where each consumer has endowment $(e_0, e_1) \in R^2_+$ and utility function $u: R^2_+ \to R$. Suppose that there is an asset that yields i units of the single commodity in every period, where $i > 0$. This problem concerns stationary equilibria, $(\overline{x}_0, \overline{x}_1, P, r, G, T)$, for this model, where $P = 1$ and $G = T = 0$. The feasibility condition for the model is

$$\overline{x}_0 + \overline{x}_1 \leq e_0 + e_1 + i. \tag{9.112}$$

Assume that $P = 1$ and $T = 0$, so that there are no taxes and the budget constraint is

$$\overline{x}_0 + \frac{\overline{x}_1}{1 + r} \leq e_0 + \frac{e_1}{1 + r}. \tag{9.113}$$

Assume that the utility function is strictly increasing and that $e_1 = 0$. Because $e_1 = 0$, the young cannot have negative savings. That is, they cannot borrow against future income. They can only invest, lend, or buy land.

a) Show that if a stationary equilibrium with no taxes exists, then its interest rate is positive, so that its allocation is Pareto optimal.

b) Calculate a stationary spot price equilibrium with no taxes when

$$u(x_0, x_1) = \ln(x_0) + \ln(x_1) \text{ and } e_0 = 1.$$

The equilibrium will depend on the asset yield i.

c) Make a drawing showing the set of feasible stationary allocations and the budget set of a consumer in a stationary equilibrium with no taxes and when $e_0 = i = 1$.

d) Prove that if $e_0 = 0$, then no stationary spot price equilibrium without taxes exists.

Answer: a) Since the utility function is increasing, the budget constraint holds with equality. Since $e_1 = 0$, it follows that

$$\overline{x}_0 + \frac{\overline{x}_1}{1 + r} = e_0 + e_1 = e_0 .$$

Hence

$$\overline{x}_1 = (1 + r)(e_0 - \overline{x}_0). \qquad (A)$$

Because $-1 < r < \infty$, $(1 + r)^{-1} > 0$, so that

$$e_0 - \overline{x}_0 = \frac{\overline{x}_1}{1 + r} \geq 0 .$$

Because the $P = 1 > 0$, the feasibility inequality holds with equality, so that

$$\overline{x}_0 + \overline{x}_1 = e_0 + i.$$

If we substitute equation (A) into this equation and cancel like terms, we obtain the equation

$$r(e_0 - \overline{x}_0) = i.$$

Since $i > 0$ and $e_0 - \overline{x}_0 \geq 0$, it follows that $r > 0$.

Since the utility function is strictly increasing, it is locally non-satiated with respect to x_0 and x_1 separately. Hence corollary 9.15 (in section 9.3) implies that the stationary equilibrium allocation is Pareto optimal if $r > 0$.

Answer: b) The equations that determine the equilibrium allocation are

$$x_0 + x_1 = e_0 + e_1 + i$$

$$(1 + r)\frac{\partial u(x_0, x_1)}{\partial x_1} = \frac{\partial u(x_0, x_1)}{\partial x_0}.$$

On substituting the actual values for the endowment and utility function, these equations become

$$x_0 + x_1 = 1 + i$$

$$\frac{1 + r}{x_1} = \frac{1}{x_0}.$$

Hence

$$x_1 = (1 + r)x_0$$

and so

$$x_0 = \frac{1 + i}{2 + r} \text{ and } x_1 = \frac{(1 + r)(1 + i)}{2 + r}.$$

On substituting these equations into the budget equation

$$x_0 + \frac{x_1}{1 + r} = 1,$$

we obtain

$$\frac{1 + i}{2 + r} + \frac{1 + i}{2 + r} = 1,$$

so that $r = 2i$. Hence

$$x_0 = \frac{1}{2} \text{ and } x_1 = \frac{1 + 2i}{2}.$$

In summary, the equilibrium is

$$((\bar{x}_0, \bar{x}_1), P, r, G, T) = \left(\left(\frac{1}{2}, \frac{1 + 2i}{2}\right), 1, 2i, 0, 0\right).$$

<u>Answer</u>: c) If $i = 1$, then $\bar{x}_0 = 1/2$, $\bar{x}_1 = 3/2$, and $r = 2$. The appropriate diagram is below. The heavy line is the set of feasible stationary allocations. The shaded triangle is the budget set. The point $\bar{\mathbf{x}} = (1/2, 3/2)$ is the equilibrium allocation. The endowment is inside the feasibility line because of the earnings of $i = 1$ from the asset.

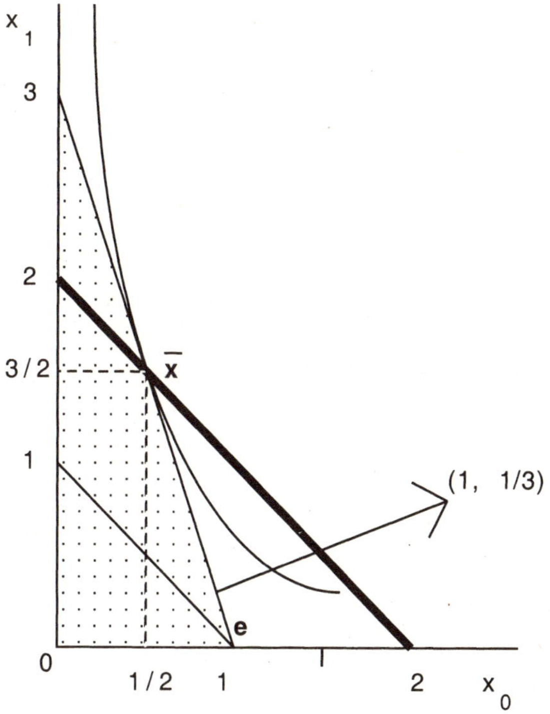

Answer: d) Since $e_0 = e_1 = 0$, the budget constraint is

$$x_0 + \frac{x_1}{1 + r} \leq 0.$$

Since $x_0 \geq 0$, $x_1 \geq 0$, and $(1 + r)^{-1} > 0$, it follows that $x_0 = x_1 = 0$. Since i units of the commodity are available in every period and i > 0, there is excess supply, and so the price P must be 0. Since the price of the single commodity cannot be 0 in equilibrium, there exists no equilibrium.

Answer to Homework Problems for Chapter 10, Problem #1

Problem: 1) Consider the Diamond model with utility function

$$u(x_0, x_1) = \ln(1+x_0) + \ln(1+x_1)$$

and with production function

$$f(K_t, L_{t+1}) = \sqrt{L_t K_{t-1}},$$

for all time periods t. (Recall that the supply of labor equals 1 in the Diamond model.)

a) What is the set of feasible stationary allocations?

b) Which of these are Pareto optimal?

c) Find a stationary spot price equilibrium, $(\overline{x}_0, \overline{x}_1, \overline{K}, \overline{L}, P, W, r, G, T)$, with $T = 0$.

d) Is the allocation of this equilibrium Pareto optimal?

e) Find the stationary spot price equilibrium, $(\overline{x}_0, \overline{x}_1, \overline{K}, \overline{L}, P, W, r, G, T)$, with $P = 1$ and such that its allocation maximizes the social welfare function

$$(1.1)\,u(x_{-1,0}, x_{-1,1}) + \sum_{t=0}^{\infty} (1.1)^{-t} u(x_{t0}, x_{t1})$$

among feasible allocations, where $x_{-1,0}$ and K_{-1} are given. Notice that you have to choose $x_{-1,0}$ and K_{-1}, so that the equilibrium is stationary. Is the allocation of this equilibrium Pareto optimal?

f) Answer question (e) with the social welfare function equal to

$$2u(x_{-1,0}, x_{-1,1}) + \sum_{t=0}^{\infty} 2^{-t} u(x_{t0}, x_{t1}).$$

Compare the capital stocks in problems e and f. Which is bigger?

Answer: a) Since $x_0 + x_1 + K = \sqrt{K}$ and $x_0 + x_1 \geq 0$, it follows that $K \leq \sqrt{K}$ and so $0 \leq K \leq 1$. Therefore the set of feasible stationary allocations is

$$\{(x_0, x_1, K, L) \mid x_0 \geq 0,\ x_1 \geq 0,\ 0 \leq K \leq 1,\ L = 1,\ x_0 + x_1 \leq \sqrt{K} - K\}.$$

Answer: b) The stationary allocations which are Pareto optimal are those that are the allocations of stationary spot price equilibria with non-negative interest rates. I calculate these. By profit maximization

$$1 + r = \frac{\partial}{\partial K}\sqrt{K} = \frac{1}{2\sqrt{K}},$$

so that output, y, is

$$y = \sqrt{K} = \frac{1}{2(1 + r)}.$$

Hence

$$K = \frac{1}{4(1 + r)^2}.$$

By feasibility,

$$x_0 + x_1 = y - K = \frac{1}{2(1 + r)} - \frac{1}{4(1 + r)^2} = \frac{2(1 + r) - 1}{4(1 + r)^2} = \frac{1 + 2r}{4(1 + r)^2}.$$

Utility maximization subject to the budget constraint implies that

$$(1 + r)\frac{\partial u(x_0, x_1)}{\partial x_1} = \frac{\partial u(x_0, x_1)}{\partial x_0},$$

which means that

$$\frac{1 + r}{1 + x_1} = \frac{1}{1 + x_0}$$

and so

$$(1 + r)(1 + x_0) = 1 + x_1$$

and hence

$$x_1 = r + (1 + r)x_0.$$

It follows that

$$(2 + r)x_0 + r = x_0 + (1 + r)x_0 + r = x_0 + x_1 = y - K = \frac{1 + 2r}{4(1 + r)^2}$$

and so

$$(2 + r)x_0 = \frac{1 + 2r}{4(1 + r)^2} - r = \frac{1 + 2r - 4r(1 + 2r + r^2)}{4(1 + r)^2} = \frac{1 + 2r - 4r - 8r^2 - 4r^3}{4(1 + r)^2}$$

$$= \frac{1 - 2r - 8r^2 - 4r^3}{4(1 + r)^2}.$$

Therefore

$$x_0 = \frac{1 - 2r - 8r^2 - 4r^3}{4(1 + r)^2(2 + r)},$$

and so

$$1 + x_0 = \frac{1 - 2r - 8r^2 - 4r^3 + 4(1 + 2r + r^2)(2 + r)}{4(1 + r)^2(2 + r)}$$

$$= \frac{1 - 2r - 8r^2 - 4r^3 + 8 + 4r + 16r + 8r^2 + 8r^2 + 4r^3}{4(1 + r)^2(2 + r)}$$

$$= \frac{9 + 18r + 8r^2}{4(1 + r)^2(2 + r)},$$

and hence

$$x_1 = (1 + r)(1 + x_0) - 1 = \frac{9 + 18r + 8r^2}{4(1 + r)(2 + r)} - 1$$

$$= \frac{9 + 18r + 8r^2 - 8 - 12r - 4r^2}{4(1 + r)(2 + r)} = \frac{1 + 6r + 4r^2}{4(1 + r)(2 + r)},$$

provided $x_0 > 0$. If $x_0 = 0$, then

$$x_1 = y - K = \frac{1 + 2r}{4(1 + r)^2}.$$

Let $\bar{r}$ be such that

$$1 - 2\bar{r} - 8\bar{r}^2 - 4\bar{r}^3 = 0.$$

Then $\bar{r} \cong 0.247491$, and $x_0 > 0$ if $0 \le r \le \bar{r}$.

In summary, the set of Pareto optimal allocations is

$$\left\{(x_0, x_1, K, L) = \left(\frac{1 - 2r - 8r^2 - 4r^3}{4(1+r)^2(2+r)}, \frac{1 + 6r + 4r^2}{4(1+r)(2+r)}, \frac{1}{4(1+r)^2}, 1\right) \middle| \, 0 \le r \le \bar{r}\right\}$$

$$\cup \left\{(x_0, x_1, K, L) = \left(0, \frac{1 + 2r}{4(1+r)^2}, \frac{1}{4(1+r)^2}, 1\right) \middle| \, r \ge \bar{r}\right\}.$$

Answer: c, d) In order to calculate stationary spot price equilibria, we need formulas for the wage, government debt, and tax. The wage is

$$W = \frac{\partial}{\partial L}\sqrt{KL}\Big|_{L=1} = \frac{\sqrt{K}}{2}.$$

Substituting for $\sqrt{K}$, we obtain

$$W = \frac{1}{4(1+r)}.$$

Government debt, G, satisfies the equation

$$(1+r)(G+K) = x_1,$$

so that

$$G = \frac{x_1}{1+r} - K = \frac{x_1}{1+r} - \frac{1}{4(1+r)^2}.$$

The tax is simply

$$T = rG$$

or

$$T = W - x_0 - \frac{x_1}{1+r}.$$

One stationary spot price equilibrium with no taxes is that with $r = 0$. This equilibrium is

$$((\bar{x}_0, \bar{x}_1, \bar{K}, \bar{L}), P, W, r, G, T) = ((1/8, 1/8, 1/4, 1), 1, 1/4, 0, -1/8, 0).$$

The allocation of this equilibrium is Pareto optimal.

Another possibility is to calculate an equilibrium with $0 \leq r \leq \bar{r}$. To do so, I use the second equation above for the tax.

$$T = W - \left(x_0 + \frac{x_1}{1+r}\right) = \frac{1}{4(1+r)} - \frac{1 - 2r - 8r^2 - 4r^3 + 1 + 6r + 4r^2}{4(1+r)^2(2+r)}$$

$$= \frac{1}{4(1+r)} - \frac{2 + 4r - 4r^2 - 4r^3}{4(1+r)^2(2+r)} = \frac{2 + 3r + r^2 - 2 - 4r + 4r^2 + 4r^3}{4(1+r)^2(2+r)}$$

$$= \frac{-r + 5r^2 + 4r^3}{4(1+r)^2(2+r)} = \frac{r(4r^2 + 5r - 1)}{4(1+r)^2(2+r)}.$$

The tax is zero when $r = 0$ or when

$$r = \underline{r} = \frac{-5 + \sqrt{41}}{8} \cong 0.17539.$$

The other root is

$$r = \frac{-5 - \sqrt{41}}{8} \cong -1.425,$$

which is less than -1 and so is not a valid interest rate. Since the tax is zero and the interest rate is positive and we know that $T = rG$, it must be that $G = 0$. Since $0 < \underline{r} < \bar{r}$, we know that $x_0 > 0$ and we should use the corresponding formula for x_1. In summary, the stationary equilibrium is

$$((\bar{x}_0, \bar{x}_1, \bar{K}, \bar{L}), P, W, r, G, T)$$

$$= \left(\left(\frac{1 - 2\underline{r} - 8\underline{r}^2 - 4\underline{r}^3}{4(1+\underline{r})^2(2+\underline{r})}, \frac{1 + 6\underline{r} + 4\underline{r}^2}{4(1+\underline{r})^2(2+\underline{r})}, \frac{1}{4(1+\underline{r})^2}, 1\right),\right.$$

$$\left. 1, \frac{1}{4(1+\underline{r})}, \underline{r}, 0, 0\right).$$

The allocation of this equilibrium is Pareto optimal, because the interest rate is positive.

Another possibility is for there to be an equilibrium without tax when $r > \bar{r}$. In this case, the interest rate would be positive, so that an equilibrium without tax would also be one without government debt. The debt equals

$$G = \frac{x_1}{1+r} - K = \frac{1+2r}{4(1+r)^3} - \frac{1}{4(1+r)^2} = \frac{1+2r-1-r}{4(1+r)^3} = \frac{r}{4(1+r)^3},$$

so that G can be zero only if r = 0 and hence less than $\bar{r}$. It follows that there is no stationary spot price equilibrium with no tax and interest rate exceeding $\bar{r}$.

Answer: e) Because $0.1 < \bar{r}$, we can use the formulas from part a to calculate the allocation of the stationary spot price equilibrium. The formulas for the other parts of the equilibrium have already been given. Therefore, when r = 0.1

$$x_0 = \frac{1-2r-8r^2-4r^3}{4(1+r)^2(2+r)} \cong 0.07044.$$

$$x_1 = \frac{1+6r+4r^2}{4(1+r)(2+r)} \cong 0.17749.$$

$$K = \frac{1}{4(1+r)^2} = \frac{1}{4.84} \cong 0.20661.$$

$$W = \frac{1}{4(1+r)} \cong 0.22727.$$

$$T = \frac{r(4r^2+5r-1)}{4(1+r)^2(2+r)} \cong 0.004526.$$

$$G = \frac{T}{r} \cong 0.04526.$$

In summary, the equilibrium is

$$((\bar{x}_0, \bar{x}_1, \bar{K}, \bar{L}), P, W, r, G, T) = ((0.07044,\ 0.17749,\ 0.20661,\ 1), 1,$$

$$0.22727,\ 0.1,\ 0.04526,\ 0.004526).$$

The allocation of this equilibrium is Pareto optimal, because it maximizes a welfare function that gives a positive weight to every consumer's utility.

Answer: f) The interest rate is now 1, which exceeds $\bar{r}$, so that $x_0 = 0$, and $x_1 = y - K$. The equilibrium variables may be calculated as follows.

$$x_0 = 0.$$

$$x_1 = \frac{1 + 2r}{4(1 + r)^2} = \frac{3}{16}.$$

$$K = \frac{1}{4(1 + r)^2} = \frac{1}{16}.$$

$$W = \frac{1}{4(1 + r)} = \frac{1}{8}.$$

$$T = \frac{r(4r^2 + 5r - 1)}{4(1 + r)^2(2 + r)} = \frac{1}{6}.$$

$$G = T = \frac{1}{6}.$$

In summary, the equilibrium is

$$((\bar{x}_0, \bar{x}_1, \bar{K}, \bar{L}), P, W, r, G, T) = ((0, 3/16, 1/16, 1), 1, 1/8, 1, 1/6, 1/6).$$

The allocation of this equilibrium is Pareto optimal, because it maximizes a welfare function that gives a positive weight to every consumer's utility.

Answer: g) The capital stock when $r = 0.1$ is 0.20661, which is greater than $0.625 = 1/16$, which is the capital stock when $r = 1$. Therefore the capital stock of part e is larger than that of part f.

Answer to Homework Problems for Chapter 10, Problem #2

Problem: 2) Consider a Diamond model with the price of the produced good equal to one, when the production function is

$$f(K, L) = 2\sqrt{KL}$$

and the utility function of each consumer is

$$u(x_0, x_1) = 2\ln(x_0) + \ln(x_1).$$

Remember that the only endowment consumers have is one unit of labor in youth.

a) Compute a stationary spot price equilibrium

$$(x_0(r), x_1(r), K(r), L(r), P, W(r), r, G(r), T(r)),$$

where $P = 1$ and $r > -1$.

b) Graph the function $T(r)$.

c) How many values of r satisfy the equation

$$T(r) = -\frac{1}{32}?$$

d) Over what range of values of r is the utility of a typical consumer increasing in r and over what range is the utility of a typical consumer decreasing in r?

e) For what values of r is the equilibrium allocation Pareto optimal?

f) Suppose that the lump-sum tax is maintained at level $T(\bar{r})$ and that an infinitesimal amount of pay-as-you-go social security is introduced. Social security changes the equilibrium interest rate to r. Will r exceed $\bar{r}$ or be less than $\bar{r}$, when

i) $\bar{r} = 0$,

ii) $\bar{r} = 2$?

Answer: a) The equation

$$\frac{\partial f(K, 1)}{\partial K} = 1 + r$$

becomes

$$\sqrt{\frac{1}{K}} = 1 + r,$$

so that

$$K = \frac{1}{(1 + r)^2}$$

and total output is

$$y = f(K, 1) = 2\sqrt{\frac{1}{(1 + r)^2}} = \frac{2}{1 + r}.$$

Output net of capital input is

$$y - K = \frac{2}{1 + r} - \frac{1}{(1 + r)^2} = \frac{2(1 + r) - 1}{(1 + r)^2} = \frac{1 + 2r}{(1 + r)^2}.$$

The equation

$$(1 + r)\frac{\partial u(x_0, x_1)}{\partial x_1} = \frac{\partial u(x_0, x_1)}{\partial x_0}$$

becomes

$$\frac{1 + r}{x_1} = \frac{2}{x_0},$$

so that

$$x_1 = \frac{1 + r}{2}x_0.$$

On substitution into the feasibility equation,

$$x_0 + x_1 = y - K,$$

we obtain

$$x_0 + \frac{1 + r}{2}x_0 = \frac{1 + 2r}{(1 + r)^2},$$

so that

$$\frac{3 + r}{2} x_0 = \frac{1 + 2r}{(1 + r)^2}$$

and hence

$$x_0 = \frac{2(1 + 2r)}{(3 + r)(1 + r)^2},$$

and

$$x_1 = \frac{1 + r}{2} x_0 + \frac{1 + 2r}{(3 + r)(1 + r)}.$$

Since $P = 1$,

$$W = \frac{\partial f(K, 1)}{\partial L} = \sqrt{K} = \frac{1}{1 + r}.$$

The government debt is

$$G = \frac{x_1}{1 + r} - K = \frac{1 + 2r}{(3 + r)(1 + r)^2} - \frac{1}{(1 + r)^2} = \frac{1 + 2r - 3 - r}{(3 + r)(1 + r)^2}$$

$$= \frac{-2 + r}{(3 + r)(1 + r)^2}.$$

The tax is

$$T = rG = \frac{r(-2 + r)}{(3 + r)(1 + r)^2}.$$

In summary, the equilibrium is

$$((x_0(r), x_1(r), K(r)), L(r), P, W(r), r, G(r), T(r))$$

$$= \left(\left(\frac{2(1 + 2r)}{(3 + r)(1 + r)^2}, \frac{1 + 2r}{(3 + r)(1 + r)}, \frac{1}{(1 + r)^2}, 1\right), 1, \frac{1}{1 + r}, r,\right.$$

$$\left.\frac{-2 + r}{(3 + r)(1 + r)^2}, \frac{r(-2 + r)}{(3 + r)(1 + r)^2}\right),$$

if $r > -1/2$. If $-1 < r \leq -1/2$, then there is no meaningful equilibrium, for output net of capital, $y - K$, is less than or equal to 0.

Answer: b)

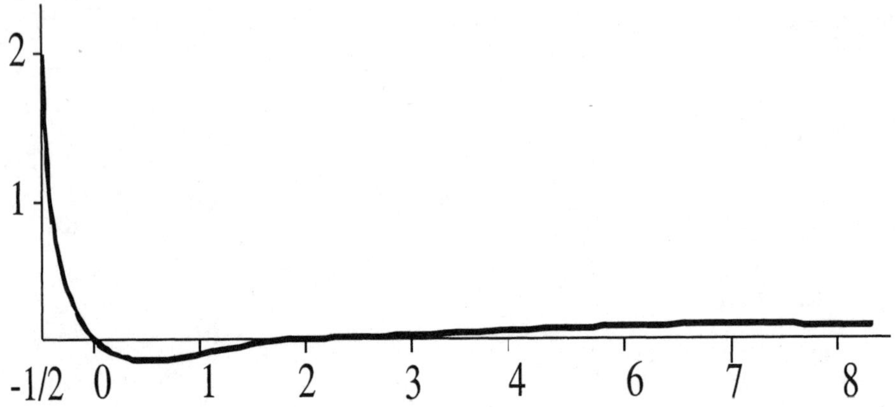

Answer: c) Two. They are $r = 0.0545673$ and $r = 1.428625$.

Answer: d) The utility of a consumer is

$$2\ln\left(\frac{2(1+2r)}{(3+r)(1+r)^2}\right) + \ln\left(\frac{1+2r}{(3+r)(1+r)}\right)$$

$$= \ln(4) + \ln\left(\frac{(1+2r)^3}{(3+r)^2(1+r)^5}\right)$$

$$= \ln(4) + 3\ln(1+2r) - 3\ln(3+r) - 5\ln(1+r).$$

The derivative of this function with respect to r is

$$\frac{6}{1+2r} - \frac{3}{3+r} - \frac{5}{1+r} = -\frac{10r(2+r)}{(1+2r)(3+r)(1+r)}.$$

It follows that the utility of a consumer is increasing if $-1/2 < r < 0$ and is decreasing if $r > 0$. It reaches a maximum at $r = 0$.

Answer: e) For $r \geq 0$.

Answer: f) We know that

$$T(r) = \frac{r(-2 + r)}{(3 + r)(1 + r)^2},$$

so that

$$\frac{dT(\bar{r})}{dr} = \frac{-\bar{r}^4 + 4\bar{r}^3 + 17\bar{r}^2 + 6\bar{r} - 6}{(3 + \bar{r})^2(1 + \bar{r})^4}.$$

The sign of $\frac{dT(\bar{r})}{dr}$ is the same as that of its numerator.

(i) If $\bar{r} = 0$, $\frac{dr}{dT_0} = \left(\frac{dT(\bar{r})}{dr}\right)^{-1} \frac{\bar{r}}{1 + \bar{r}} = 0$, so that r does not change.

(ii) If $\bar{r} = 2$, the numerator of $\frac{dT(\bar{r})}{dr}$ is $90 > 0$, so that $r > \bar{r}$.

Answer to Homework Problems for Chapter 10, Problem #3

Problem: 3) Consider the Diamond model with utility function

$$u(x_0, x_1) = \ln(x_0) + \ln(x_1)$$

and production function is

$$f(K, L) = 4K^{1/4}L^{3/4}.$$

a) Compute a spot price equilibrium,

$$(x_0(r), x_1(r), K(r), L(r), P, W(r), r, G(r), T(r)),$$

when $r \geq 0$ and $P = 1$.

b) What is the stationary equilibrium interest rate when the lump-sum tax on youth, T, equals 0.15? What are the levels of capital and of consumption in youth and old age?

c) Suppose that a social security program is introduced that taxes youth 0.1 and pays a benefit of 0.1 to the old. The lump-sum tax of 0.15 on youth is continued after the social security is introduced, so that youths pay 0.25 in total taxes. What is the stationary equilibrium interest rate? What are the levels of capital and consumption in youth and old age?

d) Suppose that when the social security program of part (c) is introduced, the lump-sum tax of 0.15 paid by youth is changed to a new level, T, so that the introduction of social security does not change the interest rate. What is this new level of the lump-sum tax?

Answer: a) The equation

$$\frac{\partial f(K, 1)}{\partial K} = 1 + r$$

becomes

$$K^{-3/4} = 1 + r,$$

so that

$$K = (1 + r)^{-4/3}$$

and total output is

$$y = 4(1 + r)^{-1/3}.$$

Output net of capital input is

$$y - K = \frac{4}{(1 + r)^{1/3}} - \frac{1}{(1 + r)^{4/3}} = \frac{3 + 4r}{(1 + r)^{4/3}}.$$

The equation

$$(1 + r)\frac{\partial u(x_0, x_1)}{\partial x_1} = \frac{\partial u(x_0, x_1)}{\partial x_0}$$

becomes

$$\frac{1 + r}{x_1} = \frac{1}{x_0},$$

so that

$$x_1 = (1 + r)x_0.$$

The feasibility equation

$$x_0 + x_1 = y - K$$

becomes

$$(2 + r)x_0 = \frac{3 + 4r}{(1 + r)^{4/3}},$$

so that

$$x_0 = \frac{3 + 4r}{(2 + r)(1 + r)^{4/3}}$$

and

$$x_1 = \frac{3 + 4r}{(2 + r)(1 + r)^{1/3}}.$$

It follows that government debt is

$$G = \frac{x_1}{1 + r} - K = \frac{3 + 4r}{(2 + r)(1 + r)^{4/3}} - \frac{1}{(1 + r)^{4/3}} = \frac{1 + 3r}{(2 + r)(1 + r)^{4/3}}.$$

The tax is

$$T = \frac{r(1 + 3r)}{(2 + r)(1 + r)^{4/3}}.$$

The wage is

$$W = 3K^{1/4} = \frac{3}{(1 + r)^{1/3}}.$$

In summary, the equilibrium is

$$((x_0(r), x_1(r), K(r)), L(r), P, W(r), r, G(r), T(r))$$

$$= \left(\left(\frac{3 + 4r}{(2 + r)(1 + r)^{4/3}}, \frac{3 + 4r}{(2 + r)(1 + r)^{1/3}}, \frac{1}{(1 + r)^{4/3}}, 1\right), 1, \frac{3}{(1 + r)^{1/3}}, r,\right.$$

$$\left.\frac{1 + 3r}{(2 + r)(1 + r)^{4/3}}, \frac{r(1 + 3r)}{(2 + r)(1 + r)^{4/3}}\right).$$

<u>Answer</u>: b)

$r = 0.25922.$

$K = 0.735413.$

$x_0 = 1.31407.$

$x_1 = 1.654703.$

<u>Answer</u>: c) The equation to be solved for r is $T(r) = 0.25 - 0.1/(1 + r)$, where

$$T(r) = \frac{r(1 + 3r)}{(2 + r)(1 + r)^{4/3}}.$$

The solution of this equation is $r = 0.297068$. At this interest rate,

$K = 0.706941,$

$x_0 = 1.288974.$

$x_1 = 1.671886.$

Answer: d) The new tax level is

$$T = 0.15 - 0.1 + \frac{0.1}{1.25922} = 0.1294142406.$$

(The calculations of this problem can be done with a hand held calculator or an Excel spread sheet.)

Answer to Homework Problems for Chapter 10, Problem #4

Problem: 4) Consider the Diamond model with

$$u(x_0, x_1) = \ln(x_0) + \ln(x_1)$$

and $f(K, L) = \dfrac{4KL}{K + L}$.

a) Compute the stationary spot price equilibrium,

$$(x_0(r), x_1(r), K(r), L(r), P, W(r), r, G(r), T(r)),$$

with $P = 1$ and for those non-negative interest rates, r, for which the stationary capital stock exists and is positive. For which interest rates is the stationary equilibrium capital stock defined and positive?

b) Compute the equilibrium for $r = 1$.

c) Suppose the economy is in a stationary spot price equilibrium with a non-negative interest rate for which the capital stock is positive and that a small amount of pay-as-you-go social security, (T_0, T_1), is introduced. Will the new stationary capital stock be higher or lower? Does the answer depend on the interest rate?

Answer: a) The equation

$$\frac{\partial f(K, 1)}{\partial K} = 1 + r$$

becomes

$$1 + r = 4\frac{d}{dK}\left(\frac{K}{K + 1}\right) = 4\left(\frac{K + 1 - K}{(K + 1)^2}\right) = \frac{4}{(K + 1)^2},$$

so that

$$K = \frac{2}{\sqrt{1 + r}} - 1 = \frac{2\sqrt{1 + r}}{1 + r} - 1.$$

The capital stock is positive if

$$K = \frac{2}{\sqrt{1 + r}} - 1 > 0,$$

Which occurs if $r < 3$.

Output is

$$y = 4\left(\frac{\dfrac{2-\sqrt{1+r}}{\sqrt{1+r}}}{\dfrac{2}{\sqrt{1+r}}}\right) = 4\left(\frac{2-\sqrt{1+r}}{2}\right) = 4 - 2\sqrt{1+r}.$$

Output net of capital input is

$$y - K = 4 - 2\sqrt{1+r} - \frac{2\sqrt{1+r}}{1 = r} + 1 = 5 - \frac{2(2+r)\sqrt{1+r}}{1+r}.$$

The stationary capital stock is well-defined if output net of capital is nonnegative. This occurs if

$$y - K = 5 - \frac{2(2+r)}{\sqrt{1+r}} \geq 0,$$

which is the same as

$$5\sqrt{1+r} \geq 2(2+r),$$

that is,

$$25(1+r) \geq 4(4 + 4r + r^2) = 16 + 16r + 4r^2.$$

This inequality is the same as

$$4r^2 - 9r - 9 \leq 0.$$

The roots of the equation

$$4r^2 - 9r - 9 = 0$$

are 3 and $-3/4$, so that K is well-defined and positive if and only if

$$-3/4 \leq r < 3.$$

The equation

$$(1+r)\frac{\partial u(x_0, x_1)}{\partial x_1} = \frac{\partial u(x_0, x_1)}{\partial x_0}$$

becomes

$$\frac{1+r}{x_1} = \frac{1}{x_0},$$

so that

$$x_1 = (1+r)x_0.$$

Therefore

$$(2+r)x_0 = x_0 + x_1 = y - K = 5 - 2\left(\frac{2+r}{\sqrt{1+r}}\right),$$

so that

$$x_0 = \frac{5}{2+r} - \frac{2\sqrt{1+r}}{1+r}$$

and

$$x_1 = \frac{5(1+r)}{2+r} - 2\sqrt{1+r}.$$

$$G = \frac{x_1}{1+r} - K = x_0 - K = \frac{7+r}{2+r} - \frac{4\sqrt{1+r}}{1+r}$$

and so

$$T = rG = \frac{r(7+r)}{2+r} - \frac{4r\sqrt{1+r}}{1+r}.$$

The wage is

$$W = \frac{\partial}{\partial L}\left(\frac{4KL}{K+L}\right)\Bigg|_{L=1} = 5 + r - 4\sqrt{1+r}.$$

In summary, the equilibrium is

$$((x_0(r), x_1(r), K(r)), L(r), P, W(r), r, G(r), T(r))$$

$$= \left(\left(\frac{5}{2+r} - \frac{2\sqrt{1+r}}{1+r}, \frac{5(1+r)}{2+r} - 2\sqrt{1+r}, \frac{2\sqrt{1+r}}{1+r} - 1, 1\right),\right.$$

$$\left. 1, 5 + r - 4\sqrt{1+r}, r, \frac{7+r}{2+r} - \frac{4\sqrt{1+r}}{1+r}, \frac{r(7+r)}{2+r} - \frac{4r\sqrt{1+r}}{1+r}\right)$$

<u>Answer</u>: b) $((x_0(1), x_1(1), K(1)), L(1), P, W(1), 1, G(1), T(1))$

$$= \left(\left(\frac{5}{3} - \sqrt{2}, \frac{10}{3} - 2\sqrt{2}, \sqrt{2} - 1, 1\right), 1, 6 - 4\sqrt{2}, \frac{8}{3} - 2\sqrt{2}, \frac{8}{3} - 2\sqrt{2}\right).$$

<u>Answer</u>: c) The derivative of the tax with respect to r is

$$\frac{dT(r)}{dr} = \frac{d}{dr}\left(\frac{r(7+r)}{2+r} - \frac{4r\sqrt{1+r}}{1+r}\right) = \frac{r^2 + r + 14}{(2+r)^2} - \frac{4(0.5r^2 + 1.5r + 1)}{(1+r)^{5/2}}.$$

The sign of this derivative depends on r. For instance, if $r = 0$, the derivative $-1/2$, which is negative. If $r = 10$, then the derivative is 0.203268,, which is positive. If the derivative is negative, the small amount of pay-as-you-go social security reduces the interest rate and hence increases the capital stock. If the derivative is positive, the social security increases the interest rate and hence reduces the capital stock.

Answer to Homework Problems for Chapter 10, Problem #5

Problem: 5) One might imagine that if the government fixed the lump-sum tax to be equal to T, then the economy would eventually settle into a stationary equilibrium,

$$(x_0(r), x_1(r), K(r), L(r), P, W(r), r, G(r), T(r)),$$

with an interest rate, r, determined by the equation $T(r) = T$. In this statement, I am assuming that the price of the produced good is one, so that T is the real value of the tax. The following problem is meant to show that we cannot necessarily assume that the stationary equilibrium interest rate is a function, r(T), of the tax, T.

Let production function f(K, L) satisfy assumptions 10.1 - 10.5 and let the utility function $u(x_0, x_1)$ satisfy assumption 10.5. Let

$$(x_0(r), x_1(r), K(r), L(r), P, W(r), r, G(r), T(r))$$

be a stationary spot price equilibrium for the Diamond model with production function f and utility function u and where $r > 0$ and $P = 1$.

a) Show that $f(K(r), 1) = (1 + r)K(r) + W(r)$.

Hint for parts b – e: Use the equation of part (a) as well as the equations

$$T(r) = W(r) - x_0(r) - \frac{x_1(r)}{1 + r} \text{ and}$$

$$x_0(r) + x_1(r) = f(K(r), 1) - K(r).$$

b) Show that $T(0) = 0$.

c) Show that $\lim_{r \to \infty} (1 + r) K(r) = 0$, $\lim_{r \to \infty} f(K(r), 1) = 0$, and $\lim_{r \to \infty} W(r) = 0$.

d) Show that $\lim_{r \to \infty} T(r) = 0$.

e) Show that $T(r)$ is a continuous function of r.

f) Show that if from some positive number r, $T(r) \neq 0$, then for some value of T, the equation $T(r) = T$ has more than one positive solution.

Answer: a) By profit maximization in the spot price equilibrium,

$$\frac{\partial f(K(r), 1)}{\partial K} \leq 1 + r,$$

with equality if $K(r) > 0$, and

$$\frac{\partial f(K(r), 1)}{\partial L} = W(r).$$

If $K(r) = 0$, then $f(K(r), 1) = 0 = W(r)$, so that

$$f(K(r), 1) = (1 + r)K(r) + W(r).$$

If $K(r) > 0$, then by Euler's equation for linearly homogeneous functions,

$$f(K(r), 1) = \frac{\partial f(K(r), 1)}{\partial K}K(r) + \frac{\partial f(K(r), 1)}{\partial L} = (1 + r)K(r) + W(r).$$

<u>Answer</u>: b) By feasibility,

$$x_0(0) + x_1(0) + K(0) = f(K(0), 1).$$

By part a,

$$f(K(0), 1) = K(0) + W(0).$$

Therefore

$$x_0(0) + x_1(0) + K(0) = f(K(0), 1) = K(0) + W(0),$$

so that

$$x_0(0) + x_1(0) = W(0)$$

and hence

$$T(0) = W(0) - x_0(0) - x_1(0) = 0.$$

<u>Answer</u>: c) Since $f(K, 1)$ is strictly concave, $\frac{\partial f(K, 1)}{\partial K}$ is strictly decreasing. Therefore the condition

$$\frac{\partial f(K(r), 1)}{\partial K} \leq 1 + r,$$

with equality if $K(r) = 0$, implies that $K(r)$ is a non-increasing function of r. Hence

$$0 \leq K(r) = \frac{f(K(r), 1) - W(r)}{1 + r} \leq \frac{f(K(r), 1)}{1 + r} \leq \frac{f(K(0), 1)}{1 + r},$$

if $r \geq 0$. Since

$$\lim_{r \to \infty} \frac{f(K(0), 1)}{1 + r} = 0,$$

it follows that

$$\lim_{r \to \infty} K(r) = 0,$$

Since f is continuous,

$$\lim_{r \to \infty} f(K(r), 1) = f(0, 1) = 0.$$

Since

$$0 \leq (1 + r)K(r) = f(K(r), 1) - W(r) \leq f(K(r), 1),$$

it follows that

$$\lim_{r \to \infty} (1 + r) K(r) = 0.$$

Since

$$W(r) = f(K(r), 1) - (1 + r)K(r),$$

it follows that

$$\lim_{r \to \infty} W(r) = 0.$$

Answer: d) By feasibility,

$$\lim_{r \to \infty} [x_0(r) + x_1(r)] = \lim_{r \to \infty} [f(K(r), 1) - K(r)] = 0.$$

Since $x_0(r) \geq 0$ and $x_1(r) \geq 0$, it follows that

$$\lim_{r \to \infty} x_0(r) = 0 = \lim_{r \to \infty} x_1(r).$$

Therefore

$$\lim_{r \to \infty} T(r) = W(r) - x_0(r) - \frac{x_1(r)}{1 + r} = 0.$$

Answer: e) Since $\frac{\partial f(K, 1)}{\partial K}$ is strictly decreasing, continuous, and positive and $\lim_{K \to \infty} \frac{\partial f(K, 1)}{\partial K} = 0$, it follows that the condition

$$\frac{\partial f(K(r), 1)}{\partial K} \leq 1 + r,$$

with equality if $K(r) > 0$, defines $K(r)$ as a continuous function. (In fact, $K(r)$ is continuous even if $\frac{\partial f(K, 1)}{\partial K}$ is not continuous.)

The function $x_0(r)$ is defined by the condition

$$\frac{du_0(x_0(r))}{dx} - (1 + r)\frac{du_1(f(K(r), 1) - K(r) - x_0(r))}{dx} \leq 0,$$

with equality if $x_0(r) > 0$. I will show that $x_0(r)$ is continuous at any $r = \bar{r} > -1$. Assume that $x_0(\bar{r}) > 0$, so that the above weak inequality is an equation. A similar argument applies if $x_0(\bar{r}) = 0$.

The function

$$\frac{du_0(x)}{dx} - (1 + r)\frac{du_1(f(K(r), 1) - K(r) - x)}{dx}$$

is strictly decreasing in x, though not necessarily continuous in x. Let $\varepsilon > 0$. Then

$$0 < 2\gamma_L = \frac{du_0(x_0(\bar{r}) - \varepsilon)}{dx} - (1 + \bar{r})\frac{du_1(f(K(\bar{r}), 1) - K(\bar{r}) - x_0(\bar{r}) + \varepsilon)}{dx},$$

and

$$0 > 2\gamma_R = \frac{du_0(x_0(\bar{r}) + \varepsilon)}{dx} - (1 + \bar{r})\frac{du_1(f(K(\bar{r}), 1) - K(\bar{r}) - x_0(\bar{r}) - \varepsilon)}{dx}.$$

Since $f(K(r), 1) - K(r)$ is a continuous function of r, there is a $\delta > 0$ so small that

$|r - \bar{r}| < \delta$ implies that

$$|f(K(r), 1) - K(r) - f(K(\bar{r}), 1) + K(\bar{r})| < \varepsilon.$$

In addition, I may assume that δ is so small that $|r - \bar{r}| < \delta$ implies that

$$\gamma_L < \frac{du_0(x_0(\bar{r}) - \varepsilon)}{dx} - (1 + r)\frac{du_1(f(K(\bar{r}), 1) - K(\bar{r}) - x_0(\bar{r}) + \varepsilon)}{dx}$$

and

$$\gamma_R > \frac{du_0(x_0(\bar{r}) + \varepsilon)}{dx} - (1 + r)\frac{du_1(f(K(\bar{r}), 1) - K(\bar{r}) - x_0(\bar{r}) - \varepsilon)}{dx}.$$

If $|r - \bar{r}| < \delta$, then

$$0 < \gamma_L < \frac{du_0(x_0(\bar{r}) - \varepsilon)}{dx} - (1 + r)\frac{du_1(f(K(\bar{r}), 1) - K(\bar{r}) - x_0(\bar{r}) + \varepsilon)}{dx}$$

$$< \frac{du_0(x_0(\bar{r}) - 2\varepsilon)}{dx} - (1 + r)\frac{du_1(f(K(r), 1) - K(r) - x_0(\bar{r}) + 2\varepsilon)}{dx},$$

where the third inequality holds because

$$x_0(\bar{r}) - \varepsilon > x_0(\bar{r}) - 2\varepsilon$$

and

$$f(K(\bar{r}), 1) - K(\bar{r}) - x_0(\bar{r}) + \varepsilon < f(K(r), 1) - K(r) - x_0(\bar{r}) + 2\varepsilon.$$

Similarly, if $|r - \bar{r}| < \delta$, then

$$0 > \gamma_R > \frac{du_0(x_0(\bar{r}) + \varepsilon)}{dx} - (1 + r)\frac{du_1(f(K(\bar{r}), 1) - K(\bar{r}) - x_0(\bar{r}) - \varepsilon)}{dx}.$$

$$> \frac{du_0(x_0(\bar{r}) + 2\varepsilon)}{dx} - (1 + r)\frac{du_1(f(K(r), 1) - K(r) - x_0(\bar{r}) - 2\varepsilon)}{dx},$$

where the third inequality holds because

$$x_0(\bar{r}) + 2\varepsilon > x_0(\bar{r}) + \varepsilon$$

and

$$f(K(r), 1) - K(r) - x_0(\bar{r}) - 2\varepsilon < f(K(\bar{r}), 1) - K(\bar{r}) - x_0(\bar{r}) - \varepsilon.$$

It follows that

$$x_0(\bar{r}) - 2\varepsilon < x_0(r) < x_0(\bar{r}) + 2\varepsilon,$$

if $|r - \bar{r}| < \delta$, so that $x_0(r)$ is continuous at $\bar{r}$.

Since $x_0(r)$ is continuous, $x_1(r) = f(K(r), 1) - K(r) - x_0(r)$ is so as well.

Since $f(K, L)$ is continuously differentiable at $(K, L) \neq 0$,

$$W(r) = \frac{\partial f(K(r), 1)}{\partial L}$$

is continuous.

We may conclude that

$$T(r) = W(r) - x_0(r) - \frac{x_1(r)}{1 + r}$$

is continuous.

Answer: f) Assume that $T(r) > 0$. (A similar argument applies if $T(r) < 0$.) Call this value of r, r_1, so that $T(r_1) > 0$ and let T be such that $0 < T < T(r_1)$. Since $T(0) = 0 < T < T(r_1)$ and T is continuous, the intermediate value theorem implies that $T(r_0) = T$, for some r_0 such that $0 < r_0 < r_1$.

Since $\lim_{r \to \infty} T(r) = 0$, there is an r_3 such that $r_3 > r_1$ and $T(r_3) < T$. Again by the intermediate value theorem, there is an r_2 such that $r_1 < r_2 < r_3$ and $T(r_2) = T$. Since $r_0 < r_2$, the equation $T(r) = T$ has at least two solutions.

Answer to Homework Problems for Chapter 10, Problem #6

Problem: 6) Let $(\overline{C}_t, \overline{K}_t)_{t=0}^{\infty}$ be a solution of the problem

$$\max_{\substack{C_t \geq 0,\, K_t \geq 0,\\ \text{for } t = 0, 1, \ldots}} \sum_{t=0}^{\infty} \beta^t \gamma^{-1} C_t^{\gamma}$$

$$C_t + K_t = \alpha^{-1} K_{t-1}^{\alpha},$$

where $\overline{K}_{-1}$ is a given positive number and where $0 < \alpha < 1$, $0 < \beta < 1$, and $0 < \gamma < 1$.

a) Show that $\lim_{t \to \infty} K_t$ and $\lim_{t \to \infty} C_t$ exist.

b) Calculate $\lim_{t \to \infty} K_t$ and $\lim_{t \to \infty} C_t$ in terms of α, β, and γ.

Answer: a) The turnpike theorem implies that

$$\lim_{t \to \infty} (\overline{C}_t, \overline{K}_t) = (\overline{C}, \overline{K}),$$

where $(\overline{C}, \overline{K})$ is the modified golden rule stationary program with discount factor β.

Answer: b) the equation defining $\overline{K}$ is

$$\frac{dF(\overline{K})}{dK} = \beta^{-1}.$$

On substituting for F, this equation becomes

$$\overline{K}^{\alpha - 1} = \beta^{-1},$$

so that

$$\overline{K} = \beta^{\frac{1}{1-\alpha}}.$$

Then

$$\overline{C} = F(\overline{K}) - \overline{K} = \alpha^{-1}\beta^{\frac{\alpha}{1-\alpha}} - \beta^{\frac{1}{1-\alpha}} = \alpha^{-1}\beta^{-1}\beta^{\frac{1}{1-\alpha}} - \beta^{\frac{1}{1-\alpha}} = \left(\frac{1 - \alpha\beta}{\alpha\beta}\right)\beta^{\frac{1}{1-\alpha}}.$$

Answer to Homework Problems for Chapter 10, Problem #7

Problem: 7) In an optimal growth model, let the production function be

$$y_{t+1} = 20\sqrt{K_t}$$

and let the one period utility function be

$$u(C_t) = 3C_t^{1/3},$$

for all t.

a) Find the golden rule allocation for this model.

b) Let $(C_t, K_t)_{t=0}^{\infty}$ be a program that has initial capital $K_{-1} = 1$ and is optimal with respect to the catching up criterion. What is the first period t such that $|K_t - \overline{K}| \leq 10$, where $\overline{K}$ is the golden rule capital stock?

Answer: a) The equations defining the golden rule program $(\overline{C}, \overline{K})$ are

$$\frac{dF(\overline{K})}{dK} = 1$$

and

$$\overline{C} = F(\overline{K}) - \overline{K}.$$

On substituting for F, we find that

$$\frac{10}{\sqrt{\overline{K}}} = 1,$$

so that $\overline{K} = 100$ and $\overline{C} = 20\sqrt{100} - 100 = 100.$

Answer: b) The Euler equation for the optimal program is

$$\frac{du(C_t)}{dC} = \frac{du(C_{t+1})}{dC}\frac{dF(K_t)}{dK}.$$

On substituting for u and F, this equation becomes

$$C_t^{-1/3} = C_{t+1}^{-2/3}10K_t^{-1/2}.$$

so that

$$K_t^{1/2} = 10\left(\frac{C_t}{C_{t+1}}\right)^{2/3}$$

and hence

$$K_t = 100\left(\frac{C_t}{C_{t+1}}\right)^{4/3}.$$

Assume that

$$C_t = c20\sqrt{K_{t-1}},$$

for all t, where c is some number between 0 and 1. Then

$$K_t = 100\left(\frac{\sqrt{K_{t-1}}}{\sqrt{K_t}}\right)^{4/3} = 100\left(\frac{K_{t-1}}{K_t}\right)^{2/3}$$

and so

$$K_t^{5/3} = 100K_{t-1}^{2/3}$$

and hence

$$K_t = (100)^{3/5}K_{t-1}^{2/5}.$$

I use this formula to compute K_t inductively. By assumption,

$$K_{-1} = 1.$$

Therefore

$$K_0 = 100^{3/5} \cong 15.85.$$

$$K_1 = 100^{3/5}(100^{3/5})^{2/5} = 100^{(3/5 + 6/25)} = 100^{21/25} \cong 47.86.$$

$$K_2 = 100^{3/5}(100^{21/25})^{2/5} = 100^{(3/5 + 42/125)} = 100^{117/125} \cong 74.47.$$

$$K_3 = 100^{3/5}(100^{117/125})^{2/5} = 100^{(3/5 + 234/625)} = 100^{609/625} \cong 88.88.$$

$$K_4 = 100^{3/5}(100^{609/625})^{2/5} = 100^{(3/5 + 1218/3125)} = 100^{3093/3125} \cong 95.39.$$

Therefore the answer is t = 4, since $|K_3 - \overline{K}| = |88.88 - 100| > 10$ and $|K_4 - \overline{K}| = |95.39 - 100| < 10$.

Answer to Homework Problems for Chapter 10, Problem #8

Problem: 8) Consider the growth model with

$$u(C_t) = \ln(C_t)$$

and

$$F(K_t) = \min((1 + a)K_t, b),$$

where $a > 0$ and $b > 0$. Find a program that is optimal with respect to the overtaking criterion given an arbitrary, positive, initial capital stock $\overline{K}_{-1}$.

Hint: The answer depends on whether

$$(1 + a)\overline{K}_{-1} \geq b$$

or

$$(1 + a)\overline{K}_{-1} < b.$$

The harder case is where $(1 + a)\overline{K}_{-1} < b$. For this case, you may use Euler's equation, feasibility, the production function, and backwards induction on time to calculate an optimal program with initial capital equal to any one of an infinite decreasing sequence of stocks, where the sequence starts with $(1 + a)^{-1}b$ and converges asymptotically to zero. The capital of an optimal program starting at one of these points reaches $(1 + a)^{-1}b$, after finitely many periods, and then stays at this level forever. If the initial capital is between two points in this sequence, then relative to the smaller of these two points there is an extra amount of output to be consumed and invested over finitely many periods until the capital stock reaches $(1 + a)^{-1}b$. Again use Euler's equation, feasibility, and the production function to see how this extra consumption and capital should evolve. Verify that the program that you calculate in this manner is optimal by showing that it is part of a program equilibrium with interest rate zero.

Answer: The graph of the production function $y = F(K)$ is the heavy line in the diagram below. The diagonal $y = K$ is also shown. It should be clear from the diagram that the golden rule program is $(\overline{C}, \overline{K}) = \left(\frac{ab}{1 + a}, \frac{b}{1 + a}\right)$ and output in the golden rule program is $\overline{y} = b$.

Notice that F is differentiable everywhere except at $K = \overline{K} = b/(1 + a)$ and that $\frac{dF(\overline{K})}{dK-} = 1 + a$ and $\frac{dF(\overline{K})}{dK+} = 0$. It follows that the Euler conditions for an optimal program are

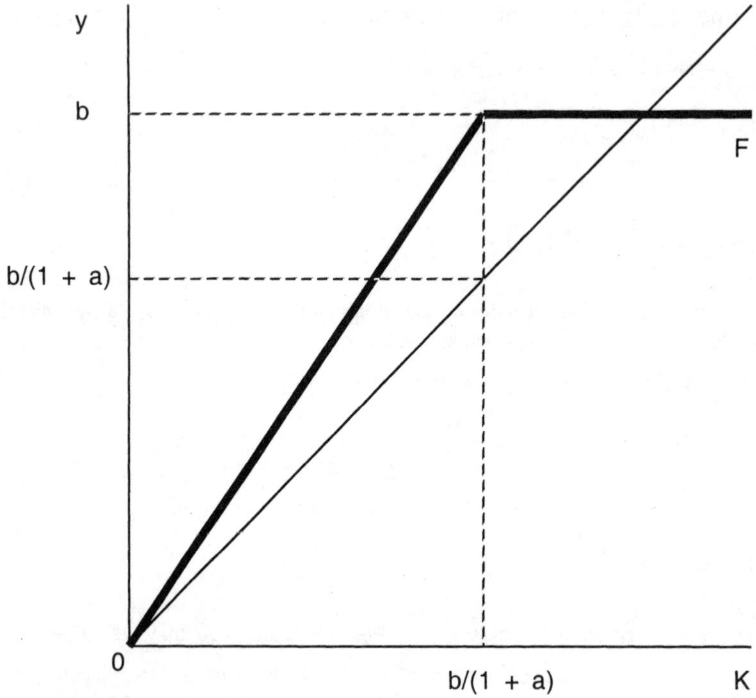

$$\frac{du(C_t)}{dC} = \frac{dF(K_t)}{dK}\frac{du(C_{t+1})}{dC},$$

if $C_t > 0$ and $K_t \neq \overline{K} = b/(1 + a)$, and

$$\frac{dF(K_t)}{dK+}\frac{du(C_{t+1})}{dC} = 0 \leq \frac{du(C_t)}{dC} \leq \frac{dF(K_t)}{dK-}\frac{du(C_{t+1})}{dC} = (1 + a)\frac{du(C_{t+1})}{dC}, \qquad (*)$$

if $C_t > 0$ and $K_t = \overline{K} = b/(1 + a)$. In fact, the Euler conditions are inequality (*) at any values of C_t and K_t, since the left and right-hand derivatives of F are equal where it is differentiable. At the golden rule program,

$$\frac{dF(\overline{K})}{dK+}\frac{du(\overline{C})}{dC} = 0 < \frac{du(\overline{C})}{dC} = \frac{1 + a}{ab} < \frac{(1 + a)^2}{ab} = \frac{dF(\overline{K})}{dK-}\frac{du(\overline{C})}{dC},$$

so that the golden rule program satisfies the Euler conditions.

I show that a feasible program $(C_t, K_t)_{t=0}^{\infty}$ is optimal according to the catching up criterion if it obeys the Euler conditions (*) and if C_t remains bounded away from 0 as t varies. Let $p_t = \frac{du(C_t)}{dC}$, for all t. I show that the Euler conditions imply that the feasible program $(C_t, K_t)_{t=0}^{\infty}$ and the price vectors p_t form a program equilibrium with interest rate zero. The definition $p_t = \frac{du(C_t)}{dC}$ implies that C_t solves the problem

$$\max_{C \geq 0} [u(C) - p_t C],$$

for all t. The Euler conditions

$$\frac{du(C_{t+1})}{dC}\frac{dF(K_t)}{dK+} \leq \frac{du(C_t)}{dC} \leq \frac{du(C_{t+1})}{dC}\frac{dF(K_t)}{dK-}$$

imply that $p_{t+1}\frac{dF(K_t)}{dK+} \leq p_t \leq p_{t+1}\frac{dF(K_t)}{dK-}$. Because F is concave, these inequalities in turn imply that $K = K_t$ solves the problem

$$\max_{K \geq 0} [p_{t+1}F(K) - p_t K],$$

for all t. Hence $(C_t, K_t)_{t=0}^{\infty}$ is a program equilibrium with interest rate zero. Since the C_t are bounded away from zero, the prices $p_t = \frac{du(C_t)}{dC}$ are bounded, and hence theorem 10.77 implies that the program $(C_t, K_t)_{t=0}^{\infty}$ is optimal according to the catching up criterion.

By the reasoning just described, the golden rule stationary program $(\overline{C}, \overline{K})$ is optimal according to the catching up criterion.

I now turn to the construction of an optimal program. If the initial output is $y_0 = (1 + a)K_{-1} \geq b$, let $C_0 = y_0 - b + \overline{C}$, let $K_0 = \overline{K}$, and for $t \geq 1$, let $C_t = \overline{C}$ and $K_t = \overline{K}$. Then

$$0 \leq \frac{du(C_0)}{dC} = \frac{1}{y_0 - b + \overline{C}} \leq \frac{1}{\overline{C}} = \frac{du(\overline{C})}{dC} < \frac{dF(\overline{K})}{dK-}\frac{du(\overline{C})}{dC} = \frac{dF(K_1)}{dK-}\frac{du(C_1)}{dC},$$

so that C_0, K_0, and C_1 satisfy the Euler conditions. Since $(C_t, K_t) = (\overline{C}, \overline{K})$, for $t \geq 1$, it follows that C_t, K_t, and C_{t+1} satisfy the Euler conditions for $t \geq 1$. Since the consumptions C_t are bounded away from zero, the program $(C_t, K_t)_{t=0}^{\infty}$ is optimal according to the catching up criterion.

I now define an optimal program when output in period 0 is $y_0 = (1 + a)\bar{K}_{-1} < b$. I begin the construction as follows. Suppose that the output in period 0 is $\underline{y}_0 = (1 + a)\bar{K}_{-1} = b$. That is, suppose that $\bar{K}_{-1} = b/(1 + a)$. Imagine that the optimal program begins at time $-T < 0$, and let $(\underline{C}_t, \underline{K}_t)_{t=-T}^{\infty}$ be the optimal program that begins at time $-T$ and is such that $\underline{K}_{-1} = \bar{K}_{-1} = b/(1 + a)$. For $t \geq 0$. Let $\underline{C}_t = \bar{C} = ab/(1 + a)$ and let $\underline{K}_t = \bar{K} = b/(1 + a)$. Assume that for each $t > 0$, $\underline{K}_{-t} > 0$ and $\underline{C}_{-t} > 0$. Then the Euler equation for $t > 0$ is

$$\frac{du(\underline{C}_{-t})}{dC} = \frac{dF(\underline{K}_{-t})}{dK}\frac{du(\underline{C}_{-t+1})}{dC},$$

which implies that

$$\frac{1}{\underline{C}_{-t}} = \frac{1 + a}{\underline{C}_{-t+1}}$$

and hence

$$\underline{C}_{-t} = \frac{\underline{C}_{-t+1}}{1 + a}.$$

Let $\underline{y}_t$ be total output in period t, so that $\underline{y}_t = \underline{K}_t + \underline{C}_t$. I find formulas for $\underline{y}_{-t}$ and $\underline{K}_t$ by induction on t, starting with $t = 0$. We know that $\underline{y}_0 = b$, $\underline{K}_0 = \frac{b}{1 + a}$, and $\underline{C}_0 = \left(\frac{a}{1 + a}\right)b$. Hence

$$\underline{C}_{-t} = \left(\frac{a}{(1 + a)^{t+1}}\right)b,$$

for all $t \geq 0$. Assume by induction on t that

$$\underline{y}_{-t} = \left(\frac{1 + (t + 1)a}{(1 + a)^{t+1}}\right)b \text{ and } \underline{K}_{-t} = \left(\frac{1 + ta}{(1 + a)^{t+1}}\right)b.$$

These formulas are clearly valid for $t = 0$. The nature of the production function implies that

$$\underline{K}_{-t-1} = \frac{\underline{y}_t}{1 + a} = \left(\frac{1 + (t + 1)a}{(1 + a)^{t+2}}\right)b$$

and hence

$$\underline{y}_{-t-1} = \underline{K}_{-t-1} + \underline{C}_{-t-1} = \left(\frac{1 + (t+1)a}{(1+a)^{t+2}}\right)b + \left(\frac{a}{(1+a)^{t+2}}\right)b = \left(\frac{1 + (t+2)a}{(1+a)^{t+2}}\right)b.$$

This verifies the inductive step and hence the above formulas for $\underline{y}_{-t}$ and $\underline{K}_{-t}$, for $t \geq 0$. Observe that $\underline{y}_{-t} > 0$, for $t \geq 0$, $\lim_{t \to \infty} \underline{y}_{-t} = 0$, and

$$\underline{y}_{-t-1} = \left(\frac{1 + (t+2)a}{(1+a)^{t+2}}\right)b < \left(\frac{1 + (t+1)a}{(1+a)^{t+1}}\right)b = \underline{y}_{-t},$$

since

$$1 + (t+2)a < 1 + (t+2)a + (t+1)a^2 = (1 + (t+1)a)(1+a)$$

and this is the inequality obtained by cross multiplying in the previous inequality. Observe that for $t \geq 0$, $\underline{K}_{-t} > 0$ and $\underline{C}_{-t} > 0$, so that the assumptions on which the construction was based are valid.

The program $(\underline{C}_t, \underline{K}_t)_{t=-T}^{\infty}$ clearly obeys the Euler conditions, for each t. Since the consumptions $\underline{C}_t$ remain bounded away from zero as t varies, $(\underline{C}_t, \underline{K}_t)_{t=-T}^{\infty}$ is optimal by the argument made earlier.

I now construct an optimal program $(\hat{C}_t, \hat{K}_t)_{t=-T}^{\infty}$ with outputs $(\hat{y}_t)_{t=-T}^{\infty}$ such that

$$b > \hat{y}_{-1} \geq \underline{y}_{-1} = \left(\frac{1+2a}{(1+a)^2}\right)b.$$

For $t \geq 0$, let

$$(\hat{C}_t, \hat{K}_t) = (\underline{C}_t, \underline{K}_t) = (\overline{C}, \overline{K}) = \left(\frac{ab}{1+a}, \frac{b}{1+a}\right).$$

Let

$$\hat{C}_{-1} = \hat{y}_{-1} - \underline{y}_{-1} + \underline{C}_{-1} = \hat{y}_{-1} - \left(\frac{1+2a}{(1+a)^2}\right)b + \left(\frac{a}{(1+a)^2}\right)b = y_{-1} - \left(\frac{1}{1+a}\right)b$$

$$= y_{-1} - \underline{K}_{-1}.$$

Let $\hat{K}_{-1} = \dfrac{b}{1+a} = \underline{K}_{-1} = \overline{K}$. I now show by induction on t that for $t \geq 1$

$$\hat{C}_{-t} = \left(\frac{1}{(1 + a)^{t-1}}\right)(\hat{y}_{-1} - \underline{y}_{-1}) + \underline{C}_{-t}$$

$$\hat{K}_{-t} = \left(\frac{t-1}{(1 + a)^{t-1}}\right)(\hat{y}_{-1} - \underline{y}_{-1}) + \underline{K}_{-t}$$

$$\hat{y}_{-t} = \left(\frac{t}{(1 + a)^{t-1}}\right)(\hat{y}_{-1} - \underline{y}_{-1}) + \underline{y}_{-t}.$$

These formulas are valid for $t = 1$. Suppose they are valid for $t > 1$. Then by Euler's equation,

$$\hat{C}_{-(t+1)} = \frac{\hat{C}_{-t}}{1 + a} = \left(\frac{1}{(1 + a)^{t}}\right)(\hat{y}_{-1} - \underline{y}_{-1}) + \frac{\underline{C}_{-t}}{1 + a}$$

$$= \left(\frac{1}{(1 + a)^{t}}\right)(\hat{y}_{-1} - \underline{y}_{-1}) + \underline{C}_{-(t+1)}.$$

By the nature of the production function,

$$\hat{K}_{-(t+1)} = \frac{\hat{y}_{-t}}{1 + a} = \left(\frac{t}{(1 + a)^{t}}\right)(\hat{y}_{-1} - \underline{y}_{-1}) + \frac{\underline{y}_{-t}}{1 + a}$$

$$= \left(\frac{t}{(1 + a)^{t}}\right)(\hat{y}_{-1} - \underline{y}_{-1}) + \underline{K}_{-(t+1)}.$$

By feasibility,

$$\hat{y}_{-(t+1)} = \hat{C}_{-(t+1)} + \hat{K}_{-(t+1)} = \left(\frac{1}{(1 + a)^{t}}\right)(\hat{y}_{-1} - \underline{y}_{-1}) + \underline{C}_{-(t+1)}$$

$$+ \left(\frac{t}{(1 + a)^{t}}\right)(\hat{y}_{-1} - \underline{y}_{-1}) + \underline{K}_{-(t+1)}$$

$$= \left(\frac{t + 1}{(1 + a)^{t}}\right)(\hat{y}_{-1} - \underline{y}_{-1}) + \underline{C}_{-(t+1)} + \underline{K}_{-(t+1)}$$

$$= \left(\frac{t + 1}{(1 + a)^{t}}\right)(\hat{y}_{-1} - \underline{y}_{-1}) + \underline{y}_{-(t+1)}.$$

This completes the induction and the verification that the formulas for $\hat{C}_{-t}$, $\hat{K}_{-t}$, and $\hat{y}_{-t}$ are correct according to the conditions characterizing an optimal program.

I now verify that $(\hat{C}_t, \hat{K}_t)_{t=-T}^{\infty}$ is optimal according to the catching up criterion. Since the consumptions $\hat{C}_t$ are bounded away from zero, it is sufficient, by the reasoning made earlier, to show that this program satisfies the Euler conditions. By construction, it satisfies these conditions everywhere except possibly at t = –1. In that period,

$$\frac{du(\hat{C}_{-1})}{dC} = \frac{1}{\hat{y}_{-1} - \underline{y}_{-1} + \underline{C}_{-1}} \leq \frac{1}{\underline{C}_{-1}} = \frac{du(\underline{C}_{-1})}{dC}$$

$$\leq \frac{dF(\underline{K}_{-1})}{dK} \frac{du(\underline{C}_{0})}{dC} = \frac{dF(\hat{K}_{-1})}{dK} \frac{du(\hat{C}_{0})}{dC},$$

since $\hat{C}_0 = \underline{C}_0$ and $\hat{K}_{-1} = \underline{K}_{-1}$ and the program $(\underline{C}_t, \underline{K}_t)_{t=-T}^{\infty}$ satisfies the Euler conditions. Hence the program $(\hat{C}_t, \hat{K}_t)_{t=-T}^{\infty}$ is optimal according to the catching up criterion.

I complete the construction of an optimal program. For every initial output y_0 such that $0 < y_0 < b$, either $\underline{y}_{-1} \leq y_0$ or there is a unique integer T such that $T \geq 2$ and $\underline{y}_{-T} \leq y_0 < \underline{y}_{-(T-1)}$. If $\underline{y}_{-1} \leq y_0 < b$, let $(C_t, K_t) = (\hat{C}_{t-1}, \hat{K}_{t-1})$, for t = 0, 1, 2, ... If $\underline{y}_{-T} \leq y_0 < \underline{y}_{-(T-1)}$, let $(C_t, K_t) = (\hat{C}_{t-T}, \hat{K}_{t-T})$, for t = 0, 1, 2, ... The program $(C_t, K_t)_{t=0}^{\infty}$ obeys the Euler conditions because the program $(\hat{C}_t, \hat{K}_t)_{t=0}^{\infty}$ does so. Because the consumptions $\hat{C}_t$ are bounded away from zero, the same is true of the consumptions C_t. Therefore the program $(C_t, K_t)_{t=0}^{\infty}$ is optimal according to the catching up criterion.